A
BEGINNERS
COLLECTION

of

EMERGENCY
PREPARATION
PRINCIPLES

Volume One

by

L.G. Wellington

Copyright through United States Copyright Office - 2012 by L.G. Wellington

ISBN-13: 978-1491067697
ISBN-10: 1491067691

Hello there!

Basically, there are two types of survivalists. The first survivalist is the person who can go into a forest with a piece of string and a match stick and construct a shopping mall. These individuals live off the land – eat spiders and centipedes – climb trees and eat coconuts - forage in the underbrush for edible twigs, sticks and rocks and build a shelter on top of a cactus. This type of survivalist should be envied – respected – and admired. But this type of survivalist is not me.

The second survivalist is the person who purchases supplies <u>in advance</u> for emergency pantries that can be used during a disaster – and hopefully, this survivalist can live through the disaster <u>in their home</u> *without* eating bugs, climbing trees and eating coconuts, living on top of a cactus or scrounging for twigs, sticks and rocks to prepare the next meal. *I am this type of survivalist.*

There are sixteen important elements affected by consequences that occur during a disaster. In this book, I will introduce you eight of them with the remaining elements being covered in Volumes 2 and 3 of this series. In addition to learning about basic emergency principles, you will be given a <u>candid</u> assessment of important strategies, insights, tips, guidelines and lists on the EMOTION, OPERATION, MEDICATION, IMMUNIZATION, COMMUNICATION, DOCUMENTATION and RECREATION Elements that can be impacted by a crisis. So let's be clear – I am not always going to tell you what you WANT to hear – but I <u>will</u> tell you what you NEED to learn in order to *prepare in advance* for future disasters.

As you begin the journey, at first it may seem overwhelming – there is so much to learn and so much to do. Based on your individual situation, you can review the information and make a *realistic* and *smart* decision on what would be good choices for your family. And in many cases, much to your surprise, you will discover that you already have many of the suggested supplies in and around your house!

As a beginning student to emergency preparation – it seems like the hardest part is taking that first step. And since you are reading this book, it tells me that you are serious and committed to getting your emergency pantries in order. We all have to begin somewhere – sometime. <u>The time is right</u>. <u>The time is now</u>. So let's get crackin!

TABLE OF CONTENTS

CHAPTER ONE - INTRODUCTION 5

CHAPTER TWO - EMOTION... 45

CHAPTER THREE - OPERATION 51

CHAPTER FOUR - MEDICATION 87

CHAPTER FIVE - IMMUNIZATION 105

CHAPTER SIX - COMMUNICATION 111

CHAPTER SEVEN - DOCUMENTATION............................ 121

CHAPTER EIGHT - RECREATION 125

SUMMARY 133

APPENDIX A 135

This book is dedicated to my best friend, *Sandy Checketts*, for her continued loyalty, support, encouragement and friendship throughout my lifetime and during some very trying times. Thank you Sandy for all that you do for me.

TERMS

TERM	DEFINITION
Consequence	Produced by a cause (disaster) having important affects or influence over the earth and its inhabitants. Examples include disruption of electrical power, flooding of neighborhoods, destruction of homes and hospitals or broken bridges and roads.
Disaster	A state of extreme ruin and misfortune. An act that has consequences. An unexpected natural or man-made catastrophe of substantial extent causing significant physical damage or destruction, loss of life or permanent change to the natural environment. Examples include *earthquake, thunderstorm, nuclear meltdown* or *volcanic eruption*.
Element	Components essential to our survival on this planet and standard of living. These elements are made up of various agencies and organizations that provide goods and services to the human population. Examples include *Administration, Operation, Sanitation, Transportation, Communication, Nutrition, Medication, Immunization, Financial Institution, Documentation, Commercialization* and *Protection*.
Health	*Physical, Mental, Emotional, Psychological* and *Spiritual* well being for all living creatures on earth.
Survival Team	Individuals in the group who purchases and consumes supplies in emergency pantries and will share in responsibilities and duties associated with implementing the overall emergency plan. Examples include a family living in a home.
Layers	Alternatives for an element. If one type of alternative isn't realistic or possible for a specific situation, another alternative could possibly be used. Examples of layered supplies that provide light include a *candle, lantern, flashlight,* and *lamp*.
Level	A classification of disaster scenario based on the elements that are affected, the severity of the consequences and the duration the element is compromised or disrupted. There are three emergency levels including Level 1, Level 2 and Level 3.
Pantry	A facility, room or container used to store various sources and items assigned to each element. Examples are pantries located in the *primary residence, place of refuge, auto, work* or an *evacuation* kit.
Place of Refuge	An alternative location for the survival team in the event the primary residence is damaged or destroyed or the pre-selected primary location for team members to reside during the disaster. A place of refuge could be a *motor home, trailer house, camper, cabin, summer home* or some other location (including a *church, school* or designated *public shelter*) pre-determined by the survival team.
Primary Residence	The building or structure and location where the survival team members will store, use and consume emergency preparation supplies and items. During a disaster, the team will congregate and remain at this location as long as the residence is habitable.
Resource	A manmade or natural source that is available to us for use in emergency preparation. Examples include the *sun, water, wood, wind* and *rain* or a *grocery store*.
Supply	A man-made or commercial product or service that is available to us for use in emergency preparation. Examples include *flashlights, clothes, radio, grain,* and *gloves*.

CHAPTER ONE

INTRODUCTION

OSTRICH SYNDROME

Whenever an ostrich senses danger, instead of facing the threat – he immediately buries his head in the sand. If he cannot see the danger – then the danger cannot see him. Only a very small percentage of citizens in this country are concerned about being prepared, educated or ready for any crisis. Some people don't believe that any disaster is going to happen here in the United States. Others believe that disasters may affect only those people who live outside of the country. Still others believe that disasters may happen but they are powerless to do anything about it. There are countless individuals throughout the world and here at home – including right in your backyard, who are not worried about any type of disaster happening to them. They truly believe that it is best to eat, drink and be merry – for tomorrow they <u>still</u> won't die! These individuals are convinced that in the event of any unlikely disaster – the government, church, employer, charities, relatives, friends, neighbors and co-workers will shoulder this burden for them.

Regardless of individual opinions about possible future disasters, it is important for all citizens to recognize the following:

NO PERSON OR GROUP IS RESPONSIBLE FOR THE SAFETY, WELL-BEING OR HEALTH OF YOUR HOUSEHOLD DURING A DISASTER. IF YOU ARE NAIVE ENOUGH TO BELIEVE THAT OTHERS ARE GATHERING SUPPLIES AND MAKING PREPARATIONS SO THAT DURING A DISASTER, YOU CAN MAGICALLY APPEAR ON THEIR DOORSTEP EXPECTING SANCTUARY AND THEY WILL BE ECSTATIC TO SHELTER, FEED, WATER, CLOTHE AND MEDICATE YOU AND YOUR HOUSEHOLD – THINK AGAIN.

Survival planning is nothing more than realizing a disaster could happen that would put everyone in a survival situation and with that in mind, take steps to increase chances of survival. Although helping others is certainly meaningful, worthwhile, and in some cases, necessary – the main emphasis for all survival team members should be to *purchase*, *gather*, and *store* resources and supplies for your own team members. Everyone must be encouraged and expected to provide for themselves. We have been encouraged through religious, education, scientific and government media to prepare for these future events.

Survival planning means being organized, having survival supplies and knowing how to use them. Emergency preparation requires *physical*, *mental*, *emotional*, *psychological*, *spiritual* and *monetary* sacrifice, but in the end, survival planning is essential.

Ahh – this bird appears to have lost his head! I'm so glad it isn't you!

PROBLEM

There are many types of emergencies and disasters that can occur in your city, county, state, country or around the world. Depending on the type and location of the disaster, the consequences can affect each of us in a *direct* or *indirect* manner. The disaster could have long-range affects on many people or only on a single individual or household. For example, extremely cold weather in Florida and California or tornadoes in the wheat belt would indirectly affect all of us due to probable loss of crops. A war in the Middle East would affect oil prices which in turn will directly affect the price of gasoline at the gas pumps. A fire could engulf a single household and would directly affect the family whose house was damaged or destroyed. A major disaster anywhere in the world has the distinct possibility of directly or indirectly affecting all of us here in our own country.

APPROACH

Because of the thousands of scenarios and possibilities that can take place during a disaster, my approach to disaster planning focuses not on the actual disaster but on the *consequences* to the elements that most likely will occur as a result of the disaster and the *length of time* those consequences will remain in place.

> *Now this is not the end. It is not even the beginning of the end. But it is, perhaps, the end of the beginning.*
>
> - **Winston Churchill**

ELEMENTS

Although there are sixteen total elements, in this first volume, we will discuss seven significant *elements* that can be damaged or destroyed by consequences that happen during a disaster. All of these elements are essential to our survival on this planet and to our current standard of living. Without these elements in our society and in our personal lives, we would find our existence on earth to be difficult to endure if not impossible to survive. These elements include:

ELEMENT	WHAT IT COVERS
Communication	Public, private and commercial communication modes including land line phones, cell phones, ham radios, television, radio, newspapers, written correspondence, postal service, satellite, Internet and written correspondence.
Documentation	Legal and personal documentation including birth certificates, death certificates, marriage certificates, home and auto titles, mortgages, leases, wills and living wills.
Emotion	Human reaction to stress, anxiety, fear, confusion, anger and depression that becomes prevalent during a crisis – both as individuals, groups and entire populations.
Immunization	Vaccinations required to minimize the possibility of contracting diseases.
Medication	Hospitals and medical centers, medical care providers, first responders, insurance carriers, prescription and over-the-counter drugs and first aid supplies.
Operation	Basic shelter, electricity, light, heat, clothing, tools and water needs.
Recreation	The means of providing enjoyment, pleasure and relief from stress during a disaster including games, music, books and sports.

It does not matter what <u>type</u> of disasters (earthquake, flood, wind) are involved – the focus is on what happens to our **health** as a consequence of that disaster. For example, during a hurricane, one family received ample warning and was able to seek refuge in an underground shelter. Once the hurricane passed through the area, all family members were able to leave the shelter and come to the surface. The family was now safe, alive and their health was preserved.

On the other hand, another family was unable to reach the underground shelter in time. As a result of flying debris, one family member was struck in the leg by a metal stake and another family member received severe head injuries. In this case, after the hurricane passed through the area, both families are safe and alive – but health is threatened for the second family who did not seek shelter in time. Again - there is one and only one goal or objective for each of us to have during any level of disaster:

> # PRESERVE AND MAINTAIN OUR PHYSICAL, MENTAL, EMOTIONAL, PSYCHOLOGICAL AND SPIRITUAL <u>HEALTH</u>

ALTERNATIVES OR LAYERS

Another important strategy in emergency preparation planning is to have numerous choices and options in providing for the various elements. <u>The more layers – the better chance of maintaining health and safety during an emergency.</u> For example, for the **OPERATION** Element and to have light during an emergency, you could include a *flashlight, lamp, lantern* and *candles* in emergency preparation pantries. For the **COMMUNICATION** Element, you could include a solar powered and hand-crank *radio*, a *walkie-talkie* and perhaps a *ham radio system*. For the **MEDICATION** Element, you could include *bandages, antibiotics* and *alcohol wipes*. Again, when purchasing and preparing for each element, include an assortment of supplies to meet your needs – and if possible, purchase supplies that do <u>not</u> require electrical power, batteries or other fuel sources. During many disasters, electricity, water and fuel will not be available for short-term and long-term scenarios.

LEVELS

When making an analysis of disaster scenarios, it is obvious there are millions of possibilities. As a result of any disaster scenario, there will likely be consequences that take place to one or more of the elements. For example, a disaster could be a 4.2 earthquake in Kansas that causes minimal damage or a 9.7 earthquake in Los Angeles, California that takes out many of the power lines. The <u>consequence</u> of the 9.7 earthquake was disruption of electricity (and possibly water) for many residents. This earthquake was the direct cause of the **OPERATION** Element (electricity/water) being disrupted.

On the other hand, the residents in Kansas did not have any disruption in services. Instead of attempting to prepare an emergency plan based on a <u>specific</u> disaster or combination of disasters, it is more prudent to <u>classify</u> disasters into three <u>levels</u> (1-3) based on (1) the elements that are affected; (2) the severity of the consequences and (3) the duration the element is compromised or disrupted.

The disaster levels are outlined in the table below:

LEVEL	DURATION
1	*1 hour to 7 days*
2	*7 days to 1 month*
3	*1 month to 1 year*

CONCEPT

	DISASTER	CONSEQUENCES	ELEMENTS	DURATION SEVERITY	LEVELS
EXPLANATION	Disaster occurs that includes one or more types i.e. flood, earthquake etc.	And as a result of the disaster, there are consequences	Consequences can affect one or more of the 16 elements maintaining our *health*	Depending on the length of time and the severity of the consequences on the affected elements	The disaster is categorized into 3 distinct levels: Level 1 is minimum and Level 3 is maximum
EXAMPLE	**Earthquake**	Takes out some power lines but alternatives are available	**OPERATION**	2 weeks	2
		Hospital damaged but alternate sites are available	**MEDICATION**	10 weeks	3

DISASTER TIMELINE

Depending on the point in time of the disaster – the less or more resources will be required to sustain the health and well-being of the survival team members. For example, if the duration of the disaster is between one month and one year, one must recognize that there will be different types and amounts of resources that will be needed at the beginning of this disaster (one month) versus at the end of this disaster (one year). As the length of time increases in a disaster and more elements are compromised or disabled – there will be less resources available and public dissention and violence could escalate to dramatic proportions.

> *Man was made at the end of the week's work when God was tired.*
>
> **- Mark Twain**

← Less Resources Needed **LEVEL THREE DISASTER TIMELINE** More Resources Needed →

| One Month BEGINNING | Three Months | Six Months | Nine Months | One Year END |

PRIMARY RESIDENCE

The primary residence is generally the main residence or house occupied by a majority of the survival team members. The primary residence could also be a cabin, motor home, trailer house, camper, office or other structure available to survival team members. In some cases, all team members (an entire family) will already reside at the primary residence. Team members may also reside in homes within a few miles of one another.

Regardless of the circumstances, it is generally advisable to select <u>one</u> residence or building to serve as the primary residence. This structure will be used to store a <u>majority</u> of the emergency supplies and items. <u>The primary residence is the principal location where team members will gather and reside during</u> *some* <u>short-term but</u> *most* <u>medium-term and long-term disasters.</u>

For short-term disasters lasting only a few hours or even a few days, team members who do not permanently reside at the designated primary residence may choose to stay in their own homes and should have basic supplies stored in the home for such emergency situations. This eliminates the need to travel to the primary residence site if circumstances do not warrant the move.

On the other hand, for Level 2 (lasting a month) and Level 3 disasters, it may be better for all team members to converge at the primary residence – where a majority of the emergency supplies should be stored to support disasters lasting a longer duration of time.

When evaluating the location for the primary residence, consider the following criteria as part of the selection process:

- The building is easily accessible for all survival team members to gather during a disaster. All persons will be able to walk (or with assistance - get there) to the location. <u>Everyone agrees that this location will be the best place to designate as the primary residence.</u>

- The legal ownership of the structure is under the control and management of at least one of the survival team members.

- A large or significant amount of resources are already available at the location, i.e., fireplace, wood-burning stove, solar panels, orchard, root cellar, natural water sources, large capacity and environmentally sound storage spaces (basement), etc.

- There is enough room in the structure to comfortably accommodate all survival team members, i.e., spacious kitchen, adequate sleeping areas, bathrooms, laundry facilities and a room to serve as the designated "shelter-in-place location.

- The building structure is sound and in good condition including the foundation, beams, roof and chimney.

- There are no obvious hazards in and around the structure or surrounding area including items that can move, fall or break during an emergency situation.

- The location is clean, uncluttered and free of debris in and around the building.

- The structure accommodates any handicapped or disabled team members.

- The utilities supporting the structure (water, gas, electricity, sewer/septic tank) have infrastructure in good condition and able to withstand damage that could occur during a disaster. For example, all large appliances including the water heater have been secured to wall studs, all electrical panels and wiring meets or exceeds code requirements, water taps and lines are not corroded, rusty or have any leaks, toilets are working properly and in good condition, flexible gas and water connections are installed on all gas appliances, propane tanks have approved valves that operate properly and sewer and/or septic tanks do not have any obvious problems that could cause sewage backups.

When selecting the primary residence, attempt to select a location that offers the least amount of problems that could occur *before*, *during* and *after* a disaster. By avoiding potential damage and destruction to the primary residence, the survival team members can reduce stress, anxiety and apprehension and focus on maintaining health for the duration of the crisis.

SURVIVAL TEAM SELECTION

A <u>major</u> task when creating an emergency preparation plan is to determine who will be included in the group that will purchase and consume the supplies in the emergency pantries and will also share in the responsibilities and duties of implementing the overall emergency plan. All survival team members should contribute to the overall emergency preparation plan – both with ideas and actions. Although discussion is certainly reasonable and warranted – all team members must agree and understand *in advance* on all or most of the emergency plan to be utilized by survival team members *before*, *during* and *after* a disaster.

The team will generally include all individuals living at the primary residence – or in other words - the family members. However, other individuals may also be included as part of the survival team when creating the emergency plan. For example, if elderly parents, children, siblings, friends, relatives, neighbors or other individuals who <u>live in close vicinity</u> to the physical primary residence and are physically close enough to be included as part of the team, then they could be included as part of the group.

When setting up the survival team, consider skills and talents that could be used by each team member in an emergency. There may be some members who will be more active in emergency preparation *prior* to the emergency, i.e., purchasing and storing supplies. Other members will become important *during* and *after* the disaster, i.e., lifting and carrying heavy items or providing medical assistance. As a disaster reaches Level 3 proportions, individual survival teams can then band together with other survival teams to create highly effective and successful groups that can work together for the benefit of all survival team members.

Another important consideration is to <u>carefully</u> consider the logistical probabilities of all members being able to congregate at the designated primary residence either *before*, *during* or *after* the disaster. A good rule to follow would be to ask the following question of candidates under consideration to join the team:

HOW FAR AWAY DOES THE CANDIDATE LIVE FROM THE DESIGNATED PRIMARY RESIDENCE AND DURING ANY DISASTER THAT <u>IMPEDES TRANSPORTATION</u> – COULD THE CANDIDATE(S) REASONABLY TRAVEL <u>ON FOOT</u> TO THE PRIMARY RESIDENCE WHERE EMERGENCY PREPARATION SUPPLIES ARE STORED OR COULD ANOTHER MEMBER OF THE SURVIVAL TEAM BRING THE CANDIDATE ON FOOT TO THE PRIMARY RESIDENCE?

If the answer is **NO** – then as hard as it may be – these individuals should set up their own survival team and store all emergency supplies at their own primary residence. To ignore this important principle is to leave individuals with no emergency supplies because they are not realistically able to travel to the designated primary residence of the team. This would include candidates that simply live too far away or who are handicapped or disabled and would not be able to walk the distance.

In a <u>small</u> town – it may be realistic to include anyone who lives in the community, providing they are healthy and able to walk to the designated primary residence. However, anyone living in towns and cities that are further away should set up their own survival team. As a <u>general</u> rule, if there is at least five to ten miles separating a possible candidate and the designated primary residence – the candidate should set up his/her own survival team.

Encourage all other family members, relatives, friends and neighbors to set up their own respective teams to guarantee that everyone is included in a survival team. This will eliminate serious problems during a disaster when non-survival team members come knocking on the door seeking sanctuary – and request or even demand that your survival team members provide them with needed resources and supplies during the term of the disaster.

> *If patience is worth anything, it must endure to the end of time. And a living faith will last in the midst of the blackest storm.*
>
> **- Mahatma Gandhi**

Carefully evaluate the willingness and ability of all members to get along with one another and be able to work together as a cohesive unit – as a strong and unified team. It is during a serious disaster that human dynamics release hidden negative attitudes and destructive opinions can surface between team members. If there is any likelihood that some members will not be able to work together as a unit – the time is before a disaster occurs to make arrangements for separate survival teams and a different primary residence for those members.

I cannot stress enough the importance of serious consideration and deliberation in determining who will belong to the survival team. Make absolutely certain that all team members understand the significance of the survival team concept, the responsibilities and duties that come with their inclusion in the team and their ability to support and contribute to the overall team *before*, *during* and *after* a disaster.

COMBINING SURVIVAL TEAM SUPPLIES

Depending on the level of the emergency, individual survival teams will begin to band together to form highly efficient and incredibility strong groups that can work together to maintain the overall health of all members. This is where community, church, and neighborhoods really show their stuff!

Although it is certainly practical to work with other survival teams to prepare for future emergencies, there are several considerations and conditions that merit careful scrutiny before combining forces. During "good" times, most team members would be willing to give a cup of sugar to a neighbor who came to the door and asked for the favor. No problem. But during "disaster" times - the line of generosity is not so clear.

There are specific emergency supplies where combining forces with other survival teams to gather and purchase items would be sensible. For example, when purchasing medical supplies and first aid items, it may be sensible for several survival teams to go in together and purchase an entire box or carton of bandages and then split the contents equally between the survival teams. No one team would be given the entire carton of bandages to store in their primary residence. Instead, each survival team would store their share of the bandages in their own respective primary residence.

There are some so-called "emergency" items that could legitimately be divided among several survival teams, and during a disaster, the teams could exchange and share the supplies with each other. For example, although survival teams having recreation supplies in emergency pantries is an important consideration, the ultimate survival of the survival team is not contingent on a badminton set, horseshoes, board games or the soccer ball.

In the case of recreation supplies, and in order to help tight emergency preparation budgets for individual teams - by all means - combine forces! Each survival team could be assigned to gather specific recreational items with the agreement that all teams would share the supplies among each other during the disaster. If one team decides to keep the soccer ball for themselves and not share - the rest of the teams will still live to see another day.

Another area where combining forces is good, and will more than likely be required is actually protecting team members and possessions during a serious disaster. Survival teams can combine together and set up schedules where each team will take turns in guarding the area or standing watch over team members, property and supplies.

Due to the overall cost of some emergency preparation supplies and equipment, individual survival teams may decide it would be smart to combine with other survival teams to purchase higher priced items and share the cost. For example, instead of a survival team purchasing a solar powered generator costing several thousand dollars, several teams could go into together and buy one - that way, no one team would have to pay the entire price and the cost would be spread over several teams. On the surface, this plan would seem like a good idea. But then the questions must be asked: (1) where will the generator actually be stored, (2) which team will be responsible for the safety and security of the item, (3) what happens if one team moves to another location, (4) what happens if the generator gets stolen or damaged - who pays for the repairs, *and more importantly* (5) <u>during a disaster</u>, how will the schedule be set up for each survival team to use the generator at their primary residence.

This is where serious problems can erupt in a very short period of time. For example, depending on the severity and duration of the disaster, the team who actually has *physical* possession of the generator may not be as willing to abide by the sharing and scheduling agreement created between teams when the generator was purchased. Parents may resist giving up the generator because of the belief their need for electric power is greater than that of other survival teams who have an equal, justifiable and legitimate right to also use the generator.

In order to avoid explosive confrontations and volatile situations, survival teams should plan to purchase, gather and store <u>most</u> emergency supplies at their own primary residence, and with very few exceptions, avoid sharing the cost, sharing the supplies and sharing the storage with other teams. By following this rule, if a survival team decides to share supplies with other teams, they will maintain the freedom of choice and power to do so.

EMERGENCY PREPARATION PRINCIPLES

As with all emergencies, it is essential to *prepare in advance* of a crisis and eliminate excessive stress, anxiety and pressure. By addressing needs and concerns <u>prior to any emergency</u>, issues can be eliminated in getting essential supplies and resources during a disaster situation. For example, depending on the severity of the disaster, our water supply could be contaminated. By *planning in advance*, we can have water stored in containers that would be available for us during the crisis.

There are thirty-one <u>general</u> principles that should be incorporated into the overall emergency plan to prepare for and in some cases eliminate problems and issues that become prevalent during a disaster situation. These general principles apply to *all* elements:

- **Create a comprehensive emergency preparation plan** for the survival team.

- *Plan in advance* of an emergency to substantially improve your chances of a healthy survival.

- When gathering and purchasing supplies, it is essential to **follow-through** and **drill down** (analyze) to make sure all supplies and equipment are kept safe and secure, properly stored, operating correctly and you know how the supplies and/or equipment will be used in a <u>disaster</u> environment. Do not confuse the way the supply or equipment is used in a "normal" environment with the way it will be used in a "disaster" environment.

- **Buy on sale and buy in bulk** whenever possible.

- **Get out of debt** and live within your means.

- **Become simple minded and uncomplicated**. When planning, attempt to utilize simple and uncomplicated procedures, processes and methods when purchasing, gathering, processing and storing emergency supplies.

12

- **Purchase supplies (whenever possible) that do <u>not</u> require electrical power (including batteries), water or fuel (including gas and propane)**. Attempt to purchase equipment that can be <u>solar</u> or <u>manually</u> operated.

- **Know your inventory and where it is stored**. Know how many supplies you have and make sure they are readily available and logistically located for easy access and transport.

- Survival teams should plan to **purchase, gather and store <u>most</u> emergency supplies at their own primary residence** and with very few exceptions, avoid sharing the cost, sharing the supplies and sharing the storage with other teams.

- **All items should be packaged and stored in the appropriate packing materials or containers**. Whenever practical, package like items together and on each container, label what is inside. Alphabetize the contents on the label for ease in identifying the items in the container.

- **Analyze risks and assess talents and skills needed to deal with emergencies**. On a continual basis, be aware of your surroundings, what is happening in the world and how any changes could affect you and your team.

- **Learn to become proficient in life-saving skills** by becoming CERT certified or proficient in CPR and other life-saving techniques, knowing how to start a fire, growing a garden, bottling fruits and vegetables, baking bread, preparing a meal using a campfire or using herbs for medicinal purposes.

- **Maintain consistent order and cleanliness** by keeping the primary residence and surrounding buildings in good repair; appliances and other mechanical, electronic or electrical equipment in good condition; gas tanks full in cars being used regularly, and keep the yard clean and free of debris and trash at all times.

- **Anticipate fears** and begin thinking about what would frighten you the most if forced to survive alone. The goal is to build confidence in your ability to function despite your fears.

- **Be realistic** in planning and remember that during disaster, the environment, atmosphere and surroundings will be different – plan accordingly for easy and uncomplicated tasks and actions. Don't be afraid to make an honest appraisal of situations.

- **<u>All</u> team members must be expected to fulfill their assigned tasks, duties and responsibilities based on the overall emergency plan.** Exceptions would be small children, the elderly, injury, death or unavailability at the primary residence or place of refuge in the event of evacuation. <u>Women and older children should understand that they must carry their own weight and can not depend on spouses, boyfriends or other male members of the team to shoulder their responsibilities.</u>

- **Every person has different priorities, values and morals** as circumstances change based on new situations and events that occur in our lives. As we move towards higher disaster levels, we will continue to change our outlook on life, death and survival issues. <u>Our priorities will change.</u>

- **Not everyone is as wholesome, sincere, nice, kind, honest, non-violent, upstanding and truthful as you are during and after a disaster.** As individuals become more stressed and fearful of a situation, and as the level of disaster increases, recognize not only what you are – but also what you are not – for better or for worse.

- **Adopt a positive attitude and have faith in a spiritual force**. Learn to see the potential good in everything. Looking for the good not only boosts morale but is excellent for exercising imagination and creativity.

- **Investigate and include alternatives, layers and options** when gathering resources and supplies.

- **Remind yourself what is at stake** and remember that failure to prepare yourself psychologically to cope with survival leads to reactions such as depression, carelessness, loss of confidence, poor decision-making and a feeling of hopelessness. All team members would be expected to accomplish assignments and tasks in an expedient and thorough manner.

- Always **hope for the best but expect the worst case scenario** - that way, if things are better, you can smile, but if things are worse, you have *planned in advance* - and you can still smile. WIN/WIN

- **Conduct practice drills** on a semi-annual basis so plans and tasks are done in an efficient and expedient manner.

- **Do not overly publicize your overall emergency preparation plan** to others or divulge the location of resources and supplies.

- If teams find themselves in the middle of a disaster, they may be **the last to know what is really going on**. The rest of the world will likely be informed via public media and access to information for those in the middle of the disaster may be sparse or unavailable.

- **The main emphasis for the survival team is to support the needs of its members**. Although charity, sharing and compassion are important, it may not be feasible or realistic to provide emergency supplies to others outside of your team circle during a serious and long-term disaster. Everyone is responsible to prepare themselves for these events.

- **Prioritize, purchase, gather and store supplies needed** for efficient operations during an emergency using a regimented plan *appropriate for the circumstances of your family*. Know the difference between a *need* and a *want* but recognize that in many cases, *want* items can make the difference between a healthy mental and psychological outlook or severe depression and anxiety during a disaster.

- While making preparations for these future events – **live in the present**. Appreciate every single leaf on the trees, every drop of rain falling to the ground and every sunbeam that shines on our world. Every day, get down on your knees and thank God for what you have - *and* what you don't have.

- Every single day as you **perform a task** - step back and ask yourself *if* and *how* this task would be performed during a disaster situation. Analyze every single step it takes to perform the task and make sure you are prepared to do these steps in a disaster environment.

- When considering any type of emergency supply, **drill down** (analyze) and consider any other complement items that would be required to utilize or consume the supply, i.e. for flashlights that require batteries, you will also need to purchase rechargeable batteries and possibly a solar-powered battery charger in order to recharge the batteries.

- Depending on the type of disaster, intensity, season, weather, time of day, or location – **government assistance to individual citizens may not be available**.

It is up to each citizen to recognize that **SELF SUFFICIENCY** is a key factor for survival. As a minimum, citizens should plan on taking care of themselves for no less than seven days and up to a year in the event of a serious and long-term disaster. Government officials, workers and first responders will be assigned roles to perform during emergencies. The focus will be on ensuring that overall utilities are working, fires are controlled, medical services are available and roads are passable. First priority will not be to support individual citizens. Depending on the severity and length of the disaster, government personnel may not reach entire towns and/or individuals for days, weeks or even months after the disaster.

NORMAL VERSUS DISASTER ENVIRONMENT

One of the most important concepts when *preparing in advance* for a disaster is to (1) examine the way you perform simple everyday tasks in this <u>normal</u> environment, (2) consider whether or not these same tasks could or would *realistically* need to be done in a <u>disaster</u> environment, and then (3) analyze how these same tasks could be done in a <u>disaster</u> environment - and especially without the use of *electricity*, *fuel* and *water*. For example:

- In a *normal* environment, and if we want a loaf of bread, we simply get in our car, buy a loaf of bread at the store and bring it home - walla! We have bread! In a *disaster* environment (and without electricity, fuel and water) - the market would be closed and we will either go without bread, barter for bread or make our own bread at home. If the team decides to make homemade bread, it will be necessary to purchase whole wheat (or flour) and it must be properly stored to avoid spoilage, a good manual wheat grinder (if using wheat) will have to be purchased, additional ingredients will have to be properly stored in order to make bread, you must know how to make homemade bread, and more importantly, some means of baking the bread *without* electricity and fuel will have to be considered.

- In a *normal* environment, we take a bath or shower and then dry ourselves with a large bath towel. After using the towel a few times, we throw it in the laundry hamper and later wash and dry the towel using the washing machine (requires electricity/fuel and water) and the dryer (requires electricity/fuel). In a *disaster* environment, that large bath towel will have to be washed by hand and dried using some other alternative other than the clothes dryer. As part of *planning in advance*, the team should consider some other alternative other than using a large bath towel - perhaps a paper towel that can be either thrown away after use, used again to wipe up spills or as a fire starter.

- In a *normal* environment, if we want to contact someone down the street, in another city or state, or even somewhere else in the world, we simply grab our cell phone or access email and within minutes we have immediate communication. If we want to see and hear important local, national or world news - again, we get on the Internet or cell phone, read the newspaper or simply turn on our television sets or listen to the radio. In a *disaster* environment, there may be no land line phone, no cell phone, no Internet, no post office, no television and no radio. Teams must recognize the severe limitations and restrictions that may be placed on any and all communication. There may be no way of knowing what is happening on the other side of town or in another state or country. As part of *planning in advance*, team members must consider other means to contact and communicate with individual members using primitive means of communication such as (are you ready) talking and writing hand-written notes.

The above examples are several of thousands of possible scenarios that can affect every element. As part of *planning in advance* - the practice of **continually** and **regularly** examining normal everyday tasks and analyzing how these same tasks could be performed in a disaster environment without electricity, fuel or water is absolutely critical. All team members must *step back*, *think through* and *drill down* to find alternative methods and processes to simple everyday tasks that will work in a disaster environment.

PANTRIES AND KITS

An emergency preparation plan is not just about storing food in a food pantry. When *planning in advance* for a disaster, it is impossible to guess every scenario that will occur during the crisis or where you will be located when disaster strikes the area. It is necessary to prepare several different types of emergency pantries – or kits – so that you will be ready for whatever consequence may come your way during an emergency situation.

> *Every choice you make has an end result.*
> - **Zig Ziglar**

There are seven <u>types</u> of emergency pantries or kits that should be considered as part of the overall emergency preparation plan:

1.   **PRIMARY RESIDENCE** – the major emergency pantry will be at the designated primary residence and will include the largest and most diverse supplies to accommodate *short*, *medium* and *long-term* disasters.

2.   **WORK** – this emergency kit would be located at your place(s) of employment and would include basic supplies that would be helpful to accommodate *short-term* emergencies.

3.   **AUTO** – this emergency kit would be located in your automobile and would include basic supplies that would be helpful to accommodate *short-term* emergencies. Depending on the size of the car and the space available to store emergency items, this kit can include basic essentials and luxury items as well.

4.   **PLACE OF REFUGE** - this emergency pantry could be a fully stocked cabin or summer home, camper, motor home, trailer house, or even hidden survival supplies at a predetermined location in the mountains or desert. It could also be a public shelter in the event the survival team has no other options. It is the place of refuge for the team if the primary residence has been damaged or destroyed or the pre-selected primary location for team members to reside during the disaster. It could be used for both short and long-term emergencies.

5.   **EVACUATION** – the evacuation kit (sometimes referred to as the 72-hour kit) contains basic supplies for each survival team member to survive a minimum of *seven days*. This particular kit should be ready, accessible and easy to transport. Team members could seek shelter at the place of refuge or sites such as a church, school or approved public shelter in the vicinity.

6.   **FIRST AID** – the emergency kit includes medical and first aid supplies and is part of the five pantries and kits listed above. Depending on the kit, first aid supplies will include basic or more advanced items.

7.   **DOCUMENTATION** – the kit includes important documentation and is part of the six pantries and kits listed above. The documentation to be added will differ depending on the specific pantry or kit.

PRIMARY RESIDENCE PANTRY

The Primary Residence Pantry is the pantry containing a majority of the goods and supplies. In many cases, survival team members could live in different residences other than the primary residence such as a house, apartment, condominium or even a trailer in a trailer park. Although all pantries are important, this pantry is the most important pantry to begin preparing as a beginning student to emergency preparation.

> *Some say the world will end in fire – some say in ice.*
>
> **-Robert Frost**

Remember – the primary residence would be the main residence or house occupied by a majority of the survival team members and would be the principal location where team members would gather and reside during *some* short term emergencies, *most* middle-term disasters and *all* long-term disasters. The priorities of each survival team are going to be unique depending on their respective circumstances. Throughout this book is detailed information on each element (**Operation, Medication, Documentation** etc.) and the supplies and items that could be included as part of that element.

At the conclusion of most chapters, I provide a summary list of supplies for that respective element. The items identified in **bold UPPERCASE** are those items that I consider to be *high priority* supplies due to the critical part they play in our overall health. The items identified in **bold** are *important* supplies. As a beginning student, I would recommend that you begin purchasing and gathering items identified in **bold UPPERCASE** and then **bold** - and if additional financial resources become available, other items can be included in the Primary Residence Pantry.

In some cases, supplies will serve multiple uses. For example, on these lists, you will see a shovel and axe are listed several times, but it is not necessary to purchase several shovels or axes. One good shovel and axe will suffice to serve all purposes. However, you may notice that some items may be listed more than once, i.e., buckets, but will have an **asterisk** (*). **This means that you will need to purchase several buckets for _different_ purposes**. Remember in some cases, the amount needed for each item will be determined by the number of survival team members.

WORK AND AUTO KITS

These kits could perhaps hold more and heavier items because a larger space may be available for storage. Depending on how many items are included in the auto kit, they can be stored in a duffle bag, box, plastic container or large plastic tote. A small tote or hard plastic container could be used at work to store emergency supplies. If you have a locker or other assigned area, the storage container would have to accommodate the assigned space allocation.

> **If funds for emergency preparation are scarce, do not spend a fortune on the auto and work kits! Buy or gather only the basics! This list is not intended to infer that all items should be included – or are even necessary. If you already have items on the list that could be included – by all means – do so, but don't spend money to stock an auto kit on "luxury" items when the money could be spent on more important supplies.**

AUTOMOTIVE

I recognize that based on the auto list, not all items will be practical for all individuals. For example, if you live in a region where the temperature never drops below 90 degrees – you probably don't need to worry about having anti-freeze or a heavy-duty coat, hat, socks and gloves. On the other hand, everyone should have a heavy-duty pair of gloves for work, a hat to protect from sunburn and a light pair of clean socks. Most men won't need to bother about having hair ties – this item is reserved for persons with long hair to keep it out of their face. If you use a sleeping bag – you probably won't need blankets. You get the idea.

> *It's easier to resist at the beginning than at the end.*
>
> **-Leonardo da Vinci**

I would also strongly recommend that you purchase solar powered flashlights and lanterns and a solar/hand-crank radio – that way you don't have to store batteries. Try to avoid items requiring batteries – when the time comes to use the auto kit – the batteries would probably be dead. Finally, plan for the worst case scenario – always assume that you will NOT be able to continually leave the car running and that the car will sit dormant during the disaster; there will be no heat or light supplied by the car.

Survivalists may wonder about the solar garden light. No – I wasn't suggesting that you create a lovely yard around your stalled car. Place the garden light outside during the day and then bring it back into the car at night for an all-night light source. You can use the light to drink the mixture of baking soda, salt and water – a recipe to reduce shock. The hammer, twine, tarp and nails may be needed to make a tent shelter if the car can not be used.

AUTO KIT

Anti-Freeze	**Map** (surrounding areas including driving and topical)
AXE	**MATCHES**
Baby Supplies (formula, diapers, etc.)	**MEDICAL EQUIPMENT** (oxygen, walker, inhaler)
Baking Soda	**MEDICATION** (prescription/over-the-counter drugs)
Binoculars	**Motor Oil**

BLANKETS	Nails
BOOTS	**NOTEPAD**
BUCKET * (heavy-duty plastic, folding or collapsible)	**PAPER AND PENCILS**
Cards, Games, Books	Paper Towels
Cash and Coins (for telephone calls)	**PLASTIC GROCERY BAGS** (human waste)
Cell Phone	Plastic Ties
CLOTHES (practical change of clothes)	**POCKET KNIFE**
Coat (heavy-duty and/or warm)	**RADIO** (solar/hand crank)
Comb/Brush	**RAIN GEAR**
Compass	**ROPE/CORD/TWINE** (towing, rescue, shelter etc.)
Cup (paper and/or metal)	**Safety Glasses**
DOCUMENTATION (See Documentation List)	**SALT** and/or sand
Dust Mask	Scissors
Eating Utensils – Plastic (knife, fork, spoon)	Sewing Kit
Eyeglasses and Eyeglass Repair Kit (if applicable)	**SHOES – STURDY**
Fan (hand held)	**SHOVEL** (collapsible)
Feminine Hygiene Products	**SIGNAL DEVICE** (light sticks, mirror, flasher)
Fire Starter	**SLEEPING BAG**
FIRST AID KIT AND MANUAL (See First Aid List)	Soap
Flag (fluorescent distress)	**SOCKS** (one warm pair PLUS one light pair)
FLASHLIGHT (solar powered)	**SOLAR GARDEN LIGHT**
Flint Striker	**SPARE TIRE**
FOOD*(non perishable - meat, vegetables, fruits, jerky, bars)	Sunglasses
FUNNEL – 2 (one for gas and one for water)	**TARP/TARP CLIPS** (tent if car unavailable)
Fuses	**Tire Chains**
GARBAGE BAGS – heavy-duty (3)	**Tire Pressure Gauge**
Gas Can	**Tissues** (facial)
GLOVES (one warm pair PLUS one heavy-duty pair)	**TOILET** (collapsible commode, bucket*, etc.)
Hair Ties	**TOILET PAPER**
Hand Sanitizer	**TOOLS** (pliers, wrench, hammer, screwdriver)
Hand Warmer	Toothbrush / Toothpaste
HAT (warm and/or light)	Toothpicks/Floss
INSECT REPELLENT	**Tow Chain**
JACK	**TOWELETTES** (pre-moistened)
JUMPER CABLES	**WATER**
Keys (extra set for home)	**Water Purification Tablets**
Lantern (solar powered)	Weapon/Ammo
Lip Balm	**Windshield Scraper**
Lotion	

* food should include easy open cans and require no cooking

WORK

Depending on the type of disaster, the electrical power may be out, the water may be shut off and the plumbing could be damaged or destroyed. Restaurants and other commercial markets may also be experiencing the same utility problems. Transportation could be severely impacted and you may be forced to remain at work for several days.

WORK KIT

BLANKET	Keys (extra set for home and car)
Bucket with lid (you guessed it – a toilet)	**Lantern** (solar powered)
Cards, Games and Books	**Lip Balm**
Cash and Coins	Map (detailed of local area)

Cell Phone	**MEDICATIONS**
CHANGE OF CLOTHES (casual/work)	**Plastic Bags – heavy-duty** (for the bucket)
Comb/Brush	**RADIO** (solar/hand crank)
Cup	**Sleeping Bag** (light weight)
Documentation (see **DOCUMENTATION** List)	**SOAP**
Dust Mask	**SOLAR GARDEN LIGHT** (used for light)
Eating Utensils (plastic)	**STURDY SHOES**
Eyeglasses / Contact Lens Solution	**TOILET PAPER**
FEMININE HYGIENE SUPPLIES	**Toiletries** (Miscellaneous)
First Aid Kit (small)	**Toothbrush**
FLASHLIGHT (solar/hand crank)	**Toothpaste**
FOOD* (nonperishable items)	**Towelettes** (pre-moistened)
Hand Sanitizer	**WATER** (bottled)
Jacket or Sweatshirt (cold months)	Whistle

* food should include flip-top cans and require no cooking

Keep in mind that you should be able to store more and heavier items at work, regardless of whether you have an office, cubicle or locker. Depending on how many items you choose to include in the work pantry kit and where you plan to store them, they could be stored in a drawer, duffle bag, box, plastic container or plastic tote - or in the bucket to be used as a toilet. Although not all items on this list will be practical for all individuals, it provides some good selections of both *needs* and *wants* on the priority list. If you drive a car to work - remember you should also have emergency supplies in your car out in the parking lot.

Why are soap, toilet paper and feminine supplies on the WORK list? During an emergency, your co-workers may not be as prepared as you but will realize they need these items. Unless you can run to the restroom faster than they can – they will get it all –you will get none. And the bucket? To be used for broken toilets and damaged sewer lines that would make using the restroom a real problem!

EVACUATION KIT

As part of evacuation from the primary residence, an emergency evacuation kit will provide each family member with food, water and other necessary items to survive during the time the team remains at a refuge location. Although planning for a three-day evacuation from the home is good, it is more likely your stay at the place of refuge may be longer, and since smart planning includes "*worst case scenario*" - attempt to prepare 7-10 day emergency evacuation kits for each member of the team.

Parents should recognize that although it is necessary to show young children compassion and understanding while preparing the child's kit and during the evacuation process, it is critical for children to follow instructions and meet their responsibilities – even if strong words and a firm hand are required.

As a team, include children in the planning process and attempt to make the project appear as an adventure and not a fearful challenge for younger team members. Practice *in advance* with children so they are familiar with the process and understand their role in an evacuation. Once in a public shelter, <u>management and other refugees will demand that parents manage and control their children for the benefit of all who are housed in the facility</u>. When preparing emergency kits for children, always consider what items will serve to calm and comfort the child during this time, including comfort foods, blankets, games, books and favorite toys.

When preparing evacuation kits, families should remember disasters can occur at any time - during any season - during any temperature. Hot or cold. Wet or dry. Depending on the weather conditions and temperature, it makes a huge difference on what would be needed in the kits - especially for meal preparation. For example, in the winter, many areas experience sleet, hail, rain and snow as well as frigid temperatures and survival would depend on finding an inside shelter. For safety and security reasons, public shelters will <u>not</u> allow fire or fuel inside the buildings so cooking would have to be done outside. In the middle of the winter, this could prove to be a problem. Each kit should contain food items that do not require cooking and can be eaten right out of the package or can.

On the other hand, during summer months, teams may be able to camp outside on the grounds adjacent to a public shelter and have a small fire to prepare meals. In this case, kits could include a small butane stove, fire starter, flint striker, cooking utensils and food requiring heat or cooking. Remember - even though a healthy human being can survive without food for up to three weeks, living in a public shelter for a week and eating beef jerky and hard candy can prove to be very stressful - especially for small children. Teams should attempt to prepare for all contingencies when selecting food items, but to be safe, think of the <u>worst case scenario</u> (middle of winter) and include food that can be opened using the hand and does not require heating - if space is limited, this eliminates the need to carry can openers and items used for heating and/or cooking the food.

<u>**Every survival team member should have their own emergency evacuation kit and with few exceptions, should be expected to carry it during the evacuation.**</u> Only very small children, the disabled, or senior citizens in poor health should be assisted in carrying their kit. The emergency kits should be stored in a location that is easy to access, easy to carry, easy to identify and easy to transport out of the primary residence and to the designated place of refuge. As part of *planning in advance*, every kit should be <u>clearly marked and identified as to ownership</u> and every team member should know where the kits are located, recognize their own kit, know how to carry it and be able to carry it to a place of refuge. Someone should also be assigned to carry the bag containing pet supplies, if applicable. Most public shelters will not allow pets inside the building - consider other options for your pets and/or livestock including pet shelters, friends, neighbors or other family members or restraining your pet on the grounds outside of the shelter.

The items for the emergency kit must be stored in a <u>water-proof</u> backpack, duffle bag, suitcase, box or plastic container. If the storage unit is not water-proof, make sure that it is completely covered with a <u>heavy-duty</u> garbage bag in the event it rains during the evacuation. This kit is generally the most complicated to prepare because of conflicting priorities and limited space. To be forced to choose between taking one item and leaving another is a difficult – even excruciating process. When evaluating whether or not to include any item in the kit – ask yourself this question:

> **WILL THIS ITEM BE REQUIRED TO PRESERVE AND MAINTAIN MY *PHYSICAL*, *MENTAL*, *EMOTIONAL*, *PSYCHOLOGICAL* AND *SPIRITUAL* HEALTH FOR THE DURATION OF THIS SHORT-TERM DISASTER AND IS IT SO IMPORTANT THAT I AM READY, WILLING AND ABLE TO CARRY IT – ALONG WITH ALL OTHER ITEMS - TO THE NEW LOCATION? IF THE ANSWER IS NO – LEAVE IT BEHIND. IF THE ANSWER IS YES – INCLUDE THE ITEM IN THE KIT.**

When gathering supplies to be included in emergency evacuation kits, **THINK SMALL**. This kit provides supplies for a <u>short-term</u> emergency – up to 7-10 days. If lotion and hand sanitizer are items to be included in your kit – buy travel size bottles – that's all you will need. Whenever possible, avoid any item that requires batteries! Unless the kits are inspected on a regular basis and batteries are replaced, your team may discover that during an emergency, battery-powered items no longer work because of dead batteries. ALWAYS attempt to purchase or gather solar-powered items.

Not every survival team member must have identical items in their packs. For example, a collapsible shovel is an important item to include in an evacuation kit, but not every survival team member must have one in their individual pack. Only one shovel would be needed – simply designate which team member will carry it in their pack. Analyze other items to see if only one is needed or if everyone should have the item in their individual pack.

One of the biggest challenges will be to have enough water in the kit. Water is heavy – one gallon weighs eight pounds. Every person should have one gallon of water per day for a minimum of <u>at least</u> three days – that's twenty-four very heavy pounds of water to carry with you. For even a seven day supply, each member would require seventy-two pounds - which is unrealistic and even a hefty male would find it difficult to carry a three day supply of water plus other supplies in a duffle bag. The amount of water to be included in the evacuation kit for each person depends on several rather prejudicial but realistic factors, including:

- **Gender** (men and boys can lift and carry more than women and girls – face it)
- **Age** (very young children and very old adults will not be able to carry as much – face it)
- **Strength** (men and boys generally have more <u>physical</u> strength than women and girls – face it)
- **Fitness** (this is where equality levels out – females can be as physically fit as males)
- **Disabled** (a majority of disabled or handicapped individuals will have trouble - face it)

Due to the "heavy" requirement of needing <u>at least</u> three gallons of water in addition to all the other supplies, it is wise to get some sort of device to carry and transport the kits. For example, a sturdy and light-weight garden trolley used to carry garden tools and supplies around the yard is perfect. I found it on the Internet and was able to load (<u>and securely strap</u>) all emergency items, including a sleeping bag, small tent and water on the cart. I discovered that by using this cart, I was able to include more supplies, including water, than I would have been able to carry using a duffle bag. It is easy to turn and moves over bumps and crevices. I have the cart stored in a closet by the front door of my home. There are other alternatives for transporting the kits including a handcart, wagon, moving dolly, wheelbarrow, duffle bag or suitcase stroller – anything that allows for easy and quick escape from the primary residence.

When preparing my own evacuation kit – it took me several days to get all the supplies I wanted to include in the kit. Many of the supplies I already had at the house and others I had to buy at the local department store. I removed any packaging materials from supplies that were in original packaging and cut out any instructions on the packaging that was important and attached it to the item using a twist tie.

> **You would be surprised at the <u>weight</u> and <u>space</u> needed for packaging materials! By removing the packaging materials, you reduce weight and space, make sure the item is not broken and is working and you have the opportunity to LEARN HOW TO USE THE ITEM! During an emergency is <u>not</u> the time to discover the item is broken or have to spend time learning how to use it!**

In a local sporting goods store, I purchased a collapsible heavy-duty plastic bucket used to carry water. The cost was around ten dollars. Since a bucket is an important item to be included in an evacuation kit – check out your local sporting goods store to see if you can find such an item. Good investment!

I spent several hours organizing the supplies into groups, for example, *toiletries*, *clothing*, *cooking*, *food*, *medical*, *operations* (shelter, light, fuel) and *miscellaneous* supplies. After I had sorted all of my supplies into proper groups, I put the supplies for each group into plastic bags, plastic containers or other storage units. It took me quite some time to fit the grouped items into their proper storage container. Once the supplies were all placed in the storage containers, I typed up labels for each of the groups (listing the supplies in <u>alphabetical</u> order) and attached the appropriate label to the respective container. By alphabetizing the lists, it is easy to see which supplies are in the container.

As part of my plan, I had an extra large duffle bag and placed all the storage containers (including my water) into the duffle bag and then put the duffle bag in a heavy-duty garbage bag to protect my supplies from rain. I strapped the bag to the garden cart. The cart had several shelves where I strapped down a light-weight tent and a sleeping bag (which were also placed in heavy-duty garbage bags prior to securing them to the cart). Although the entire process took several days, I am now confident my supplies are organized and easy to locate if I ever need to utilize my evacuation kit.

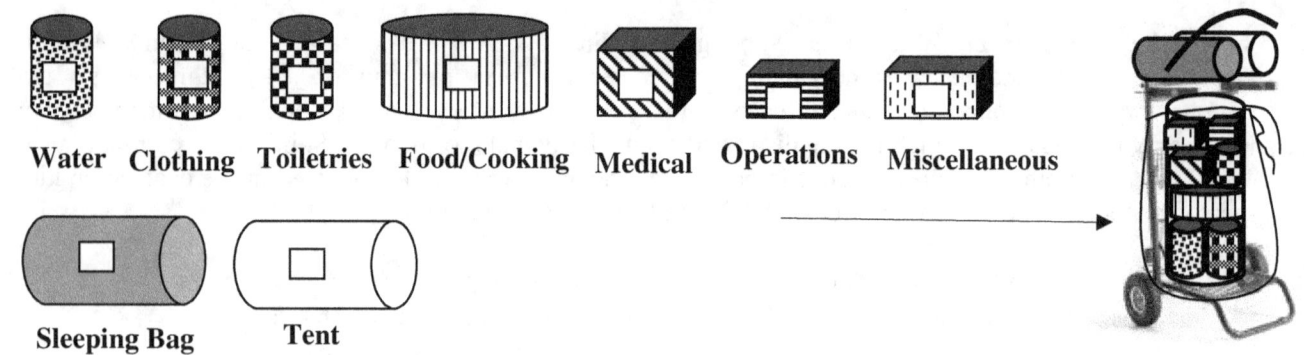

Water   Clothing   Toiletries   Food/Cooking   Medical   Operations   Miscellaneous

Sleeping Bag   Tent

As part of your overall emergency evacuation plan from the primary residence, make sure all survival team members understand that regardless of the emergency compromising the primary residence – all family members should take their evacuation kit when evacuating the home – NO EXCEPTIONS.

REMEMBER! Every team has different needs and not all supplies will be needed by all members. Depending on the chosen location as the place of refuge, not all items would be needed. For example, if your team plans to take refuge in the desert, the fishing pole probably wouldn't be a required item. If you don't have a baby or pets - I wouldn't worry about any baby or pet supplies either - right?

If your team plans to evacuate to a church, government building or designated public shelter, and depending on the circumstances and the extent of the disaster, officials <u>may</u> be equipped to provide <u>some</u> amenities including a heat source, water, medication, sanitation facilities and even food. However, since no one knows exactly what will be damaged or destroyed during an emergency, it is wise to <u>assume</u> that the facility would be able to provide <u>shelter only</u> with no electricity, heat or water - you should plan to provide your own water, food, light, heat, medication and sanitation supplies. (In the event a public shelter has a water fountain available, a funnel may be necessary to transfer the water from the faucet on the fountain into your own water container).

Remember that in a public shelter, there will no doubt be many people - privacy and space will be very limited. In order to provide a means of privacy for team members, a *pop-up tent* (with no stakes) is great. It doesn't need to be expensive - just simple to set up. This tent provides limited privacy when changing clothes and/or sleeping. Another important addition to the kits is a *solar garden light*. Instead of using candles, put the solar garden light outside and let the sun do its work. At night, bring the light inside and the team has a reliable light source for the entire evening. Another important item is a *tarp* <u>or</u> *heavy duty (2 mil) 55 gallon trash bag* that can be placed <u>under</u> the sleeping area (whether inside or outside) and will serve to "stake out" your team's space in the building. Remember that in public shelters, fire and fuel will not be allowed. It is important to select alternative methods for heat (blankets/sleeping bag, clothes), light (solar powered lantern, flashlight, garden light) and cooking (food not requiring fuel/fire for cooking i.e., meat, vegetables, fruits, jerky, bars, mix, powdered beverages).

Another important factor to remember if staying in a public shelter - it is also possible hardened criminals, pick-pockets, child molesters, thieves, drug dealers, addicts and gang members may also choose to take shelter in these places. Special care and precautions should be taken by team members at all times while staying in any type of public shelter - watch your children carefully and guard your supplies. On the other hand, the simple fact that there are a large number of people in the shelter would discourage thugs and gang members from challenging any one individual - there really is strength in numbers.

If the team decides to take shelter outside in the mountains, desert, or field, supplies should include items needed to survive in an outside environment, including an axe, tarp/clips (for making a tent or to serve as flooring), ropes, flint striker, fishing pole, fire starter, insect repellent, etc. Some of these same items could also prove useful if staying in a public shelter - especially if the shelter has only limited amenities. If you live in a region with four seasons and an emergency occurs during the cold season, it will be important to have basic winter apparel in the kits - at the very least, a warm pair of socks, gloves, thermal underwear, a jacket, and a hat. Don't forget sleepwear (for the kids) and a light pair of house slippers for all team members.

EVACUATION KIT

Axe	Lip Balm
Baby Supplies (formula, diapers, etc.) - if needed	**Lotion**
Baking Soda	**Map** (surrounding areas including driving and topical)
BLANKET	**MATCHES**
Bowl (used for personal hygiene)	**MEDICAL EQUIPMENT** (inhaler)
BUCKET* (heavy-duty plastic, *folding or collapsible*)	**MEDICATION** (prescription/over-the-counter drugs)
Cards, Games and Books	Nails
Cash and Coins (for telephone calls)	**Napkins (paper)**
Cell Phone	**NOTEPAD AND PENCIL**
CLOTHES (practical change of clothes)	**PAPER TOWELS**
Clothes Line and Pins	**PLASTIC BAGS**
Coat (heavy-duty and/or warm) - if applicable	**PLASTIC TIES**
Comb/Brush	**POCKET KNIFE**
Compass	**RADIO** (solar/hand crank)
Cookware (sauce pan/skillet)- if needed	**RAIN GEAR**
Cup (paper and/or metal)	**ROPE/CORD/TWINE** (towing, rescue, shelter etc.)
DOCUMENTATION (See Documentation Pantry List)	**SALT**
Duct Tape	**Sewing Kit**
Dust Mask	**SHOES – STURDY**
Eating Utensils – plastic (knife, fork, spoon)	**SHOVEL** (collapsible)
Eyeglasses and Eyeglass Repair Kit	**SIGNAL DEVICE** (lightsticks, mirror, flasher, reflector)
Fan (hand held)	**SLEEPING BAG**
Feminine Hygiene Products	**Liquid Soap**
Fire Starter	**Socks** (one warm pair PLUS one light pair)
FIRST AID KIT AND MANUAL (See First Aid List)	**SOLAR GARDEN LIGHT** - for light at night
FLASHLIGHT (solar/hand crank)	**Sunglasses**
Flint Striker	**TARP/TARP CLIPS**
FOOD* (non perishable - meat, vegetables, fruits, jerky, bars)	**TENT** – pop up, waterproof and easy to assemble
FUNNEL – (water)	**Tissues** (facial)
GARBAGE BAGS – 55 gallon heavy-duty (1)	**TOILET PAPER**
GARBAGE BAGS - 13 gallon heavy-duty (2-3)	**TOOLS** (pliers, hammer, screwdriver)
GARBAGE BAGS - 33 gallon heavy-duty (1)	**TOOTHBRUSH**
GLOVES (one warm pair PLUS one heavy-duty pair)	**TOOTHPASTE**
Hair Ties (pull hair back out of the face)	Toothpicks/Floss
Hand Warmer	**TOWELETTES** (pre-moistened)
Hand Sanitizer	**WATER** - minimum of a three day supply per person/pet
HAT (warm and/or light)	**WATER PURIFICATION TABLETS**
Insect Repellent	Weapon/Ammo
Keys (extra set for home)	**Whistle**
Lantern (solar powered)	

* food should include flip-top cans and require no cooking

IMPLEMENTING A PLAN

An emergency preparation plan requires organization, knowledge of inventory control and an effective money management program. A fully stocked emergency pantry provides protection against outside forces (economic, political, natural), and when you stock up on emergency supplies, your emergency pantries (primary residence, place of refuge, evacuation, auto and work kits) become your store.

Getting Started

The goal of fully stocked emergency preparation pantries can begin with your next paycheck. The *Emergency Preparation Worksheet* and the *Emergency Supplies List* (**APPENDIX A**) provides a method to determine what resources, items and supplies will be included in the various emergency pantries, inventory current supplies available at the house, determine wanted or needed supplies still to purchase, and estimate the overall cost of the supplies. Using the worksheet and list of supplies **and a sharpened pencil**, follow these steps:

1. Print off at least twenty pages (front and back) of the **Emergency Preparation Worksheet** located at the back of this book and identified as **APPENDIX A**.

2. Using the **ITEM** Column, and after reviewing the list of supplies in the table (also part of **APPENDIX A**), write down (on the **Emergency Preparation Worksheet**) all supplies and items the survival team wants to include in the various emergency pantries.

3. Using the **ELEMENT** Column, identify element(s) served when purchasing each item. Some items may serve more than one element. For example, an axe could serve for cutting wood to build a shelter (**OPERATIONS**), building a fire for cooking food (**NUTRITION**) or keeping warm (**OPERATIONS**).

4. Using the **NEED/WANT** Column, review supplies listed on the worksheet and add or delete items based on an assessment of basic and realistic needs for your circumstances. Be tough on yourself in determining what is a *need* is and what is a *want* or *luxury*. Identify all remaining items on the worksheet as a *need* (**N**) or *want* (**W**).

> As you work through the worksheet and inventory your home, you will be pleasantly surprised to learn that **you already have many of the items on the list!** The problem is that they are scattered all over the property! Some items are stored in the attic, others are out in the garage, many are stored in the shed and still others are located in drawers, cabinets and closets throughout the house. **GET IT TOGETHER!** Make sure you know the location of all emergency items and they are stored in areas that are easy to remember and access during an emergency situation.

5. Using the **PRIORITY** Column, use a priority rating system of 1 through 3 (1 being very important, 2 being somewhat important and 3 being not important) and rate each item on how *essential* or *vital* it is to meet the basic needs of your team, i.e., if it is very important to have toilet paper, you would rate it as a "1" priority, if it is somewhat important, you would rate it as a "2" priority, if it is not important, you would rate it as a "3" priority. If an item would definitely enhance the emergency pantry but is simply unrealistic to purchase or obtain now, you could either cross the item off the list or assign a Priority "1" rating but recognize that acquiring this item would be in the future.

6. Using the **HOUSEHOLD MEMBERS** Column, list the total number of team members in your group.

7. Using the **LENGTH OF TIME** Column, establish the duration (length of time) that you want to have supplies in your various emergency pantries. For example, as a beginner, you may consider only gathering supplies for a seven day period of time. On the other hand, in order to have adequate supplies for a Level 3 (long-term) disaster, consider emergency supplies to sustain survival team members for an entire year. *The goal is to work towards a one year supply*.

8. Using the **PRIMARY RESIDENCE, PLACE OF REFUGE, AUTO, EVACUATION** and **WORK** Pantry Columns, determine how many of each supply listed on the worksheet will be needed for each pantry (kit).

9. Using the **TOTAL ITEMS NEEDED** Column, add up the totals of each item in the worksheet shown in the pantry columns (see Number 8 above) to determine how many total supplies will be needed to fill <u>all</u> pantries.

10. On a separate piece of paper, go throughout the entire home, garage and surrounding buildings including any barns, sheds or storage facilities, and inventory all items identified on the worksheet as being necessary to fill one or more of the emergency pantries. As part of this process, the list should include the

following information: (1) description of each item, (2) how many of each item, (3) where each item will be located, i.e. auto, work, place of refuge or evacuation kit, or a specific place in the primary residence.

11. Physically move these items to the designated locations as part of your overall emergency plan. Make sure that all items are in good working condition and you know how to use them.

12. Using the **ON HAND** Column, and based on your inventory, identify and list how many of each item on the worksheet is on hand and available to add to the various pantries.

13. Using the **STILL TO PURCHASE** Column, *subtract* the number in the **ON HAND** Column from the number in the **TOTAL ITEMS NEEDED** Column. This will give you the total number of each item still needed to be purchased.

14. Using the **PACKAGING** Column, identify and list the packaging type of items on hand and still to be purchased, i.e., each, box, package or pair for each item in the worksheet.

15. Using the **UNIT COST** Column, research a practical and realistic unit cost for each item that must still be purchased. Cost should be based on sound purchasing practices, i.e., buying in bulk, buying on sale, buying as a co-op etc. Consider the legitimate necessity to purchase higher quality and more costly items versus lower quality and cheaper items, i.e. a heavy-duty bucket versus a cheap crappy bucket.

16. Using the **TOTAL COST** Column, *multiply* the number shown in the **STILL TO PURCHASE** Column with the dollar amount listed in the **UNIT COST** Column. This will give you an estimate on the total dollar amount still to be expended on each item in the worksheet.

INITIATING A BUDGET

In order to initiate an Emergency Preparation Budget, borrowing money or using credit cards is generally not a sound policy. However, there are some items that because of their high price tag may require a payment plan with the bank. If borrowing money is necessary, make sure you are using sound financial management principles.

Begin by doing the following:

- Identify net income (after taxes) including *wages*, *interest*, *dividends*, *alimony*, *child support*, etc.

- Identify fixed expenses that are the same amount every month (generally includes *mortgage*, *rent*, *car payment*, *insurance*)

- Identify variable expenses that vary in the amount every month (generally includes *utilities*, *taxes*, *food*, *charitable donations*, *gas*, *clothing*, *entertainment*, *savings*, *miscellaneous*, etc.)

- Can net income be increased or fixed/variable expenses decreased? - make the appropriate adjustments.

For most of us, and when necessary, we can increase our income by selling items no longer needed or taking on an extra job. We can also decrease our fixed and variable expenses in the same manner. For example, analyze your insurance policies to see if premiums can be reduced, practice conservative use of all utilities, be more prudent in driving the car, purchase clothing needs (not wants) at second hand stores, have shoes repaired instead of buying a new pair, attend movies during non-peak times and buy cheaper cuts of meat.

Another very abrupt and immediate method to cut expenses is to simply *cease* or drastically *reduce* the practice of what may be considered as luxuries and not necessities.

For example:

- Agree that any gift giving will include items to be added to emergency preparation pantries
- Agree with family and friends to stop or modify gift giving during special occasions
- Cancel all unnecessary memberships to the spa and health clubs
- Cancel all unnecessary subscriptions to magazines, books, and other services
- Discontinue cable or satellite television
- Discontinue Internet - use free Internet available at local libraries and schools
- Do your own housekeeping
- Do your own nails and hair (including cutting your own hair)
- Drink water (free) instead of soft drinks when at a restaurant or fast food outlet
- Eliminate or reduce all school activities requiring large cash outputs
- If working outside of the home, brown-bag your lunch instead of eating out
- Make a commitment to stop smoking and drinking alcohol, soda or caffeinated drinks
- Mow your own lawn every other week instead of every week
- Run the air conditioner a little higher and the furnace a little lower
- Select either a landline or a cell phone (if possible) but not both
- Sell cars, trailers, boats, ATV's, and snowmobiles that are not needed or being used
- Stay out of the grocery and department stores unless absolutely necessary
- Stop buying stupid stuff that you don't actually need
- Stop buying unnecessary clothes
- Stop or reduce going out to dinner at restaurants or fast-food establishments
- Stop or reduce going out to the movies
- Stop or reduce luxury massage treatments
- Stop taking laundry to the dry cleaners and do your own laundry at home
- Use coupons whenever possible to buy *needed* items
- Use the bus system (if possible) instead of driving the car
- Wash your own vehicles
- When grocery shopping, try to avoid processed or packaged foods, make a list and stick to it

> **Why don't we just take a sharp stick and poke it in our eye??? Sigh . . .**

By <u>avoiding</u> certain types of expenses, you can also manage money more effectively. For example, follow driving laws and avoid getting tickets, pay bills on time to avoid late fees, maintain the minimum amount in checking and saving accounts to avoid monthly service charges, refrain from using ATM machines charging fees, and whenever possible, repair broken items instead of buying a new one, practice preventive maintenance on yourself, home, car and other appliances to avoid more costly expenses down the road.

> *What the caterpillar calls the end of the world, the Master calls a butterfly.*
>
> - **Richard Bach**

Another possibility is to reduce or forego expensive family vacations and use the money for emergency supplies instead - remember - <u>emergency preparation requires recreational and monetary sacrifices</u>.

It is also important for <u>teenagers</u> to contribute towards emergency pantries. If teenagers are working and making wages, consider approaching them about contributing towards the dollar amount designated for emergency preparation. After all - they will certainly be using the supplies. It will also teach teens the law of budgeting, the law of contribution, the law of sacrifice and the importance of working together as a survival team to meet this very important objective. And when it comes time to use the supplies, they will be much less likely to waste since their hard earned dollars also contributed to purchasing the items.

> **Another great idea! Freeze leftover food and then have a "restaurant night" with all the leftovers. Pretend you are the waitress/waiter and take the kids' orders. Tell them what's on the menu and let them each choose different meals. Microwave your frozen leftovers and enjoy a great family dinner!**

Each survival team should determine what is *realistic* and *acceptable* for them in finding additional funds from our already stretched dollars to begin purchasing items for emergency pantries. Once the team has determined the workable amount of money from everyone's (including teenagers) paycheck that can be used to purchase items for emergency pantries, review the items on the worksheet and **TOGETHER** decide which supplies and items can be purchased on each payday. The family may decide to purchase items that are less expensive so that it can be marked off as "complete" in a sooner time period. On the other hand, you may decide to focus only on Priority 1 items or items that provide uses over multiple elements, i.e., matches or buckets.

If possible, try to purchase items from all the elements (**Operation, Medication** etc.) to guarantee you are meeting basic requirements and have several *alternatives* or *layers* available for each element. Remember, if teenagers are going to financially contribute to the emergency pantries, include them in the priority and buying decisions and shopping excursions. Whatever approach you take in stocking emergency pantries, continue to keep accurate records of the inventory. This practice will eliminate over-buying some items and not buying adequate supplies of other items. Remember to buy in bulk, pay attention to sales and consider discount drug stores, garage sales, charitable outlets, wholesale outlets, membership clubs, mass merchandisers, dollar stores or Internet sites.

WANT VERSUS NEED

When preparing emergency pantries, team members must learn the difference between a *need* and a *want*. A *need* is an item that you absolutely must have in order to survive or there are none or few alternatives, for example, shelter, food and water. A *want* is a luxury item that would be nice to have but is not absolutely necessary for survival, for example, a washing machine and personal hygiene items including toilet paper. In fact, for many items, we have become so used to having them, we consider them to be essential when in actuality – they are not absolutely necessary – just convenient. Most supplies that team members will include in emergency pantries will not be absolutely essential for survival – but they will simply make surviving more bearable. And that is alright.

A good rule of thumb is to ask if the team could realistically survive without it. If the answer is 'no' – then consider these supplies as *need* items. If the team could survive without it and there are alternatives, consider these supplies to be *want* items. Recognize that many *want* supplies, although considered as "luxury" items, are also very important to include in pantries. For example, we certainly can get along without a toothbrush and toothpaste, and there are alternatives, but these two items provide an easy, inexpensive and convenient means for dental health.

Although toilet paper is a luxury item – I consider it to be absolutely essential because I would not be willing to accept the alternatives. On the other hand, if money is an issue when making purchases (which tends to usually be the case) having cologne and makeup as a top priority would be impractical. Be cautious in your selection process and carefully analyze each item. Remember – try to avoid any supplies that require electricity, batteries and/or fuel whenever possible unless arrangements are made to provide for an electrical power source such as solar energy.

THE GOOD, THE BAD AND THE UGLY

As the team gathers supplies for emergency pantries, some items **MUST** be high-quality supplies while others may not need to be at the high end of the scale. Sometimes, a high quality item can be purchased at second hand stores, garage sales and charity outlets for less money than if purchasing a new item. On many items, it really doesn't matter if you purchase a high scale or high quality item. For example, if you buy a notebook for $100.00 and another one for $2.00 – both will serve the purpose.

It is not always the price paid for the item – what matters is what you get for your money. The reality of disaster survival focuses on the fact that there would be some supplies used over and over again and for very important functions. These specific supplies **MUST STAND UP TO CONTINUAL USE, ABUSE AND OPERATION.** When creating the overall budget for emergency supplies, the table below will serve as a guideline on items that should be good-quality and/or heavy-duty merchandise.

ITEM	DESCRIPTION	PRICE
Aluminum Foil	Although it is acceptable to purchase cheaper aluminum foil for some purposes, if used for cooking and grilling, spend the money and get the heavy duty stuff.	$5.00/roll
Axe	A good axe can make the difference in having wood for heat and cooking.	$30 - $50
Blankets/Quilts	Although it is perfectly sensible to purchase cheaper and lighter blankets, pantries should also be stocked with heavy and warm blankets as well – how much they cost is up to you.	$50 - $100
Boots	The boots should be warm and waterproof and stand up to harsh working and weather environments.	$50 - $150
Broom	Purchase a good quality broom used for sweeping in the house and outdoors. A low quality broom will begin breaking up very quickly. With no electricity – the <u>electric</u> vacuum becomes a dead item.	$10
Bucket	**HEFTY HEFTY HEFTY**. You will need (1) for carrying drinking water, (1) for cleaning and (1) for sanitation. <u>One bucket can NOT serve all three purposes – they must be separate buckets</u>. The buckets should be big enough to hold water that can be <u>easily</u> carried by adult team members. It will serve no purpose to buy a huge bucket that when filled with water, cannot be easily transported.	$10 - $20 each
Can Opener (Manual)	The manual can opener you find in a dollar store will NOT last. Do yourself a favor and get a good one – it will make the difference on opening those cans.	$6 - $8
Chain Saw	A chain saw does not need to be top of the line – but make sure it is a heavy-duty model.	$100 - $300
Clothes Line Rope	The rope used for a clothes line must be strong in order to hold up the wet clothes on the line. After spending an afternoon washing all the clothes by hand, you will not want the clothes falling in the dirt because of a wimpy clothes line.	$10 - $20
Clothes Wringer	If the team decides to invest in an old-fashioned clothes wringer that is used to wring out the wet clothes after washing, make sure that you purchase an industrial heavy-duty model.	$200- $250 (includes stand)
Dust Masks	For team members who reside in locations susceptible to volcanic eruptions, earthquakes, chemical spills or any other manmade or natural disaster that may contribute to airborne particles – buy the good stuff.	$5 - $10 (High Quality)
Fishing Pole/Line	Although the fishing pole does not need to be the best brand or the highest quality – get one that will support the weight of fish in your area. Buying good quality line can also make the difference between having fish for dinner – or not.	$50 - $100
Flashlight (at least one)	By all means, buy a variety of flashlights when they are on sale. But make sure that at least one of them is a high quality solar or hand crank flashlight.	$30 - $40

ITEM	DESCRIPTION	PRICE
Garbage Bags	**HEFTY HEFTY HEFTY.** The 13-gallon, 33 gallon and 55 gallon bags MUST be heavy duty and high mil (thickness) to support toilet and trash functions.	$5 - $10/pkg
Generator (Solar Power)	A solar-powered generator is a very important investment. Be careful and research the various models and companies to ensure that you are getting a high quality machine that provides reliable power and minimum maintenance.	$1700 - $7000
Gloves	All team members should have good-quality gloves for warmth and for work. The less expensive work gloves quickly wear out. During cold weather, warm gloves are essential.	$10 - $50
Grain Mill	Teams should have an adequate supply of whole grain stored in the pantries. The mill will be used over and over again to provide flour for the team. I purchased one online and made in Germany (which tells you it will be a good one) called the Wonder Mill Junior Deluxe Hand Grain and Flour Mill.	$100-$220
Hammer	A good hammer will provide the team with a tool that can serve multiple purchases.	$7 - $15
Hatchet	A hatchet will provide the team with a tool that can serve multiple purchases.	$15 - $20
Hoe	A good high-quality hoe will prove invaluable in the garden and in the yard.	$10 - $20
Knife	Make sure you have some good quality knives (including pocket knives) that will be used for carving and cutting operational supplies.	$5 - $50
Knife Sharpening Tool	Although most high quality knives are slow to dull –they will need to be sharpened.	$5 - $10
Laundry Tub	These plastic tubs would be used to perform laundry functions (unless you decide to use the kitchen sink or bathtub which is perfectly acceptable). The tub will be filled with water and you will bend over the tub and clean your laundry. I recommend the plastic tubs because they will not rust. These tubs come in all colors. I got mine at Wal-Mart.	$5 - $10
Plastic Sheeting	Plastic sheeting will cover broken windows and help in keeping airborne particles from entering the house or specific rooms. I would recommend purchasing an entire roll of heavy-duty plastic sheeting. (Consider sharing the roll with other survival teams)	$80 - $100/roll
Pliers	By all means, buy dozens of pliers of all shapes and sizes and at every price. But make sure that the survival team has a good quality set of pliers – a tool that serves multiple purposes and will be very important during an emergency.	$20 - $40 set

ITEM	DESCRIPTION	PRICE
Radio (hand crank)	A radio will be vital during an emergency in order to receive important information concerning the status of the disaster and applicable instructions. There are many solar and hand-crank radios on the market – make sure you get a good quality model.	$20 - $30
Rake	A rake will serve multiple purposes - include a leaf rake and medal-tong rake in the pantry.	$20 - $30
Ropes	Although it is important to have a variety of different types, sizes and grades of rope, make sure that some heavy duty rope is also included in the storage box.	Various
Saws	During a disaster, it will be useful to have a variety of saws for different types of jobs. Some saws will be used for cutting and shearing branches and twigs from shrubs and bushes while others will be used to cut lumber. The teeth on low quality saws begin to quickly wear down. Purchase good-quality saws.	$20 - $100
Screwdrivers	Make sure that the emergency pantry has a diverse set of good-quality screwdrivers that serve different functions. This is one tool where you generally get what you pay for – a cheap screwdriver will break and bend in no time.	Various
Shoes	Each team member should have a pair of good quality work shoes.	$20 - $100
Shovel	A shovel serves multiple purposes and is used in construction, gardening, yard work, snow and trash removal and even in digging a grave to bury the dead. Make sure the various types of shovels that are purchased are good quality merchandise.	$20 -$50
Sleeping Bag	If the team chooses to use a sleeping bag as an alternative to blankets and quilts in the home, the sleeping bag should be one that supports cold weather – even if used indoors. Although this sleeping bag does not need to be top of the line – it should be one that keeps the person warm and dry in cold weather conditions without a furnace.	$40 - $100
Socks	Although light socks are certainly needed during warm weather, make sure each team member has at least one pair of good quality socks for cold weather.	$10- $15
Solar Powered Battery Charger	A good solar powered battery charger will enable the team to charge batteries using the sun. These batteries can provide the means for light, communication and other vital functions. Don't forget to buy a variety of rechargeable batteries.	$30 - $60
Stapler	A heavy-duty stapler will be used to staple the plastic sheeting around windows and doors.	$20 - $30
Step Ladder	A heavy-duty metal step ladder is used for multiple purposes.	$40 - $60
Tarps	Although a variety of medium-quality tarps is certainly a good idea, make sure that good-quality tarps are included in the storage box. These tarps would be used as tents and protection from inclement weather.	$10 - $300

ITEM	DESCRIPTION	PRICE
Thermals	Every team member should have at least one pair of heavy-duty thermal underwear.	$20 - $40
Trash Can	This trashcan will be used to store human waste in the event the toilet and/or sewer system is compromised. It must be a heavy duty can with a locking lid.	$50 - $100
Wheel Barrow	Used for multiple purposes including gardening, yard work and construction.	$50 - $100
Wrenches	A good variety of wrenches will be needed for multiple purposes including plumbing functions and turning on/off gas lines.	$30 - $100

HOME HAZARDS

An important step in emergency preparation is to inspect the home and surroundings for possible hazards and then take action to lessen those hazards before the emergency. The following is a basic checklist to help identify and correct home hazards:

> *In the end, you are measured not by how much you undertake but by what you finally accomplish.*
>
> - **Donald Trump**

Rooms in the Home

Look for the following hazards in each room:

- Windows and other glass that may shatter
- Unanchored bookcases, cabinets, refrigerators, water heaters and other furniture that may topple
- Heating units, fireplaces, chimneys and stoves that could move or fall
- Areas that could be blocked by falling debris
- Hanging pictures and wall decorations that could topple from the wall

Securing Appliances

Secure large appliances with flexible cable, braided wire or metal strapping and install flexible gas and water connections on all gas appliances. This will significantly reduce the chances of having a major fire after an emergency. Brace and support air conditioners and particularly those on rooftops.

The typical water heater weighs 450 pounds when full of water. In an emergency, the floor tends to move out from under the heater, often causing it to topple. The movement can also break the gas, electric and water line connectors, posing fire or electric shock hazards, and can shatter the glass lining within the water heater.

Here are two suggestions on how to secure a water heater:

(1)   Wrap at least a ½ inch wide metal strap around the top of the water heater and attach it to wall studs with three-inch lag screws. Attach another strap about 2/3 of the way down from the top of the water heater.

(2)   Wrap steel plumber's tape around the entire water heater at least twice. Then secure the tape to two different wall studs with three-inch lag screws.

Securing Items in the Bathroom

Replace glass bottles from the medicine cabinet and around the bathtubs with plastic containers.

Hanging and Overhead Items

Inspect and anchor overhead light fixtures and chandeliers, heavy mirrors and pictures hanging above beds, chairs and other places where you sit or sleep. Analyze if the full swing of hanging lamps or plants will strike a window and if so, move them. Secure hanging objects by closing the opening of the hook and replace heavy ceramic or glass hanging planters with light-weight plastic or wicker baskets.

Shelves, Cabinets, and Furniture

Secure top-heavy and free-standing furniture such as bookcases and china cabinets. Use "L" brackets, corner brackets, or aluminum molding to attach tall or top-heavy furniture to the wall, eyebolts to secure items located a short distance from the wall, and attach a wooden or metal guardrail on open shelves to keep items from sliding or falling off. Fishing line can also be used as a less-visible means to secure an item. Place heavy or large objects on lower shelves. Secure cabinet doors by installing sliding bolts or childproof latches.

Hazardous Materials

Identify poisons, solvents or toxic materials in breakable containers and move these containers to a safe, well-ventilated storage area. Keep away from water storage and out of reach of children, pets, wildlife and livestock.

HOME STRUCTURE

Examine the structural safety of the primary residence and homes occupied by survival team members not residing at the primary residence. If the house is conventional wood construction, it is probably resistant to earthquake damage and particularly if it is a single-story structure. The following suggestions will take an investment of time and money but will add stability to the home. If you want to do the work yourself, many hardware or home improvement stores will assist with information and instructions.

Foundation

Check to see if the house or garage is securely fastened to the foundation. If the house was built before 1950, it probably does not have bolts securing the wood structure to the concrete foundation. If this is the case, use a hammer drill and carbide bit and drill a hole through the sill plate into the foundation. Holes should be approximately six feet apart. Drop a ½ x 7 inch expansion bolt into each hole and tighten the nut and washer.

Beams, Posts, Joists, and Plates

Strengthen the areas of connection between beams, posts, joists, and plates using "T" and "L" straps, mending plates, joist hangers, twin post caps, and nails and lag screws. Pay particular attention to exposed framing in garages, basements, porches and patio covers.

Roof and Chimney

Check the chimney or roof for loose tiles and bricks and repair as needed. Reinforce the ceiling surrounding the chimney with ¾ inch plywood nailed to ceiling joists. On a regular basis, make sure the chimney is cleaned to remove smoke buildup from forming on the inside walls of the chimney.

SHUTTING OFF UTILITIES

Teach all adult team members *where*, *when* and *how* to shut off utilities – **this includes all female adults and young adults old enough to understand the instructions and perform the task**. The natural gas should be turned off at the *meter only* if the in-house lines are damaged or if instructed to do so by a firefighter, police or gas company representative. Remember that if the natural gas is turned off at the main meter into the house, a professional will be required to turn it back on. If you use propane as your fuel source – it can be turned on and off at the meter on top of the tank. <u>Know where the main water meter and electrical box are located and how to turn these utilities on and off at the source.</u>

PERSONS WITH DISABILITIES

For those persons with disabilities or individuals that require special assistance during a disaster, a personal support network can help in preparing for an emergency situation. By *planning in advance*, this network group can assist in identifying and getting the resources needed to cope effectively *before*, *during* and *after* a crisis.

Those with disabilities or special needs often have unique circumstances that require more detailed planning in the event of a disaster. Consider the following actions:

- Become a member of a survival team. Investigate and seek out a suitable team that will be <u>ready</u>, <u>willing</u> and <u>able</u> to accept you (and your disability and/or special needs) as one of their members.

- Write down any specific needs, limitations and capabilities that you have and any medications you take on a regular basis. Make a copy of the list and put it in your purse or wallet.

- Provide a spare key to your home with a member of the survival team or let them know where they can find one in an emergency.

- Learn what to do in case of utility outages and personal injuries. Know how to connect and start a back-up power supply for essential medical equipment.

- Consider getting a medical alert system that will allow you to call for help if you are immobilized in an emergency. Most alert systems require a working phone line, so have a back-up plan, such as a cell phone or pager if the regular landlines are disrupted.

- If using an electric wheelchair or scooter, have a manual wheelchair as a backup.

- Teach those who may need to assist you in an emergency how to operate necessary equipment. Label equipment and attach laminated instructions for equipment use.

- Store back-up equipment (mobility and medical) at a neighbor's home, school or your workplace.

- If at work, school or area where you spend a lot of time, arrange for more than one person from your outside network group to check on you in an emergency.

- If you are vision impaired, deaf or hard of hearing, plan ahead for someone to convey essential emergency information to you if you are unable to use the television or radio.

- If using a personal care attendant from an agency, check to see if the agency has special provisions for emergencies (e.g., providing services at another location should an evacuation be ordered).

- If you live in an apartment, ask the management to identify and mark accessible exits and access to all areas designated for emergency shelter or safe rooms. Ask about plans for alerting and evacuating those with sensory disabilities.

- Learn about devices and other technology available (PDA's text radio, pagers) to assist you in receiving emergency instructions and warnings from local officials.

- Be prepared to provide clear, specific and concise instructions to rescue personnel. Practice giving these instructions clearly and quickly until you are confident of your message.

- Prepare survival team members and outside network groups to assist you with anticipated reactions and emotions associated with disaster and traumatic events (confusion, thought processing, memory difficulties, agitation, fear, panic and anxiety).

The **first** priority in preparing for an emergency would be to become a member of a survival team. This team could be close family members, relatives, friends or neighbors. If you are living alone, immobile and/or isolated from social interaction with others, you need to be included in a survival team near your place of residence. It is critical that all members of the team fully understand and accept your limitations. Be candid, open and straight-forward about your disabilities and/or requirements for special assistance during an emergency situation including all conditions and restrictions that would be involved with other team members supporting your needs.

> *I seldom end up where I wanted to go, but almost always end up where I need to be.*
>
> - **Douglas Adams**

If the disability allows you to be mobile and you are able to easily move throughout your home and/or travel to other areas, organize an outside network group as well that includes your school, workplace, volunteer site, and any other places where you spend a lot of time. Members of your network can be roommates, relatives, neighbors, friends and co-workers. They should be people you trust and who can check to see if you need assistance. Do not depend on only one person. Include a minimum of two people in your network for each location where you regularly spend a lot of time since people work different shifts, take vacations and are not always available. They should know your capabilities and needs, and be able to provide help within minutes. Make sure that the survival team is included in all discussions involving this outside network so that they can be part of the overall emergency plan involving your safety during a disaster.

The **second** priority is to complete a personal assessment and list personal needs and resources for meeting them in a disaster environment. These questions and your answers should be thoroughly discussed with all survival team members and your outside network group. Answers should describe both your current capabilities and the assistance you will need *before*, *during* and *after* an emergency. Base your plan on your lowest anticipated functioning level based on where you are physically located at the time of the disaster, the environment after the disaster, your capabilities and your limitations.

- **Adaptive Feeding Devices**. Do you use special utensils that help you prepare or eat food independently?

- **Building Evacuation**. Do you need help to leave the home or office? Can you reach and activate an alarm? Will you be able to evacuate independently without relying on auditory cues such as noise from a machine near the stairs? These cues may be absent if the electricity is off or alarms are sounding.

- **Building Exits**. Are there other exits (stairs, windows or ramps) if the elevator is not working or cannot be used? Can you read emergency signs in print or Braille? Do emergency alarms have audible and visible features (marking escape routes and exits) that will work even if electrical service is disrupted?

- **Disaster Debris**. How will you cope with debris in the home or planned exit routes following the disaster?

- **Electricity-Dependent Equipment**. How will you continue to use equipment that runs on electricity such as dialysis or electrical lifts? Do you have a back-up power supply and how long will it last?

- **Errands**. Do you need help getting groceries, medications and medical supplies? What if your caregiver cannot reach you because roads are blocked or the disaster has affected him or her as well?

- **Getting Help**. How will you call or summon for help to leave the building? Do you know the locations of text telephones and phones that have amplification? Will your hearing aids work if they get wet from emergency sprinklers? Determine how to communicate with emergency personnel if you don't have an interpreter, hearing aids aren't working, or if you don't have a word board or other communication device.

- **Mobility Aids / Ramp Access**. What will you do if you cannot find your mobility aids? What will you do if your ramps are shaken loose or become separated from the building?

- **Personal Care Equipment**. Do you use a shower chair, tub-transfer bench or other similar equipment?

- **Personal Care**. Do you regularly need assistance with personal care such as bathing and grooming? Do you use adaptive equipment to help get dressed?

- **Service Animals/Pets**. Will you be able to care for your animals (provide food, shelter, veterinary attention) during and after a disaster? Do you have another caregiver for your pet if you are unable to meet its needs? Do you have the appropriate licenses for your service animal so you will be permitted to keep it with you should you need or choose to use a public shelter?

- **Transportation**. Do you need a specially equipped vehicle or accessible transportation?

- **Water Service**. What will you do if water service is cut off for several days or if you are unable to heat water?

CHILDREN

A child may be afraid of injury, death or recurrence during and after an emergency. They may fear being separated from family or being left alone. Children may even interpret disasters as punishments for real or imagined misdeeds. A child will be less likely to experience prolonged fear or anxiety if they know what to expect and talking with children openly and *in advance* will help overcome fear or misgivings. Explain that an emergency situation is not their fault and talk about your own experiences with disasters. Encourage the child to express feelings of fear, listen carefully and show understanding. A child may need both verbal and physical reassurance that everything will be all right. Make sure the child understands the situation would not likely be permanent.

Although it is important to deal with the child's needs in a compassionate and caring environment, it is also important to understand that during an actual disaster, the adult should take whatever steps are necessary to ensure the physical safety of the child. Once the child is safe and secure, the mental and psychological aspects can be addressed. It will be comforting to the child to watch the household begin to return to normal so include a child in any clean-up activities. As part of the emergency pantry, make sure that toys, games and other important items are readily available for the children.

If children of survival team members are in school, *plan in advance* and discuss the emergency preparation plan outlined by the school with school administrators. Make sure that **EVERYONE** understands what will take place during a disaster – including the school officials, parents and children. During a disaster is the perfect time for a predator or other unauthorized adult to take advantage of a situation and abduct or remove a child from a school without authorization and during a disaster is not the time for a school official to encounter a screaming parent demanding their children be released.

Take special steps to talk to your children and in conjunction with the agreement made between school officials and the parents, discuss with the children exactly what they should do during the disaster and when and under what circumstances they will be released from the school to the parents. For very young children in school, it may be a sensible plan to have the child stay at the school. A parent should make arrangements (in advance) with the administration to pick up the child if at all possible after the disaster and then walk or drive to the designated meeting area.

EVACUATION PLANS

During some disasters, team members may need to evacuate a damaged area – *including the primary residence.* When creating, practicing and implementing evacuation plans, it is important to communicate with all survival team members *before, during* and *after* a disaster. The team will be better prepared to respond appropriately and efficiently to signs of danger or to directions by civil authorities. Take time with the survival team members to communicate various scenarios of evacuation plans and places of refuge.

Sketch a floor plan of the primary residence and walk through each room and discuss evacuation details. Plan an alternate approach to exit from each room or area, if possible. If special equipment is needed such as a rope ladder - buy it, install it and mark where it is located. On the floor plan, mark where emergency food, water, first aid kits, evacuation kits and fire extinguishers are located and mark where the utility switches, valves or meters are located so that they can be turned off. If there is time, and only if there is time, and if you have not received contrary instructions from local authorities, secure the primary residence before you evacuate the home:

- Turn off all natural gas or propane appliances, furnace and air conditioner
- Turn off the propane tanks
- Disconnect all electrical appliances including television, computer and hot water heater
- Lock all windows and doors and activate the house alarm
- Move vehicles to garage, carport, shed or driveway
- Store any perishables
- Make arrangements for pets and livestock and display the appropriate signs
- Prepare windows for breakage, i.e., plywood or plastic over the glass window or door

EVACUATION LOCATIONS

Remember that during an emergency, our preference will be to remain in our homes - or the primary residence for the duration of the disaster. However, our home and/or primary residence may be damaged or destroyed - and the survival team would need to find alternative meeting places and/or shelter sites. As part of *planning in advance*, survival teams should designate three alternate meeting places and/or shelter sites as follows:

Priority One Location

Designate a **PRIORITY ONE** area outside of the primary residence where all survival team members can *meet if the structure is damaged but the surrounding area is still safe.* Make sure the meeting place is not directly adjacent to the home. Avoid an area close to power lines, gas lines or propane tanks. This area could be in an open field, by the mail box, or by a tree near the home.

On the evacuation plan, indicate the location of the **PRIORITY ONE** emergency outdoor *meeting* place for the team. Once all family members have reached the designated location, arrangements can then be made to move to an alternate shelter site or a place of refuge. **Make arrangements for pets and livestock!**

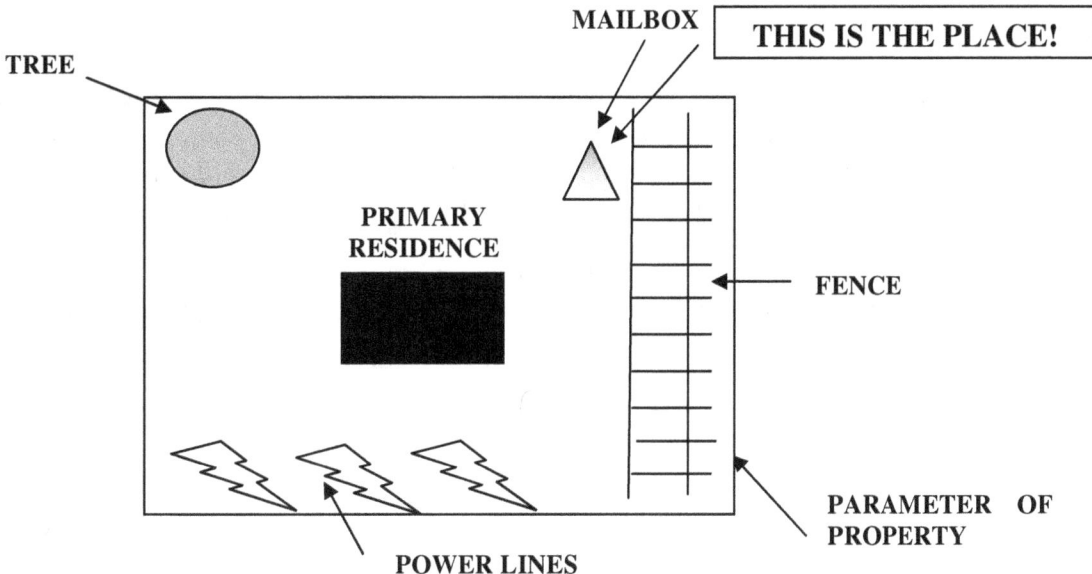

Priority Two Location

Evaluate the vicinity of the primary residence and select a **PRIORITY TWO** area <u>outside of the primary residence parameter</u> where everyone will *meet* <u>if</u> the **PRIORITY ONE** area is compromised <u>or</u> when team members meet at the **PRIORITY ONE** location and it is now time to move to an alternate shelter site or place of refuge. Make sure the area is away from power lines, gas lines or propane tanks. This area could be the home of a friend, relative or neighbor, park, church, soccer field or school.

The **PRIORITY TWO** location should be no more than one or two miles from the primary residence. As part of the overall evacuation plan, since survival team members may be at the primary residence during this emergency, make sure that all members are physically and mentally capable of reaching the **PRIORITY TWO** area <u>on foot</u>. If not, arrangements will need to be made to ensure that disabled members are able to join the rest of the survival team at the designated location. **Make arrangements for pets and livestock!**

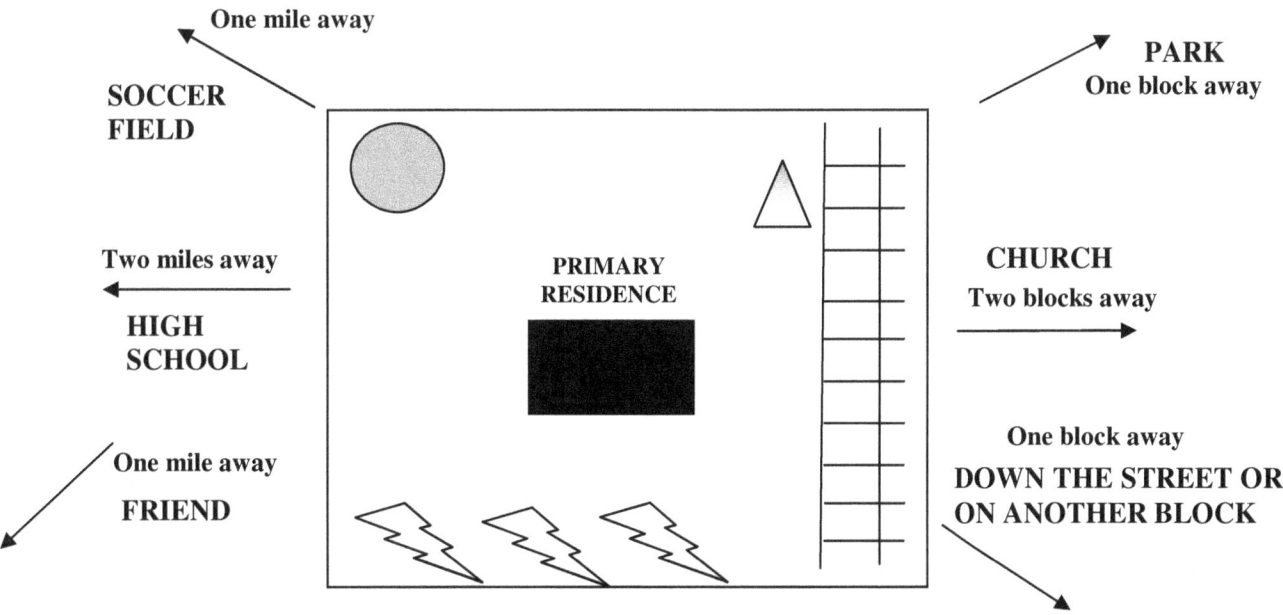

Priority Three Location

It is possible when an emergency occurs that all members of the survival team will be in different places! For example, both parents could be at work either in the same city, in another town or even in another state. The children could all be at different schools throughout the area. The teenagers could be with their friends at the movies, at a soccer game, on a picnic in the canyon or shopping at the mall. The distance between team members and the primary residence could be many miles.

The situation could present an unrealistic expectation for everyone to be able to make it back to the primary residence. For example, all roads could be impassable, power lines could be down, or a large chemical explosion could make the area restricted between team members and the primary residence. Under these circumstances, the communication systems (including cell phones and land lines) could be down and it could be virtually impossible to locate every member of the survival team. The primary residence could also be damaged or destroyed.

As a general rule, if a serious emergency happens that places the **THREAT** between the primary residence and the survival team members or if it would be obvious the primary residence is damaged or destroyed – attempt to select a meeting place in the middle where all team members have approximately the same amount of distance (and chance of success) to travel in order to reach the meeting place destination. For example, if a parent is working, the kids are in school and one of the teenagers is finally cleaning his filthy dirty room while at home as a parent stands over him with a sledge hammer – perhaps a good "middle-of-the-road" meeting place could be the *closest public building* to the primary residence. Once all team members are assembled, the team could then move to a more permanent place of refuge (public shelter or a privately owned location such as a cabin, motor home, trailer, camper or the home of a friend or relative).

If the location of the **PRIORITY THREE** destination is a government building, church, school building or building approved as a reception center or public shelter, there should be a registration system in place and *all survival team members should register as soon as they arrive at the building.* By doing so, this will assist agencies responsible for verifying missing or injured citizens and determining fatalities. It could also provide the survival team with information concerning the individual status of their team members.

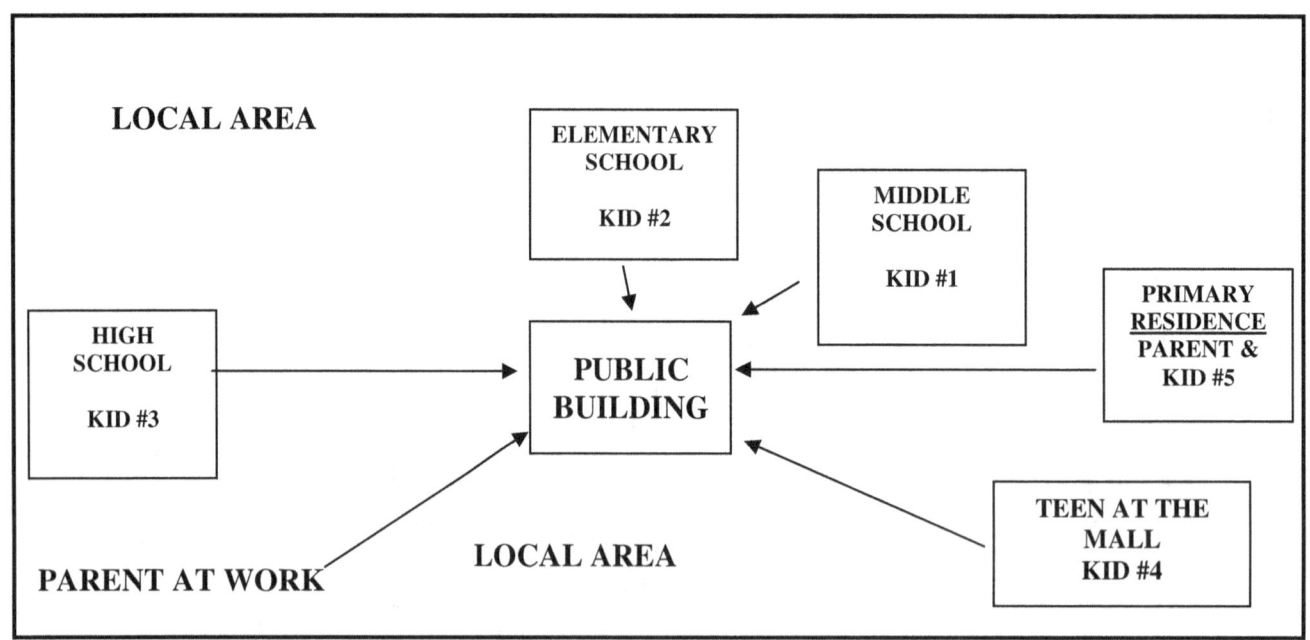

For all three priorities, all survival team members, including children, must understand the plan, scenarios of possible emergencies, what to do, when to go, where to go, and what is expected of them. **COMMUNICATE EFFECTIVELY** that once they are at the designated meeting place – they should stay there until **ALL MEMBERS** are accounted for – even if it is cold, wet or hot weather. Again - once all members arrive at the meeting place, other arrangements can be made for a more permanent, safe and secure shelter.

EVACUATION LINES

If residents are ordered to leave an evacuation perimeter, NO ONE will be allowed to cross the line and return to the evacuation area. If the primary residence or place of refuge is inside this evacuation perimeter, you would not be allowed to return to the residence. This type of evacuation is considered as a police or fire mandated evacuation and they have ultimate authority to force you out of your residence and out of the evacuation perimeter.

You would not be able to assist any other survival team members, friends or neighbors inside of the perimeter nor would you be allowed to retrieve any personal belongings, retrieve your pets or turn off any utilities that you may have forgotten in a panic to leave the area. Furthermore, if you do not know where all survival team members are at the time – you would still be required to leave the area. In these cases, it will be the first responders, including law enforcement, National Guard, military and fire fighters who will be responsible for ensuring everyone is out of the evacuation area. **As part of overall emergency evacuation plans, consider this fact about evacuation lines.**

PETS AND LIVESTOCK

When preparing pets for the possibility of a disaster, remember the basics for survival – *shelter*, *water* and *food*. Consider two kits: (1) everything your pets will need at the primary residence and (2) a light-weight smaller version if you and your pets are required to seek refuge. Be sure to review the kits regularly to guarantee the contents are fresh.

- **Collar/Tag/Harness/Leash**. The pet should wear a collar with a rabies tag and identification at all times. Include a backup leash, collar and identification tag in the pet's emergency supply kit. Place copies of the pet's registration information, adoption papers, vaccination documents and medical records in a clean plastic bag or waterproof container and add them to the kit. Consider permanent identification (microchipping or recovery database).

- **Crate/Pet Carrier**. To evacuate in an emergency situation, the ability to do so will be aided by having a sturdy, safe, comfortable crate or carrier ready for transporting your pet. The carrier should be large enough for your pet to stand, turn around and lie down.

- **First Aid**. Talk with the veterinarian about what is most appropriate for the pet's emergency medical needs. Most kits include cotton bandages, rolls, bandage tape, scissors, antibiotic ointment, flea and tick prevention, latex gloves, alcohol, eye drops and saline solution. Include a pet first aid book.

- **Food**. Keep 7-10 days of dry food in an airtight and waterproof container for each pet. Don't forget to pack the bowl.

- **Photo**. If you become separated from your pet during an emergency, a photo of you and your pet together would help to document ownership and allow others to assist in identifying your pet. Include detailed information about species, breed, age, sex, color and distinguishing characteristics.

- **Sanitation**. Include pet litter and litter box (if appropriate), newspapers, paper towels, plastic trash bags and household chlorine bleach to provide for sanitation needs. You can use bleach as a disinfectant (dilute nine parts water to one part bleach). Do not use scented or color safe bleaches or bleach with added cleaners.

- **Toys**. Include favorite toys, treats or bedding which will help to reduce stress for your pet.

- **Water**. Store at least 7-10 days of water specifically for each pet. Don't forget to pack the bowl.

In the event of evacuation from the primary residence and depending on the circumstances, make sure *advanced planning* is taken with regards to livestock. In some cases, it may be wise to contain and shelter any livestock. In other instances, it may be necessary to release livestock to give them a chance for survival.

Plan

Be prepared to assess the situation. Plan how you will assemble your pets and determine the place of refuge. If you must evacuate, take your pets with you if practical to do so. If you go to a public shelter, keep in mind your pets may not be allowed inside. Secure appropriate lodging *in advance* depending on the number and type of pets in your care.

Options may include a motel that allows pets or a boarding facility such as a kennel or veterinary hospital near an evacuation facility or pre-determined meeting place. Find out before an emergency happens if any of these facilities in your area might be good options. Plan with neighbors, friends or relatives to make sure that someone is available to care for or evacuate pets if you are unable to do so. Show them the location of pet emergency supply kits. Designate specific locations to retrieve pets after the emergency.

Gather contact information for emergency animal treatment. Make a list of contacts, addresses and phone numbers of area animal control agencies including the Humane Society or ASPCA and emergency veterinary hospitals. Keep one copy of these phone numbers with you and one in your pet's emergency supply kit. Purchase or make "**PET ALERT**" stickers and place them near all doors and/or windows *in advance* including information on the number and types of pets in the home to alert firefighters and rescue workers. Consider putting a phone number on the sticker where you could be reached in an emergency.

PET ALERT

PLEASE SAVE OUR PETS

☐ DOG ☐ CAT ☐ BIRD

☐ OTHER _____

Before evacuating and if time permits, write the words "**EVACUATED WITH PETS**" across the stickers if you are able to actually evacuate with your pets and then place the stickers on doors and/or windows. These stickers can be purchased on-line through the ASPCA and other organizations. You may decide to make your own decal. I would also recommend that the background of the sticker be **red** so responders can see it. Due to the fact that these stickers will fade over time, it would be a good idea to laminate the stickers.

The level and consequences will determine what to do with regards to your pets and livestock.

- Whether to take them with you
- Whether to leave them enclosed at the primary residence, either in the house or pet enclosure
- Whether to release them outside

- Whether to leave them with friends, neighbors or other facilities able to facilitate pets and livestock

There are so many factors to consider including:

- Probable length of time you will be away from the primary residence or home
- Whether others in the immediate vicinity will also be required to leave the area
- Whether emergency and rescue workers will be able to reach the area within a reasonable amount of time
- Type of dangers outside the home or shelter where pets are located, i.e., downed power lines
- Weather conditions and temperatures acceptable for survival

Livestock

In most cases, livestock can remain at the primary location unless there is probable danger of flooding or an emergency situation that would cause harm or death to the animals if they remain in place. Depending on the level of disaster, emergency and rescue workers as well as humane societies and other animal groups would attempt to access the damaged areas as quickly as possible to provide assistance.

As a responsible owner, you should also do whatever is possible to provide rescue for your livestock. If circumstances merit the release of livestock in order to provide them with a chance of survival – then do so. If possible, attach some type of collar or tag to your animals with the name of the owner, address and phone number so that after the crisis, livestock can be identified and returned home. In order to assist rescue workers, be sure to attach a "**LIVESTOCK INSIDE**" sticker to barn doors, sheds or other enclosures *prepared in advance* to alert them that livestock are in need of assistance.

PRACTICE DRILLS

By *planning in advance* and practicing what to do in an emergency, teams can learn to react automatically. During several types of disasters, collapsing building materials and heavy falling objects such as bookcases, cabinets, and heating units cause most deaths and injuries. Learn the "safe" and "unsafe" spots in each room of the home. The "safe" spots are under tables, desks and beds.

The "unsafe" areas are inside a doorway, by windows and mirrors, underneath or adjacent to heavy objects standing on the floors or hanging on the walls or ceilings. If there are children in the home, get the entire family to practice going to the "safe" locations. Participating in an emergency drill can help children understand what to do in case you are not with them. Make sure you and the children understand the school's emergency procedures for disasters to help coordination of *where*, *when*, and *how* to reunite with the child.

41

During a drill, get under a sturdy table, desk or bed and if none are available, cover your face and head with your arms or brace yourself in an inside corner of the house or building. Remember that many people are injured at entrances of buildings by falling debris.

Practice drills should be conducted <u>at least twice a year</u>. Another good idea is to include using the car as part of the evacuation plan. Although a car may not be available – if it is – it provides a valuable means to transport members and supplies during an evacuation. Although the practice drills do not need to actually include the evacuation of pets and livestock, make sure each team member "walks through the steps and pretends to do the motions" of handling indoor pets and outdoor pets and livestock.

STORAGE

Remember – the best place to store most emergency supplies is in a *dark*, *cool* and *dry* environment. These storage areas should be located in areas where there is minimal chance of water damage, sun damage, fire damage, heat damage, rodent damage, insect damage or theft. One of the best places to store emergency supplies is in a basement. However, due to the possibility of flooding, all items should be stored <u>above the floor</u> – on pallets or shelves and away from windows and walls. *Never* store items on a concrete floor – especially food or items stored in metal or plastic cans – the lime from the concrete can leach into the containers.

Other areas where emergency supplies could be stored include:

- Above the washer and dryer (shelving)
- Closets
- Attic
- Garage
- Back of a door (shelving)
- Against the walls in rooms (shelving)
- Under the sink
- Under a stairwell
- Under the bed
- Behind the couch or chair
- In an enclosed shed in close proximity to the primary residence
- In a room especially designed for storage
- Underground (providing proper containers are used and items will not be damaged by water, etc.)
- <u>Nearby</u> commercial storage facility

> *And know that I am with you always; yes, to the end of time.*
>
> - **Jesus Christ**

The garage can be used as a storage location – <u>but not for food items, including dehydrated or freeze-dried food</u>. The extreme heat and cold environment in a garage and the possibility of rodent and insect damage and theft are reasons why a garage may not be a good choice. If no other areas are available, items such as tools, equipment and non-perishable supplies can be stored in the garage area.

When storing emergency supplies, <u>items must be stored in the right type of containers</u>. By storing supplies properly, it eliminates waste, destruction or contamination of expensive supplies. Remember that when storing food items, the containers must be approved for <u>food</u> storage. For example, hard plastic paint buckets purchased in hardware stores are <u>not</u> acceptable for storing food items – they contain harmful chemicals that can leach into the food.

By properly organizing emergency supplies in containers, there will be less stress during an emergency – the supplies will be easy to locate and readily available. During an emergency is NOT THE TIME TO BE DISORGANIZED!

There are many places where good storage containers can be purchased or gathered other than grocery or department stores. If buying new containers, purchase them when on sale. Check out local garage sales - you would be surprised how many people are "throwing away" perfect storage containers for your emergency supplies. Another good source is local charitable organizations or dollar stores who sell items at drastically reduced prices or local restaurants and fast-food outlets. A large amount of bulk food items arrive at their doors in sturdy, heavy-duty buckets and containers that are <u>safe for food items</u>. In many cases, these containers are discarded. Make arrangements with the owner or manager to get these containers for your emergency supplies.

There are several types of storage containers that can be used for storing emergency supplies including a large tote or container, barrel, bucket, box, sack or bags just to name a few choices. For example, when storing medical supplies, you could place bandages, lotions, creams, medications, and tools (tweezers, thermometer, tongue blades etc.) in separate small containers or baggies.

On the front of each small storage unit, place a label listing the contents. Then place the smaller containers into one large tote or container and on the front of the large tote, place a label that says **MEDICAL SUPPLIES**. Using this method, and during an emergency, all medical supplies are stored together in one large tote and when opening the **MEDICAL SUPPLIES** storage container, all of the medical supplies are organized and stored in the respective small container for easy access.

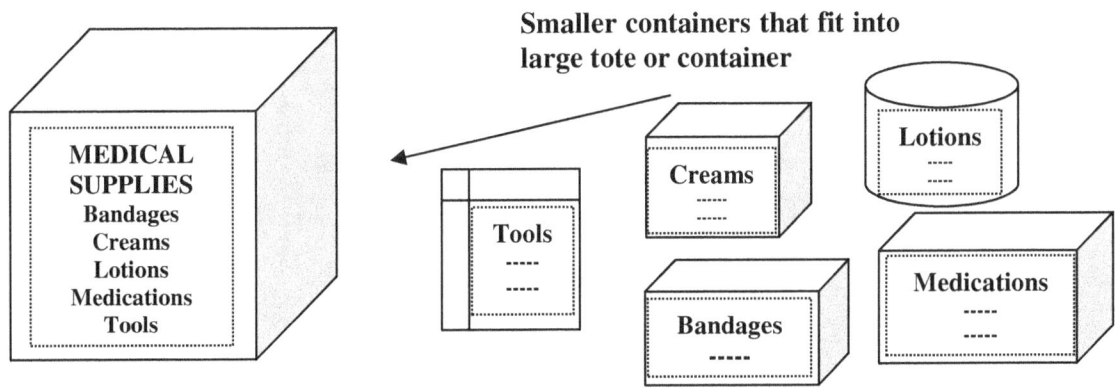

<u>Smaller Containers Holding Items</u>

- Use only containers with tight fitting lids or strong zippers
- Label all containers listing the content type and amount i.e. Razors (2)
- List contents in <u>alphabetical</u> order (to determine quickly if item is inside container)
- Place clear plastic tape over the label (so it won't be torn or come off)
- Use containers that are sturdy but light i.e. hard plastic, metal, leather, denim
- Avoid glass containers and flimsy plastic bags
- Attempt to store "like" items in the same container, i.e. tools, lotions, creams, bandages, medications

When purchasing new items:

- Remove all packaging

- Examine item to ensure you have all parts

- Make sure the item is operational

- Know how to use the item

Clear tape over label

MEDICAL
SUPPLIES
Bandages
Creams
Lotions
Medications
Tools

This chapter gave us the basic emergency preparation principles and guidelines we must follow as we begin gathering our emergency supplies for <u>all</u> elements - including those discussed in Volumes 2 and 3.

Although time-consuming, it is important to take the time to complete the worksheet at the back of this book. By doing so, you will have a solid plan of attack to begin gathering your inventory of supplies.

We have also learned preemptive measures we can take to increase our chances of survival - selecting a primary residence and survival team, determining evacuation locations, initiating practice drills and evaluating the overall safety of our residence. We have also learned some tips on storage of emergency supplies and how we can look out for our pets and livestock.

Remember! Our goal is to preserve and maintain our physical, mental, emotional, spiritual and psychological health during a disaster, and one of the best ways we can accomplish this objective is by planning in advance!

SUCCESS!!!

CHAPTER TWO

EMOTION

HUMAN FACTOR

An essential part of any disaster is the *human reaction* to stress, anxiety, fear, confusion, anger and depression that is so prevalent during a crisis. Human behavior is complex and unpredictable and would certainly escalate during a serious nuclear attack, earthquake, land invasion or other catastrophe that happens rapidly without giving the human mind time to process the events.

With the entire population reacting to the disaster instead of just a few individuals or small groups, the situation could be out of control and dangerous for all citizens. The human mob tends to act irrationally and chaos breeds more chaos. The more frantic the mob, the more difficult it is to contain the population. As human beings – we should not flatter ourselves into thinking that we are exempt from losing control during a crisis.

Reaction to disaster can take place over a considerable period of time and is not just one problem but a series of problems. The real challenge of managing a disaster can actually come from *social disorganization* and not from individual emotional behavior. A disaster can destroy or damage the physical facilities and elements upon which social organization is dependent such as electricity, fuel, communication, transportation, medication and technological developments associated with it. When these elements are damaged or destroyed, the result is social paralysis and later recovery depends on external assistance such as government agencies, or from historically more stable and honorable religious and charitable organizations.

There are many opinions and theories on how the general population will react to various types of disasters. Based on my research, it is my opinion the reaction of the general population will be based on several factors:

The <u>first</u> factor is related to **PAST HISTORY** and **FUTURE EVENTS**.

1. Disaster has <u>happened in the past or can be expected to happen in the future</u>. Although we may not have been personally involved or directly affected by a specific type of disaster, we are aware that in the past, it has occurred in our area and we understand the possibility of the same type of disaster and consequences happening in the future. For example, a power outage, wild fire, flood, hurricane, tornado, thunderstorm, lightning, landslide, drought, riot, terrorist attack, earthquake, heat wave, extreme cold, tsunami, volcano, explosion or chemical spill.

   or

2. Disaster has <u>not happened in the past or is thought to be unlikely to happen in the future</u>. Although we may be familiar with these disasters happening in other countries based on what we have viewed on television or read in the newspapers or magazines, the probability of this type of disaster occurring in our area – or in our country – is <u>believed</u> to be a remote possibility. For example, biological or chemical warfare, land invasion or nuclear war.

Although not everyone has experienced all disasters that are common and familiar in our country, we are at least knowledgeable of the consequences that occur as a result of the disaster and the means used to return to normal living conditions. For example, those individuals in New York City on 11 September 2001 can fully appreciate a terrorist attack on our nation. But through the media, the rest of the nation – and the world – were able to be a part of the crises and experience the destruction, devastation and death. We were able to share the emotions of fear, anger, confusion and loss with those that were there on that day. And over the years, we have watched the recovery of ground zero as well as the nation. In essence, as a nation, we are now familiar with a terrorist attack and have more or less worked through the healing process.

We may not have personally experienced a riot, landslide, wild fire, flood, hurricane, tornado or earthquake, but we know people who have gone through these disasters and we have watched the crisis being aired on television and read about the event in the newspapers. At some level – we are familiar with these disasters.

Our country has <u>not</u> experienced biological or chemical warfare, a nuclear attack or an enemy ground invasion on our soil. With the exception of the Revolutionary War and the Civil War, and in the case of the Pearl Harbor attack during World War II, most wars we have been involved in have been fought on foreign soil and we as a nation have not been subject to destruction and devastation of buildings, structures, natural resources and the land that comes with a war in your own country.

As a nation, we are more likely to react in a constructive way to disasters we have experienced in the past or are familiar with the consequences of these disasters. That is not to say we would not feel the negative emotions that come with any disaster, but we would be able to cope with the consequences and work towards returning to a normal lifestyle and standard of living. A disaster that is uncommon and in our opinion, unlikely, serves to escalate a negative reaction resulting in accelerated stress, apprehension, fear, anger, confusion, resentment, anxiety and sadness. Unless these emotions and feelings were managed by the citizens, an environment of social disorder, chaos and anarchy could easily prevail across the land.

The <u>second</u> factor is related to the **AMOUNT OF TIME** one has to prepare *prior* to the disaster.

1. Disaster <u>occurs immediately and there is no time to prepare for the consequences</u>. We may or may not be familiar with the disaster or the consequences that could result from the crisis. We are caught off-guard and our bodies and mind must take the necessary time to process the event. For example, we are at work and the office building begins to shake and rumble from a 9.2 earthquake; we are driving on the freeway and a truck slides off the road and dumps toxic chemicals; we are at home and the power station explodes across the street; or we are walking down Broadway in New York City and a plane flies into the World Trade Center.

   or

2. Disaster is <u>not immediate and we have a longer period of time to prepare for the consequences</u>. We may or may not be familiar with the disaster or the consequences that could result from the crisis, but we have been given warning time to prepare *prior* to the disaster and are able to focus in advance on survival techniques. In some cases, we may have less than an hour to prepare and in other cases, we may have months or even years to prepare for the disaster on our doorstep.

   For example, we have been informed that a hurricane or tornado is heading towards our city and should be in our area within an hour; heavy snowfall from winter storms is anticipated to bring flooding to the valleys in the spring; a wild fire burning on the hill and prevailing winds suggest damage to surrounding structures; news of an upcoming severe snow, rain, thunder or lightning storm; continued dry spells throughout the country taking a toll on wheat, fruit and vegetable crops or **we have been told over and over again to prepare at least a years worth of emergency supplies for what will come in the last days**.

Over the years, I have asked myself whether I would want to die suddenly or be given enough time to get my house in order, say goodbye to my family and friends and make legal and financial arrangements for my home, personal property and my pets. My personality tends to want to prepare for the event. I prefer not to be caught off-guard and have the disaster strike me from behind when I am unprepared and ill-equipped to deal with the crisis. I want to be able to face the dragon- in fact, bring it on!

I am better able to cope with disaster if I have enough time to analyze and process the anticipated consequences and plan appropriate action to survive the crisis. I recognize that others may prefer not to go through the anguish of waiting for a disaster to strike. Regardless, depending on an immediate or extended time for a disaster, each person will have to deal with the emotional and psychological fallout in their own way. Remember that although your survival team may have *prepared in advance* for future disasters – others will not. Team members must be prepared to deal with those who are <u>not</u> prepared and their reactions and behaviors that will ensue during and after the crisis.

The <u>third</u> factor is related to the **DURATION** of the disaster <u>and</u> of the **CONSEQUENCES** - a short time or an extended length of time.

1. Disaster and consequences <u>last a short amount of time – generally one hour to a month</u>. The actual disaster generally lasts for only a short period of time, for example, an earthquake only shakes the earth for a few seconds, a hurricane moves rapidly through an area, or a thunderstorm, wind storm or rain storm lasts only a few hours. Although we may experience stress, fear, anxiety or panic during the disaster, once the calamity is over, we are relieved and able to evaluate any consequences. The consequences could be nothing more than an inconvenience or annoyance to our daily schedules.

    For example, as a result of a severe thunder storm, the electrical power could go out for several hours or even an entire day or night; a severe winter storm strands us on the side of the road until morning; a lightning storm forces us to leave the golf course before we have finished the game; or a riot in the city requires stores and markets to close for a few days in order to repair damage and restock supplies.

    or

2. Disaster and consequences <u>last an extended length of time – generally one month to one year and even up to five years</u>. The actual disaster and consequences alter our life style, our standard of living and our ability to survive each day. As the length of time increases, the ability for the human psychic to cope and function rationally becomes strained. For example, a heat wave involving extreme temperatures that overcome a region over an entire season, an extended famine that reduces or eliminates many of the food sources in the area or a world-wide nuclear war that involves every country on the planet.

Although the disaster can be devastating to our bodies and mind, if the crisis is short-lived, most human beings can process the event and focus on how to manage the aftermath of consequences. A long-term disaster has a tendency to wear down our ability to battle the dragons that continue to attack our body and our mind. We may lose the will to fight and confidence we can overcome the odds we perceive are stacked against us. I believe this is where the "God Factor" becomes important – it would be by His grace that we are able to cope with the consequences and hopefully survive the overall disaster.

The <u>fourth</u> factor is related to the **SEVERITY** of the disaster and of the **CONSEQUENCES**.

1. Disaster and consequences are <u>mild to medium</u> in nature. As a result, the consequences will more than likely also be mild or medium in inconvenience, damage or destruction. For example, a wind storm passing through the area uproots only a few trees; a wildfire is quickly contained causing no structural damage or loss of life; an earthquake registering only 3.1 on the Richter Scale with very minor damage to structures; or a river overruns the bank where there is no damage to natural resources, humans or wildlife.

    or

2. Disaster and consequences are <u>severe</u> in nature. As a result, the consequences will more than likely result in severe damage, destruction and devastation to the land, natural resources, wildlife, plant life and human population. For example, a comet could literally strike the earth causing a complete and catastrophic environmental change to our entire planet; a world war lasting for years; a volcano could erupt destroying entire villages, forests, mountains, rivers, lakes, and wildlife; a hurricane could be so severe as to cause wide-spread flooding in cities and vital agricultural areas; or a drought, famine or pestilence could be so relentless and brutal as to wipe out entire civilizations, states and nations.

47

The severity of the disaster will have a direct impact on how the human population will react during the crisis. During a severe disaster, the ability to avoid stress and use our logic, common sense, judgment and reason will be stretched to the limit. There will be many persons who will become overwhelmed with anxiety, fear, confusion and anger over the circumstances. The ability to avoid panic will be difficult and challenging.

There are other factors that become prevalent *before*, *during* and *after* a disaster. For example, there are specific elements that are fundamental to survival for all living creatures. The **OPERATIONS** Element includes many sources needed for life, namely shelter and water. Without shelter from environmental (heat, cold, wet, dry) and man-made (ammunition, biological and chemical warfare, nuclear attack, bombs) elements, a living creature will be susceptible to death in a short period of time. A healthy human being can survive without drinking water for three or five days. The question one must ask is how long do you believe it would take before you took drastic action to get these fundamental survival items for you and the team members and more importantly, how long do you think others will wait?

For many centuries, societies have managed to live productive and successful lives without the use of cell phones, automobiles, computers, toilets, aspirin, McDonalds and Wal-Mart – but these advancements provide conveniences to our society we take for granted and have learned to depend on for our day-to-day living. These man-made "toys" are engrained in our lives and to be denied could result in severe and vicious withdrawal and our ability to cope with the disaster could be a problem.

The unconditional need for shelter, water and food and the desire for perceived luxuries could easily drive many human beings to behave, respond and act "as necessary" to get supplies for their ultimate survival during any disaster. The factors listed above will ultimately determine the thinking process, physical reaction and behavior of a human being in dealing with disaster scenarios and the ability of society to maintain social order.

EMOTION PHASES

There are several factors that influence the reaction we have to fear, anxiety and stress and some factors that are generally beyond our influence: (1) the disaster type, intensity and duration, (2) the duration of time between receiving a warning and the disaster event, and (3) the time of day and the season of the year. Other factors are susceptible to our influence including: (1) education, preparation and training a person takes prior to disaster situations, (2) government knowledge, competency and preparation of disaster events and what civil defense preparation has on the population, and (3) actual location of team members *before*, *during* and *after* the disaster.

A disaster generally has five phases that are part of the human ability to deal with the consequences. The mind first issues a warning to the body that a disaster is coming or in process. The disaster is then met with crash, followed by alarm, then a retreat phase and finally a healing phase.

Warning

It is important for survival team members to heed the counsel of religious leaders, scientists, government and other knowledgeable agencies about the possibility of disaster and prepare and practice a definite plan of action *in advance* of an anticipated disaster scenario. Lack of preparation causes anxiety - especially if there is knowledge that a disaster is a possibility. If the population is apathetic to danger or lacks practice and experience of warning, it fails to recognize the nearness of danger and to react in a reasonable manner. In preparing the overall emergency plan, and as a team, there should be no doubt as to the action to be taken during a disaster scenario. The plan of action for each scenario should be well understood and well rehearsed by all team members.

During any serious disaster, a large number of people will be stunned or dazed. There would be no professional, psychiatric or medical care because all physicians would be engaged in life saving treatment. The other agencies such as police, fire, military and civil defense volunteers would be assigned to re-establishing vital functions, services, systems and facilities to the nation. As a team *prepared in advance* for disaster – members will be more likely to survive the ordeal with less mental, emotional, psychological and physical repercussions than those in the population who chose not to heed the warning and are unprepared to face the crises.

Crash

Once the disaster happens, crash is the time period (generally lasting a few minutes to an hour) when the population reacts to the situation. The reaction to the impact by the population can be divided into three groups (1) the cool and collected (these people are effective), (2) the stunned, dazed or bewildered (most of the population), and (3) the confused, bewildered and anxious including those who exhibit hysterical crying (these persons are ineffective and unable to look after themselves).

Social disorganization occurs immediately at the time of crash and will be extensive throughout the population. The behavior of individuals may appear confused to the outside observer and lack of uniformity in action looks like "panic" but it is really a symptom of social disorganization.

During a serious disaster, there will be few individuals, if any, who exhibit a cool and collected demeanor. Those who do have their wits about them will more than likely be religious leaders and perhaps some community leaders. The individuals who are stunned, dazed or bewildered are typical of normal people and at some point, the stunned response will be replaced by irritability, difficulty in making up the mind, sadness or resentment of authority, muscular tension or freezing of action, sweating, rapid heart rate, rapid breathing, giddiness, nausea or even vomiting. These are normal bodily functions in preparation for fight or flight.

Team members should understand *before*, *during* and *after* a disaster, there will be a reaction to the disaster and consequences (including even rioting and general chaos) will occur as a result of the crises. By *planning in advance*, the team will be better equipped to successfully cope with these consequences unlike the population who exhibits confusing and anxious reactions.

Alarm

Flight does not mean alarm or panic because when danger is recognized, the population rightfully seeks safety by purposeful flight. Terror means blind flight and is based on the perception of danger and the impression that all escape routes are blocked. Some studies even conclude that wide scale panic is not a common finding even in large-scale disasters. I disagree.

During an actual emergency situation, orderly flight would be the only rational choice if one is to survive. For example, if a large group of people are in a burning building, it would be logical to assume that if individuals exit the building in an orderly fashion, it is more likely that everyone will be able to get out of the building. On the other hand, if everyone rushes to the exit, there are going to be people who fall and get trampled or pushed and shoved aside while other frantic persons attempt to make their escape.

Unfortunately, the human species is not known for being logical – especially during a crisis situation. It is more probable that during an actual serious disaster, there will be **MAJOR PANIC** by most of the population affected by the disaster. If an individual truly believes they are facing imminent death - calmness, good manners and compassion for others may not be at the top of their priority list.

During some types of disaster, an immediate large-scale exodus could no doubt take place and after a momentary escape, may be followed by return and purposeless activity. Team members must recognize that during an actual emergency, although they may be able to deal effectively with the crisis – others will not – and these are the individuals that team members must deal with when managing their own safety and security – and more importantly – their overall health.

Retreat

Retreat usually lasts several hours to several days as survivors achieve more awareness of what has happened. Disaster tends to lead towards dependency feelings and survivors may move toward each other for mutual protection and emotional support and begin to depend on one another for survival. The need to be with others becomes so strong that social barriers can disappear and results in a dramatic increase of social solidarity. There could be an outpouring of love, generosity and self-sacrifice in those who have experienced the disaster.

However, it is not as marked in people outside the disaster area, that is, among people who will be called upon to share home and food with disaster victims. For psychological first aid, an important healing component will be the need to ventilate and express oneself in talking through the ordeal with other team members and survival teams. The management of this phase may be of crucial significance to the subsequent overall health of all survivors.

After the disaster, survivors will spontaneously select their leaders. In general, the group will look to the "cool and collected" persons for leadership. These leaders would more than likely be known religious leaders or prominent community leaders whose role will be to foster morale, lead their groups into constructive activity and provide an atmosphere of confidence and reassurance to those individuals assigned to the group. Depending on the severity, duration, and consequences of the disaster, and the status of government, politicians and workers may or may not be available or even accepted by survivor groups.

Healing

The healing process extends from a few days after collision and after the danger has passed and may cover the rest of a person's life. The environment is no longer threatening but is somewhat predictable. The first full awareness occurs now – an awareness of what the disaster has "meant" in terms of loss and possessions, home and loved ones. The reactions can include anxiety, fatigue, depression and hysteria. It is important to allow team members to talk out the experiences and perform useful activity.

Every single person will deal with human emotions during an emergency situation in their own way - and it will be different for everyone. There will be some who will behave in a rational manner throughout the entire process. The majority of the population, however, will become frightened and confused. There is nothing more dangerous than a frightened and confused animal - and yes, we are animals as well.

There will be many citizens who will use the disaster as a convenient excuse to begin looting, stealing and even killing to take supplies they will need to survive the disaster. As the severity and duration of a disaster increases in time, even other law-abiding citizens will begin to demonstrate a lawless attitude and behavior in order to protect and provide for themselves.

However, at some point in time, the general population will no longer allow individuals, thugs or gangs to hide behind laws or convenient excuses that allow them to harm team members or steal emergency supplies. These individuals will be dealt with deliberately and swiftly to protect the overall population. The overall population will *come* together to *work* together in order to *survive* together.

CHAPTER THREE

OPERATION

One of the most important components in an emergency preparation plan is to ensure that *operational* needs and concerns are addressed <u>prior to any emergency</u> to reduce overall problems in obtaining shelter, electricity, light, heat, clothing, tools and water during a disaster situation. Depending on the severity of the disaster, our basic needs for shelter and utilities could easily be damaged or destroyed with household destruction, power outage, fuel disruption and/or contaminated water.

EMERGENCY PREPARATION PRINCIPLES

There are <u>six</u> principles that can be incorporated into the overall emergency plan to prepare for and in some cases eliminate *operational* issues that can become prevalent during an emergency situation. For example:

- Purchases for the **OPERATION** Element are a high priority – we are dealing with ultimate survival – shelter, electricity, light, heat, clothing and water.

- Know your operations inventory and where it is stored. Know how much you have of all resources, supplies and items associated with the **OPERATION** Element. Supplies should be readily available and logistically located for easy access and transport.

- A shelter-in-place is a vital component for emergency preparation. Obtain all necessary supplies and store in the designated room.

- A place of refuge is essential in the event of evacuation from the primary residence. This location could be a family-owned trailer house, motor home, trailer, camper or summer home. It could also be a public shelter, church, school or even a location in the mountains or desert. Scout out the area and make sure all members are familiar with the surroundings and a plan is in place for survival at these locations.

- Investigate all alternative shelter, electrical, heat, light and water natural resources in the area for use during a disaster.

- When creating your emergency operations plan, use methods that include *alternatives* or *layers* of sources and items so if one fails or is not available or realistic to use, another item or source may be used instead.

SHELTER

During a disaster, there are several scenarios that could happen with regards to shelter. For example:

1. A disaster has occurred but you still have the primary residence for protection and all or some utilities and other important facilities, equipment, machinery and/or tools.

2. A disaster has occurred and the primary residence is damaged or destroyed, all or part of the utilities is damaged and other arrangements must be made to provide shelter.

51

SHELTERING IN PLACE

Depending on the type of emergency, and assuming that your primary residence is alright and utilities are working, "sheltering in place" may be a proper first response to guarantee survival. A shelter-in-place can be used for several scenarios: (1) a disaster or emergency has occurred that makes residing in the entire residence impossible or impractical and (2) a disaster has occurred that requires team members to locate in the primary residence *and* an enclosed area. And once again – planning ahead for this possibility will eliminate stress and possible loss of life.

> Every home should have a designated shelter-in-place location where survival team members would reside during specific short-term emergencies or disaster situations.

A common emergency that merits the use of a shelter-in-place room is a broken furnace in the middle of winter (with below freezing temperatures) and it's going to take several days to get the part *or* a power outage in an area that could mean no heat from the furnace and no water in the taps. Until the furnace has been repaired or electricity is restored and the power comes back on - the shelter-in-place room would be a logical location to "set up camp".

Other possible disasters that could initiate this type of shelter may be a biological or chemical attack or even a chemical spill where the main security measure will be to avoid breathing in the contaminated air. In such a circumstance, you would either witness the disaster first-hand and/or be directed by the Emergency Alert System through the media to immediately take shelter and provide as much protection for the team as possible. Survival team members who reside in regions that may be susceptible to biological or chemical spills should take special precautions.

In the event of biological or chemical disasters, retreat to a room as far from outside air as possible and seal your survival team into it by covering window and door openings, air ducts and heater vents with plastic sheeting, and sealing the edges securely with tape. This room should be on an upper floor since chemical and biological agents are heavier than air and will settle to the lowest point. When selecting the room at the primary residence to serve as a "shelter-in-place" – consider using a room with little or no outside windows and doorways.

If possible, use a room with direct access to water and/or bathroom facilities. Sinks and toilet drain traps should have water in them which acts as a seal. You can use the toilet but you should **NOT** drink water from the sink or bathtub tap. More than likely, electrical power could be available and appliances requiring electricity in your room could be used providing you seal the electric plug and/or the electrical outlet being used by the appliance to avoid air from the outlet coming into the room. The team would most likely not be in the shelter for more than a few hours; however, you should plan for a minimum of three days. Listen to the television and/or radio for announcements indicating it is safe to leave your shelter.

The following items should be readily available in this designated room:

- Food - ready to eat
- Water (one gallon of water per person or pet per day in plastic bottles)
- First Aid Kit / Medications
- Bedding / Sleeping bag
- Books (Spiritual and Entertainment)
- Flashlight / Lantern (solar)
- Radio (crank-handle or solar-powered)
- Duct Tape
- Scissors (to plan ahead - have plastic pre-cut)
- Towels
- Plastic sheeting (heavy duty)
- Stapler and staples (heavy duty)
- Telephone

> My master bedroom is the "shelter-in-place" room. It has one window and door. A bathroom offers water and bath facilities. My clothes are in this area. The room has a TV (if power is available). A fireplace is in the room (which would have to be sealed off during a biological or chemical attack or chemical spill) but would be beneficial during disasters requiring other "shelter-in-place" room situations.

- Heater (if cold weather)
- Weapon/Ammo

Once the decision has been made to shelter-in-place, use the following steps:

1. Release the livestock from enclosures and pens – give them a chance to run and survive
2. Get inside the house as quickly as possible (**DON'T FORGET THE PETS**)
3. Shut and lock all outside doors and windows
4. Turn off the air conditioner, furnace and all fans
5. Go into your designated shelter-in-place room and shut the door (<u>take pets with you</u>)
6. Close all outside windows in the room
7. Shut fireplace flue and tape heavy-duty plastic over the opening of the fireplace (chemical/biological)
8. Tape heavy-duty plastic over the windows in the room
9. Use duct tape around the windows, doors and vents and make an unbroken seal
10. Seal any electrical outlets or other openings
11. Turn on television and/or radio for instructions

<u>Loss of Electrical Power</u>

A situation may occur in many areas where the electrical power is off for an extended period of time during the winter (cold) months. When electrical power is lost, the inconvenience is much greater than not being able to turn on the lights. For most households, the furnace heating the home requires electrical power. Households using underground wells for water also require electrical power to run the pump that brings water from underground into the home.

During a power outage lasting for an extended period of time, and depending on the season, weather conditions or outside temperature, <u>the main focus will be to maintain heat and warmth for the survival team and to ensure that water pipes are not frozen.</u>

> *When Thomas Edison worked late into the night on the electric light, he did it by gas lamp or candle. I'm sure it made the work seem that much more urgent.*
>
> **- George Carlin**

Again, a modified "shelter-in-place" plan can be used during this type of emergency situation. Select a room that is adjacent to an alternate heat source that has water and bath facilities if possible.

1. Using your heavy duty plastic sheeting and duct tape, seal off any outside windows and doors and construct a barrier (that allows for individuals to come in and out of the room but still keeps the heat in the room) on the inside door connecting this room with the rest of the house

2. If an alternative heat source is available in this "shelter-in-place" room, i.e., fireplace, wood-burning stove), make sure adequate fuel is available

3. Gather bedding and sleeping bags (if necessary) and put in this room – this room is where the entire survival team (and pets) can sleep for the duration of the emergency

4. Gather warm clothing for all team members to wear during the emergency, i.e. warm pants, shirts, coats, hats, gloves, socks, shoes, underwear, house slippers, robe and sleepwear

   <u>To drain water out of water pipes in the house and to keep them from freezing and breaking:</u>

5. Although the electricity is off, turn off the main electrical breaker switch to the house (usually located in the garage or utility room). If using an underground well for water, this will guarantee that the electric pump in the well will not operate to bring any water from the well into the house.

6.   Turn off the main valve bringing water into the house so no additional water gains access into the water pipes of the home.

7.   Drain the hot water heater (do not turn on the electric breaker controlling the hot water heater while the water heater is empty - it will cause serious damage to the heater).

8.   Open all taps (kitchen, sink, utility room) and allow water to drain out (you may wish to catch this water in a container for use). <u>Leave the taps open.</u>

Once the emergency is over and electrical power has been restored, (1) turn on the main electrical breaker switch, (2) turn <u>off</u> the breaker that controls the hot water heater, (3) close all open taps, (4) open the main water valve, (5) fill the hot water heater, and (6) turn <u>on</u> the breaker that controls the hot water heater. Depending on the conditions, you may wish to say in the "shelter-in-place" room until the furnace can regenerate adequate heat throughout the house.

PLACE OF REFUGE

A healthy human can survive for several weeks without food and several days without water. However, without proper shelter from the environment - especially during cold winter months, inclement weather, heat waves etc., chances of survival could be reduced to several hours. That is why it is important to *prepare in advance* for alternative shelter facilities and if necessary, know how to build an emergency survival shelter – or have a place of refuge in the event the survival team must evacuate the primary residence and find other facilities. This place of refuge would be designated as the "new primary residence" and would be considered as the location where team members could then focus on survival through the course of the emergency. In some cases, survival teams may elect to designate a location other than the primary residence as the principal place of refuge where team members will go at the very onset of the disaster (regardless of the condition of the homes where team members reside) and would remain at this location throughout the crisis.

If the main household of residence or designated primary residence is damaged or destroyed, there are many *layers* or *alternatives* that could be used for short-term, medium-term and long-term shelter purposes including:

- **Second Residence, i.e., cabin or summer home (stocked)**
- **Bomb Shelter (stocked)**
- **Motor Home (stocked)**
- **Travel Trailer (stocked)**
- **Camper (stocked)**
- **Houseboat (stocked)**
- Tent
- Sandbags
- Shed
- Barn
- Vacant Lot
- Horse Trailer
- Van/Car
- Abandoned buildings, structures or cars
- Friend or Relative
- Neighbor
- School
- Post Office (always open)
- Hotel/Motel
- Apartment/Condo

> **Depending on the circumstances, survival team members should have <u>advanced permission</u> to access and reside in buildings and/or structures they do not legally own. Owners tend to become cranky when "squatters" set up house on their property.**
>
> **Although United States Post Office buildings are always open, this should <u>not</u> be considered as an open invitation to set up a permanent household. The post office would be only a very short-term (one night) solution until more permanent arrangements could be made for the team.**

- Public Shelter
- Underground Bunker
- Igloo (during winter months)
- Caves
- Tree House
- Lean-To Structures (Tarps, Ropes, Knife)

There are countless ways to construct a temporary shelter <u>to use outside</u>. As part of your overall emergency preparation plan, attempt to make whatever arrangements are necessary to have these items available to you during a disaster (for example, include them in the evacuation kit and/or in the car(s) :

- Tarps (heavy duty)
- Ropes (heavy duty)
- Tent (heavy duty)
- Knife (heavy duty)
- Knife Sharpening Tool (heavy duty)

For some survival teams, the place of refuge may have to be a church, school or other public shelter in walking distance from the primary residence simply because they have no other alternatives available to them. However, many survival teams will have other alternative shelters in place, <u>such as a motor home, travel trailer, camper, cabin or summer house, or even an enclosed shed or barn</u>. There will be numerous teams who may decide to head for the mountains or desert to live out the disaster. Whatever location is selected by the team members, appropriate provisions should be made available *in advance* for medium to long-term emergencies.

An important factor to <u>consider</u> is the physical location of the place of refuge. As a general rule, if the place of refuge is a motor home, travel trailer or camper located on the property of the primary residence, make sure it is located as far away as possible from the primary residence - that way, if the primary residence is damaged or destroyed, there is a likelihood that your alternative place of refuge may still be available. If it is to be a cabin or summer house, the location should <u>not</u> be any more than 5-10 miles from the primary residence. It may be possible for the team to walk a longer distance but it may not be advantageous to make the journey. For example, the canyon access to a cabin could be impassable, the roads leading to the summer house could be destroyed, or there could be mobs or gangs canvassing the vicinity creating unsafe travel conditions.

Unless the place of refuge is a government or church building, the structure should be a location where at least one survival team member has legal ownership or authority to occupy the physical premises or property. Unless circumstances require immediate action, all vacant buildings or structures should be avoided as a place of refuge – property owners generally do not take kindly to perceived "squatters" occupying their property - even during disasters.

If a cabin, summer house, motor home, travel trailer or camper are to be used as the place of refuge, try to stock it *in advance* with all basic emergency supplies needed for the duration of a disaster. During an actual disaster is <u>not</u> the time to begin stocking these places of refuge with emergency supplies.

PUBLIC SHELTERS AND RECEPTION CENTERS

<u>The first preference is to remain in our homes and/or primary residence during the course of a disaster</u>. But as we have learned, that may not always be possible and alternatives may have to be made by team members. We have learned that some teams may choose to head for the mountains or desert and others will have access to recreational vehicles. However, many survival teams will not have the luxury of these amenities, including most college students, citizens and illegal aliens living off government assistance, the homeless, the elderly, newlyweds, or individuals living in apartments, condominiums or trailer courts. At some point in time during the course of an extended disaster, most citizens may have to rely on public shelters to offer shelter (in the event their home and/or

primary residence is damaged or destroyed) as well as food, water, clothing, sanitation and first aid supplies once their own supplies have been used up.

The federal government has given authority to the American Red Cross to scrutinize and designate government buildings and other public facilities that can be used as public shelters, if necessary, during an emergency. These buildings must meet stringent criteria, i.e., number of toilets, kitchen facilities and square footage, in order to be approved as being a public shelter facility. After a disaster has occurred, local emergency officials would contact the American Red Cross assigned to their region, and based on the severity and location of the disaster, the American Red Cross would approve specific structures that would serve as public shelters during the course of the emergency. The local officials would then provide this information to local citizens using communication media available in the area. As part of this plan, the Red Cross **IF POSSIBLE** would contract with local services to provide food, water, sanitation and medical support for the occupants in the public shelter. In many cases, recreation centers, stadiums, convention centers and local schools are designated as public shelters.

There are other structures that may be designated as *reception centers*. In many cases, these structures include local churches (although many churches will plan to serve as actual shelters for their congregations) or even city or county buildings. The role of a reception center is to register refugees, perform triage (determine extent of injuries), provide *basic* first aid and advise city and/or county emergency personnel of any serious medical or transportation requirements. Government officials, in turn, would attempt to make arrangements for medical and/or transportation for individuals requiring additional care. In most cases, neither the county nor city would provide any food, water, clothing, sanitation or other emergency supplies to these reception centers. Individuals would be required to provide their own emergency supplies.

It is important to recognize a few significant points about both public shelters and reception centers:

- Individuals who are housed in either a public shelter or reception center would be required to register.

- Both public shelters and reception centers will become more crowded as the length of the disaster increases, both with families who loose the use of their home or primary residence and when families and individuals run out of food, water and other emergency supplies.

- Due to safety reasons, fire and fuel of any kind would not be allowed in any public shelter or reception area. Any cooking (if allowed) would be done outside of the building.

- There would be individuals who would insist on smoking, drinking and playing loud music.

- There will be a significant diversity of people from different races, wealth, ethnic backgrounds, creeds, cultures, customs, traditions, morals and religions - count on the fact that not everyone is not going to behave in the same way that you do - get ready for some possible confrontations.

- Most refugees would be frightened, angry, confused, frustrated, stressed and discouraged - which many times will lead to quick-tempered outbursts and the inability to tolerate the behaviors of others.

- There would be a large number of children whose parents are unable or unwilling to control their children's behavior and actions. Insist on parents controlling their children.

- Privacy and space for each survival team and/or individual would be limited.

- Count on long lines at available and/or working restrooms and food lines.

- It is possible that hardened criminals, pick-pockets, child molesters, thieves, drug dealers, addicts and gang members may also choose to take shelter in these public shelters or reception centers.

- Not everyone will consider using trash receptacles and toilets - prepare for probable garbage, trash, urine and feces in and around the facility.

- Prepare for bad smells - smells from unusual or rotten food, possible sewer backups, trash and garbage, urine and feces and lack of personal hygiene including individuals who are not *able* or *willing* to shower, brush their teeth, use deodorant or wash their clothes. This may even include you.

- Prepare for continual loud noises, screaming, talking and shouting. Not everyone will maintain the same sleep schedule.

- Prepare for interrupted, reduced or no utilities, including electricity, heat, air conditioning, lights, etc.

- Depending on the severity and the duration of the disaster, food, water, sanitation and medical supplies may or may not be available - even in public shelters.

Special care and precautions should be taken by survival team members at all times while staying in any type of public shelter or reception center - watch children carefully and enforce their good behavior and guard your supplies. On the other hand, the simple fact that there are a large number of people in the shelter would generally discourage thugs and gang members from challenging any one individual - there really is strength in numbers.

As part of *preparing in advance*, contact the local officials in your city, county and state and find out about the emergency plan in your area, where the public shelters and reception centers will be located, the process to be used to notify the public about their availability and use, and rules and guidelines that will be enforced at the facility.

Light-Duty Tent

A light-duty and inexpensive tent included in the evacuation kit can provide a privacy barrier inside a public shelter or reception center. Depending on the situation, you may be able to set up the tent inside the building. This particular tent shifts its purpose from protecting you from the outside elements to providing the team with some privacy while changing clothes or sleeping. It must be a pop-tent or other small freestanding tent not requiring stakes.

HEAT (WARMTH)

If living in a region that experiences cold temperatures, and depending on the time of year when an emergency happens, survival team members must have adequate heating sources. As part of *planning in advance*, make sure the primary residence and all homes where team members reside have ample insulation in the attic and walls of the structure.

Various forms of insulation are also available for water pipes (under the sinks) and for flues attached to the furnace. Make sure all windows and doors are caulked.

> **As part of an experiment, I turned my furnace off the latter part of March - it was still very chilly outside but not cold enough to freeze my pipes. I chose not to use any other heat source and wanted to see just how I could manage having no heat in the house at all. I assumed by putting on a jacket or coat, I would be fine. WRONG! Even with warm socks, mittens and a hat, I was very uncomfortable! It was hard to move around in the house and I lost a lot of energy. I didn't seem to have the "get-up-and-go" to work on chores or even read a book. And the worst thing of all - my nose and feet were always cold! And when I was in bed, the sheets were cold too! I could never get warm! I was irritable, ornery and bad-tempered during the entire length of the experiment which lasted five weeks. I can just imagine what it would have been like with small children or elderly parents in the home! Not very funny!**

Based on the severity of the disaster, it is probable utilities including electricity, natural gas and/or propane would be disrupted. For most households, the furnace heating the home requires electrical power. During a power outage lasting for an extended period of time and depending on the season, weather conditions or outside temperature, <u>a critical factor will be to maintain heat and warmth for the team – and the pets!</u>

Again, a modified "shelter-in-place" plan could be used during this type of emergency situation.

1. Select a room that will be used for living purposes during the emergency (your "shelter-in-place" designated room would more than likely be the best choice).

2. Using your heavy duty plastic sheeting and duct tape, seal off the outside windows and doors.

3. Construct a barrier (allowing for individuals to come in and out of the room but still keeps the heat in the room) on the inside door connecting this room with the rest of the house.

4. If an alternative heat source is available in this "shelter-in-place" room, i.e., fireplace, wood-burning stove), make sure adequate fuel is available.

5. Gather appropriate bedding and sleeping bags (if necessary) and place in this room – this room is where the entire family (and pets) can sleep during the length of the emergency.

6. Gather warm clothing for all family members to wear during the length of emergency, i.e. warm pants, shirts, coats, hats, gloves, socks, shoes, underwear, house slippers, robe and sleepwear.

It is important to have several *alternatives* or *layers* of heat (warmth) available such as:

- **Fireplace** (wood-burning)
- **Wood Burning Stove**
- **Wood** (for fireplace and stove)
- **Axe** (for cutting wood)
- **Coal** (for fireplace and stove)
- **Generator and Fuel** (preferably a <u>solar</u> powered generator)
- Space Heaters (electric and/or butane)
- Catalytic Heaters
- Barbeque and Briquettes – outside only (for heating hot water for hot water bottle, drinks etc.)
- **WARM CLOTHING** (coats, shirts, pants, socks, shoes, hats, gloves, robe, sleepwear, slippers)
- **Rain Gear**
- **Thermal Underwear**
- Chemical Hand and Feet Warmers
- Hot Water Bottle
- Heating Pad
- **BEDDING** (quilts and blankets)
- **SLEEPING BAGS** (tested for cold weather)
- **Plastic** (Heavy-Duty) - place over windows/doorways
- **Stapler and Staples** (Heavy-Duty)
- Campfire
- **Matches**
- Flint Fire Starter Tool
- Fire Extinguisher
- Fire Alarm (battery operated)
- Carbon Monoxide Detector (battery operated)

> **Make sure you have an outside thermometer to read temperatures.**

> **It is easier to heat a small space than a large space. Consider setting up a freestanding pop tent inside the room where you plan to sleep. The tent would trap and conserve heat – even if it's only body heat. Another way to set up a tent is to use a card table and spread a large blanket or quilt over the top and sides. Either way, the idea is to contain all the heat you can in a small space. This concept can also be used to house and shelter pets during cold temperatures.**

- Tent (pop tent that does not require staking)
- Card Table (for making a tent)

BLANKETS AND BEDDING

There are many types of blankets on the market today. Assuming the primary residence is intact and you live there during the emergency, you may require alternative heat sources. These blankets would be <u>located</u> at the primary residence, would <u>stay</u> at the primary residence and would be <u>used</u> at the primary residence.

Virgin Acrylic Blanket	Very warm and has many of the advantages of wool. Lightweight. Squishable. Dries quickly. Good choice for evacuation kit as well.
Fleece Throws	Warm. Very affordable. Squishable. Dries quickly. Keeps you warm when wet. Good choice for evacuation kit as well.
Wool Blankets	Very warm. Very bulky. Heavy. Takes a long time to dry.
Thermal Blankets	Warm. Fairly bulky. Lightweight. Dries quickly.
Polyester/Acrylic Blankets	Fairly warm. Fairly heavy and bulky. Inexpensive.
Quilts	Very warm. Bulky. Heavy. Takes a long time to dry.
Comforters	Very warm. Bulky. Heavy. Takes a long time to dry.
Sleeping Bags (cotton/polyester)	Very warm. Water repellent. Bulky. Can be expensive.

CLOTHING

Although clothing is necessary twelve months a year – the subject merits discussion on the <u>type</u> of clothing to be stored and available for each survival team member during emergency situations.

Depending on the level of disaster (1-3), all manufacturing, wholesale and local retail clothing outlets could be damaged or destroyed within a short period of time. For example, if oil production and processing is disrupted, the manufacturing of clothing articles would be impacted since many fabrics are made from oil-based products. If electric power is disrupted, sewing machines will not operate, commercial outlets would close their doors and clothing purchases would become difficult if not impossible.

There are specific types of clothing that should be part of all survival team members' emergency pantries depending on the time of year, season, temperature and weather conditions. Obviously, team members living on the equator can dispense with the warm clothing items. Clothing articles do not need to be new items, <u>but should be well made and in good condition</u>. There are many places where used clothing can be purchased including charitable organizations, garage sales, second-hand stores, or even from relatives, friends and neighbors.

The clothing items stored for emergency purposes does *not* include prom dresses, tuxedoes, bow ties, suits, high heel shoes or hats with feathers. A disaster event is <u>not</u> the place for a fashion show. The clothing for THIS event should be manufactured for every-day use and for the work environment. Although spring and summer apparel will not be as heavy or bulky, these clothes should also be made of good quality fabric and materials that will hold up well and withstand the stress and strain of a survival environment. Consider the likelihood of growth and expansion for most survival team members – infants, children and teenagers will more than likely grow taller and adults tend to grow wider - - - sigh.

When selecting clothing for emergency pantries –spring, summer, fall or winter seasons – hot and cold temperatures – dry and wet weather - use common sense and select items that are durable, resilient, hard-wearing, long-lasting and flexible. Choose fabrics that are "wash and wear" – easy wash – quick dry – no iron! Depending on the budget, the emphasis is not to purchase emergency clothing at high-end stores but instead, to obtain clothing that is comfortable and relaxed, and can be laundered using minimum effort and resources.

Clothing articles should be distributed over several different pantries, including the following:

- The **primary residence** would obviously have clothing hanging in the closets and stuffed in vanity drawers. It is important to make sure that clothing is available at the primary residence for **ALL SURVIVAL TEAM MEMBERS** – remember that some team members may not actually reside at the primary residence but live in the vicinity.

- The **automobile**(s) should have at least one change of clothing (for hot and cold season and wet weather) for all team members using the vehicle included in this emergency pantry.

- The **evacuation** kit should have at least one change of clothing (for hot and cold season and wet weather) included in this emergency pantry.

- The **work** kit should have at least one change of clothing (for hot and cold season and wet weather) included in this emergency pantry.

- The **place of refuge** (motor home, travel trailer, camper, cabin, summer home) should have an ample supply of clothing (for all seasons, temperatures and weather conditions) stored at the location.

If applicable, the emphasis should be placed on warm clothing during cold and wet seasons. **IN COLD REGIONS, IT COULD BE WARM BEDDING AND WARM CLOTHING THAT WILL PROVIDE THE WARMTH WE NEED TO SURVIVE. PREPARE YOURSELVES**.

Listed below is a table of clothing items that could be considered as part of the emergency pantries for each survival team member supplied across the different pantries:

ITEM	TYPE
Belt	Include various types of belts with plenty of room for growth and expansion.
Boots	Boots should be heavy-duty, sturdy and comfortable. A good pair of work boots will be essential to support the survival environment. Include boots that cover the ankle and have good tread on the soles. Don't forget water-proof materials. Allow for growth and expansion. **Don't forget extra shoe laces**.
Coats	A heavy-duty coat is mandatory for every survival team member living in cold climates. This coat should be well lined and water-proof and have a heavy-duty zipper. A warm hood could also be attached to the coat. An excellent place to buy this type of coat is at the local Army/Navy outlets where coats are sold supporting arctic conditions. Allow for growth and expansion.

ITEM	TYPE
Gloves	Gloves will be essential for every survival team member. During the winter (cold) months or rainy season, include heavy-duty and water-proof gloves and/or mittens. Gloves with straps that can be tightened around the wrist are excellent to keep out the cold. Lighter gloves and mittens should also be part of the inventory. During all seasons, make sure everyone has plenty of work gloves.
Hats	During the winter (cold) months, include hats made from heavier materials including cotton, fur or wool. Make sure each team member has a warm hat that pulls down over the ears. Another good hat is the face (or ski) mask that completely covers the face except for the eyes and mouth. During the summer (hot) months, include a light-weight hat to protect the face and neck from sunburn.
House Slippers	Each survival team member should have a pair of house slippers for both winter (cold) and summer (hot months). Footies are good too! Allow for growth and expansion.
Jackets	A good-quality jacket is essential for every survival team member living in a climate that flucuates between mildly cool and gently cold temperatures. This jacket should be well lined, water-proof and have a heavy-duty zipper. A hood could also be attached to the coat. Jackets should basically accommodate spring and fall seasons and can include both heavy and light weight materials. Allow for growth and expansion.
Rain Gear	There are many types of raincoats available on the market. Each team member should have a good heavy-duty **WATER-PROOF** rain coat with hood that is large enough to accommodate growth and expansion. Light-duty rain coats could be included in the auto, work, evacuation and place of refuge kits.
Robe	Each survival team member could have a robe for both winter (cold) and summer (hot months). Allow for growth and expansion.
Shirts	During the winter (cold) months or the rainy season, include loose-fitting long and short sleeve shirts made from heavier materials including flannel or wool. During the summer (hot) months, include loose-fitting long and short sleeve shirts made from lighter materials including cotton and synthetics. Allow for growth and expansion.
Sleepwear	Each survival team member should have several pairs of pajamas for both winter (cold) and summer (hot months). Allow for growth and expansion.
Socks	During the winter (cold) months or the rainy season, include short and long length socks made from heavier materials including wool. During the summer (hot) months, include short and long length socks made from lighter materials including cotton and synthetics.
Shoes	Every survival team member <u>must</u> have adequate foot protection for a disaster environment - in all climates, seasons, temperatures and conditions. During the winter (cold) months, select shoes that are fully enclosed and made from materials that withstand bad weather conditions. The soles should be made from materials that prevent slippage. These shoes should be sturdy and comfortable fitting and would hold up in a survival environment including walking, hiking and working in less than ideal environments. A pair of steel-toed (safety) shoes would be a very good investment with emergency preparation as the main objective. The protection of the feet will be essential during a disaster with all types of dangers and challenges in getting around the area. During the summer (hot) months, sandals are great providing they are well made and support the survival environment. **NO HEELS!** Allow for growth and expansion. **DON'T FORGET EXTRA SHOE LACES!**

ITEM	TYPE
Slacks/Pants	During the winter (cold) months or the rainy season, include loose-fitting full-length pants made from heavier materials. A good choice would be some heavy-duty jeans or pants made out of polyester or wool fabrics. During the summer (hot) months, include some loose-fitting full-length pants made of lighter materials and even some shorts or capris. Allow for growth and expansion.
Sweat Shirts	During the winter (cold) months or the rainy season, include loose-fitting long sleeve shirts made from heavier materials - either pull-over or zipped. Many sweat shirts have hoodies – a perfect addition to complete the outfit! Allow for growth and expansion.
Sweaters	During the winter (cold) months or the rainy season, include loose-fitting long sleeve and short sleeve sweaters made from heavier materials including wool and wool or cotton blend fabrics. The choices include pull-over, zipped and button-down designs. Allow for growth and expansion.
Thermals	Every survival team member should have thermal underwear including tops (short and long sleeve) and bottoms. Make sure that you buy good quality and heavy-duty thermals – they can make the difference between keeping warm and staying cold. Allow for growth and expansion.
T-Shirts	During both the winter (cold) months, the rainy season, and the summer (hot) months, include long and short sleeve T-shirts. Allow for growth and expansion.
Underwear	Every survival team member should have a good supply of underwear including shorts and boxers for the men and boys and panties for the women and girls as well as under shirts, bras and halters. Don't forget to include religious apparel that may be part of your religious beliefs.

BABY SUPPLIES

If the survival team currently has or plans to have a baby in the future, planning and preparation must be made for clothing and supplies. If this is the first baby to the household, purchase a baby book providing detailed information on raising a baby. There may be an ample supply of used clothing and supplies worn and used by older children in the closet that can certainly be passed down to this new or future arrival of the household.

> *If you are in a spaceship that is traveling at the speed of light, and you turn on the headlights, does anything happen?*
>
> - **Steven Wright**

If there is any possibility of a new baby in the foreseeable future, be very cautious about donating current supplies of clothing – keep them! If this clothing is not actually used by a new arrival – the clothing can be used as a bartering tool for other items needed by the survival team during a disaster. As you review current inventory of baby and children's clothing (if any), attempt to provide for at least two to four outfits for each age, i.e., newborn, 0-3 months, 3-6 months, 6 months, 9 months, 12 months, 18 months, 2T, 3T, 4T, 5, 6, 7 and so forth. Make sure you also consider seasonal outfits to support hot and cold, wet and dry months.

Obviously, no one will actually know the gender of a future child, so if purchases are necessary to fulfill the clothing allowance of a future member of the survival team, select generic colors and styles, i.e., yellow, green, red, white, brown and even blue is worn by both boys and girls. It should be noted, however, that during a disaster – the top priority is not the color of shirt, the style of pants or whether they match as an ensemble!

Baby clothes and supplies are expensive. Even when purchasing items on sale, the sheer magnitude of purchasing clothing for the various ages of a future child and the multitude of supplies and equipment can be staggering. Check out garage sales, discount stores and charitable outlets in addition to department store sales. Remember that during disaster situations, survival teams could set up a swap meet with other teams to exchange and/or share baby supplies. The baby pantry could include the following supplies and equipment:

CLOTHING	SUPPLIES AND EQUIPMENT	
• Body Suits	• Bath Soap	• Moisture Wipes
• Coats	• Bathtub	• Oil
• Diapers (disposable)	• Bibs	• Pacifiers
• Diapers (cloth)	• Blankets	• Potty Chair
• Gloves	• Bottle/Bottle Brush	• Powder
• Hats	• Carrier	• Quilts
• Mittens	• Comb/Brush	• Rattle
• Pajamas	• Crib	• Shampoo
• Pants	• Crib Sheets	• Slurpy Cup
• Plastic Pants	• Diaper Bag	• Stroller
• Shirts	• Diaper Pins	• Swaddles
• Shoes	• Diaper Rash Ointment	• Swing
• Sleepers	• High Chair	• Teething Rings
• Socks	• Lotion	• Toys
• Training Pants	• Medicine Dropper	• Utensils
• Underwear	• Medicine Spoon	• Washcloths

Buying disposable diapers (Pampers, Huggies, Luvs) may be unrealistic. A simple mathematical calculation will quickly highlight the amount of money and the number of diapers that would need to be purchased and stored to support the child through potty-training time. The chart below displays the average weights and lengths of both boys and girls based on age increments:

AGE	WEIGHT	LENGTH	WEIGHT	LENGTH
	Boys	*Boys*	*Girls*	*Girls*
Birth	6.7 - 8.1 lbs	19.1 - 20.1 inches	6.5 - 7.8 lbs	18.9 - 19.6 inches
3 months	13.0 - 15.2 lbs	23.6 - 24.7 inches	11.8 - 14.0 lbs	23.0 - 24.1 inches
6 months	16.2 -18.8 lbs	26.1 - 27.2 inches	14.8 - 17.5 lbs	25.3 - 26.5 inches
9 months	18.2 - 21.1 lbs	27.7 - 28.9 inches	16.7 - 19.7 lbs	27.0 - 28.3 inches
12 months	19.8 - 22.9 lbs	29.2 - 30.5 inches	18.2 – 21.4 lbs	28.5 - 29.8 inches
15 months	21.1 - 24.5 lbs	30.5 - 31.8 inches	19.5 - 23.0 lbs	29.9 - 31.2 inches
18 months	22.4 - 26.0 lbs	31.7 - 33.1 inches	20.8 - 24.5 lbs	31.0 - 32.5 inches
21 months	23.6 - 27.5 lbs	32.7 - 34.3 inches	22.0 - 26.0 lbs	32.1 - 33.8 inches
24 months	24.8 - 28.9 lbs	33.8 - 35.4 inches	23.3 - 27.5 lbs	33.2 - 34.9 inches
27 months	27.0 - 31.2 lbs	34.1 - 36.1 inches	25.8 - 30.0 lbs	33.7 - 35.6 inches

AGE	WEIGHT	LENGTH	WEIGHT	LENGTH
	Boys	*Boys*	*Girls*	*Girls*
30 months	27.8 - 32.3 lbs	35.0 - 37.0 inches	26.7 - 31.1 lbs	34.6 - 36.6 inches
33 months	28.6 - 33.2 lbs	35.8 - 37.8 inches	27.6 - 32.3 lbs	35.4 - 37.4 inches
36 months	29.5 - 34.3 lbs	36.5 - 38.6 inches	28.4 - 33.4 lbs	36.0- 38.1 inches
4 years	33.3 - 39.1 lbs	39.2 - 41.5 inches	32.2 - 38.5 lbs	38.6 - 41.0 inches
5 years	37.5 - 44.7 lbs	41.7 - 44.2 inches	36.3 - 44.0 lbs	41.3 - 43.8 inches
6 years	41.9 - 50.6 lbs	44.2 -46.9 inches	40.8 - 50.0 lbs	43.9 - 46.7 inches
7 years	46.5 - 56.8 lbs	46.6 - 49.5 inches	45.6 - 56.6 lbs	46.5 - 49.4 inches
8 years	51.5 - 63.6 lbs	48.9 - 52.0 inches	50.9 - 64.3 lbs	48.8 - 51.9 inches

SOURCE: Gerber Corporation

The chart below provides an estimate on the number of disposable diapers required for each age increment if the baby was changed three times a day, four times a day or five times a day. For example, the average weight of a newborn baby is between *6-8 pounds* so the appropriate diaper size would be for a *newborn* since most newborn diapers support a baby weighing *4-10 pounds*. If the parent changed the diaper of the newborn three times a day, it would take *270* diapers from the time of birth until the baby was at the end of being three months old. The numbers are based on a thirty-day month.

AGE	AVERAGE WEIGHT OF CHILD	DIAPER SIZE	SUPPORTING DIAPER SIZE	CHANGED (3/day)*	CHANGED (4/day)*	CHANGED (5/day)*
Newborn	*6-8 pounds*	*Newborn*	*4-10 pounds*	*270*	360	450
3 Months	12-15 pounds	1	8-14 pounds	270	360	450
6 Months	15-19 pounds	2	12-18 pounds	270	360	450
9 Months	17-21 pounds	3	16-28 pounds	270	360	450
12 Months	20-22 pounds	3	16-28 pounds	270	360	450
15 Months	20-24 pounds	3	16-28 pounds	270	360	450
18 Months	21-26 pounds	3	16-28 pounds	270	360	450
21 Months	22-27 pounds	3	16-28 pounds	270	360	450
24 Months	23-29 pounds	3	16-28 pounds	270	360	450
27 Months	26-31 pounds	4	22-37 pounds	270	360	450
30 Months	27-32 pounds	4	22-37 pounds	270	360	450
33 Months	28-33 pounds	4	22-37 pounds	270	360	450
36 Months	29-34 pounds	5	> 27 pounds	270	360	450

Based on a 30-day month

Most families with children in diapers cannot afford to purchase sufficient disposable diapers to support lengthy disasters - it is unrealistic. For disposable diapers, and depending on which diaper size is purchased, the package will contain a different amount of diapers. For example, if purchasing Size 1 diapers, the package may contain 86 diapers and for Size 2, the package may contain 50 diapers. It is impossible to provide an exact estimate of cost – there are many variables. Some brands cost more than other brands even though the same amount of diapers is in the respective packages. Sale prices will affect the cost of diapers. The overall cost will also be determined by how often the baby is changed each day and when the child successfully completes potty training - during a long-term disaster – the sooner the better.

However, based on an average cost (not including tax) of diapers for each size, here are some *estimates* for the cost of purchasing enough *disposable* diapers to support a child through the age of three years old or thirty-six months (when potty training should normally be completed):

SIZE	UNIT COST	3 PER DAY	4 PER DAY	5 PER DAY	TIME PERIOD IN DIAPER	AGE OF CHILD
Newborn	.15	$40.50	$54.00	$67.50	3 months	0-3 months
Size 1	.15	$40.50	$54.00	$67.50	3 months	3-6 months
Size 2	.16	$43.20	$57.60	$72.00	3 months	6-9 months
Size 3	.16	$259.00	$346.00	$432.00	18 months	9-27 months
Size 4	.28	$226.80	$302.40	$378.00	9 months	27-33 months
Size 5	.35	$94.50	$126.00	$157.50	3 months	33-36 months
TOTALS		$704.50	$940.00	$1,174.50	3 years	3 years

If you have a baby in the home, you may find a diaper problem under emergency conditions. It is best to keep an ample supply of disposable *and* cloth diapers on hand for emergency use. In addition, any moisture resistant material can be cut and folded to diaper size and lined with absorbent material. Most families with children in diapers, however, cannot afford to purchase sufficient diapers to support lengthy disasters. During a disaster lasting for an extended period of time, parents may be forced to consider unpopular decisions on how often a diaper will be changed. Get Ready!

TOOLS

Due to the critical nature of including tools, hardware and parts in the emergency supply pantries; I have provided a list of tools that should be considered by survival team members during any disaster. These tools will be used across most every element and can and will make the difference in surviving any level of disaster.

Faith is the strength by which a shattered world shall emerge into the light.

- Helen Keller

Tools will be essential for cutting wood, turning on and off utilities, finding water and repairing and maintaining property, automotive and mechanical equipment and supplies, growing gardens and burying the dead. There should be a diversity of tools and hardware for both standard and metric projects. Although electric tools are certainly an important asset for any household, if electrical power is off, these tools will not help the survival team during an emergency unless an alternative power source is available.

There are countless types and sizes of tools and hardware. For example, when purchasing shovels, team members should consider not only the appropriate shovel for digging in the dirt – but don't forget the shovel you will need for digging in the snow! When scoping out pliers, a bewildered consumer will discover snap ring, precision, needle nose, curved jaw locking, tongue and groove joint, lineman, diagonal and long reach hose grip pliers – all tools used for different tasks! As a minimum, the team should have tools that can be used for *multiple purposes*. If the budget permits, attempt to purchase heavy-duty and high-quality tools – during an emergency is NOT the time to discover the wrench purchased at a dollar store busted while trying to repair a broken water pipe.

High quality tools can be purchased at hardware outlets and many department stores. Another possibility is to canvas garage sales and estate sales (although only intellectually challenged persons would sell good tools). In addition to tools, it is important to have a good supply of hardware including <u>nails, nuts, bolts, fasteners, screws, and washers</u>. Again, as with tools, hardware comes in a variety of types and sizes. During a disaster causing property damage and destruction, the importance of having nails, nuts, bolts and screws will be appreciated.

These supplies can be purchased at hardware outlets and department stores, but also discount tools outlets. Most families (and especially men) have a buffet of tools in every shape and size and for multiple uses. Good! But if unsure what type of tools to purchase, ask a <u>qualified and knowledgeable</u> sales person to assist when purchasing tools for emergency pantries. If you are a beginner in acquiring tools, make sure you at least get the basics. As always – purchase tools and hardware supplies on sale.

CONSTRUCTION/REPAIR/MAINTENANCE		GARDENING & YARD TOOLS
Bars	Paintbrush	**AXE**
Bolt Cutter	Planers	**HATCHET**
Bolts / Nuts	**PLIERS**	**HOE**
Cement Trials	Punch	**LAWN MOWER** (Manual)
Chisels	Putty	Lopper
Clamps	**RATCHETS/SOCKETS**	**PICK**
Crimpers	Sand Paper	**PITCH FORK**
Duct Tape	Sander	**PLOW**
Files	**SAWS**	**PRUNER**
Glass Cutter	Scrapers	**PRUNING SAW**
Glue	**SCREWDRIVERS**	**RAKES**
HAMMERS	**Screws**	**SHEARS**
KNIFE (putty, utility)	**SLEDGE HAMMER**	**SHOVEL**
KNIFE SHARPENER	Snips	Spades
LADDERS	Spikes	Weeder
Level	Squares	
Lumber	Tape Measure	**MAKE SURE ALL TOOLS AND PARTS**
Mallet (rubber)	Vise	**ARE IN THEIR PROPER PLACE –**
Miter Box with Saw	**Washers**	**ORGANIZED – EASILY ACCESSIBLE!**
Nails	**WEDGE**	
Nut Drivers	**WRENCHES**	

During an emergency situation, tools and hardware are one of the first items that will be needed by team members in order to repair damage to property and equipment and later to maintain equipment and provide sustenance for the household. A diverse selection of tools and hardware will make it easier to survive! Don't forget the ladders including: (1) escape ladder if primary residence has a second floor, (2) step stool to reach items on shelves and cabinets, (3) step ladder to reach items higher up on shelves and cabinets, and (4) extension ladder to reach the roof and high branches in trees.

ELECTRICITY

Without a doubt, other than food and water, electricity is our most valued and treasured resource on the planet and one of the prime obstacles of emergency preparation planning is attempting to work around the problem involved with not having electricity. Without electricity, there is a detrimental affect on every single element and on us.

Electricity is extremely vulnerable to most disaster types. With few exceptions, the power grid is susceptible to earthquakes, explosions, extreme cold, fire, floods, heat waves, hurricanes, landslides, lightning storms, nuclear attacks, riots, terrorist attacks, thunderstorms, tornados, tsunamis, volcanoes, war, wind and winter storms. There is no manmade resource that can totally and completely bring down an entire civilization, their standard of living, their ability to survive and their will to live like the "power" of electricity. The ultimate "power" of electricity is the ability to control the power of the other elements!

When the power is out, gasoline pumps cease to function, computers are inoperable, cash registers are shut down, garage doors will not open, television stations and household televisions are quiet, light bulbs are cold and dark, x-ray machines are lifeless, restaurants and fast food outlets are closed, banks are unable to verify accounts or handle funds, furnaces and air conditioners are silent, water taps are dry, household appliances are unresponsive, government agencies are scrambling to find data that is now inaccessible and the utility companies are frantic to restore the life-blood back into our lives.

ONE OF THE MOST IMPORTANT CONTINGENCIES TO BE MADE FOR ADVANCED PLANNING IN EMERGENCY PREPARATION IS THE ABILITY TO SECURE ELECTRICAL POWER TO BE UTILIZED ON A DAILY BASIS USING A RELIABLE AND NATURAL SOURCE TO GENERATE THE ELECTRICITY. The obvious answer is **solar power** using the sun as the natural source to generate the electricity. With *solar panels* or a *solar powered generator*, many of your electrical appliances may be able to be used during the emergency when the standard electrical grid is out.

Another positive argument for a solar power is that households relying on electrical power for running the furnace (electricity is required to run the motor), turning on all or some of the lights, running the electrical pump in an underground well used to bring water to the surface, and running medical equipment (oxygen) - will quickly discover that a solar power can provide this vital source of electricity during a disaster.

Solar power can also provide power for small electric heaters to heat individual rooms in the home and a small electric hot plate for cooking meals. Furthermore, for emergency supplies requiring batteries, unless the survival team has a solar powered battery charger and there is an ample supply of batteries – at some point in time, the batteries are going to expire or will need to be recharged – using – electricity.

Even with the use of a solar power source and when preparing for a disaster across all elements, every effort should still be made to purchase and store sources, items and supplies that does not directly or indirectly require electrical power. Be prepared for a challenge. Many items requiring manual operation are hard to find and alternatives to electrical power can be extremely expensive for the middle-class household.

If possible, it is important to have several *layers* or *alternatives* of electrical power available such as:

- **GENERATOR - SOLAR POWERED (SHORT, MIDDLE, LONG-TERM)**
- **SOLAR PANELS (SHORT, MIDDLE, LONG-TERM)**
- Wind Turbine (long-term)
- Generator and Fuel (short-term)
- **SOLAR POWERED BATTERY CHARGER (SHORT TO LONG-TERM)**

GENERATOR (SOLAR)

A solar generator is one of the most important investments that can be made by the survival team to _prepare in advance_ for any type of disaster. CONSIDER IT A HIGH PRIORITY. These generators are by far the better choice for survival team members since the operation does not rely on any type of fuel. Many of these solar-powered generators provide up to 1800 watts of electricity on demand and are made in the United States. The solar generator kit consists mainly of four main components: (1) the generator, (2) the solar panel(s), (3) batteries and (4) the charge controller.

The generator produces continuous electricity - the unit stores power and makes it available when you need it. The unit emits no fumes and runs with no noise. The generator is recharged constantly by the sun allowing you to use the system and charge it at the same time. Simply roll it to whatever location needs the power and begin plugging in appliances. It will run both AC and DC appliances. The generator can run either a small refrigerator, sump pump, well pump, shortwave radio, AM/FM radio, television set, lamp, fireplace fan, furnace motor, computer, printer, power tool, trimmer, blower, coffee maker, alarm clock, security system and cell phone recharger. They are easy to transport and can be taken anywhere. For example, if the primary residence is damaged or destroyed, the generator can be transported to a safer or alternative location.

Depending on the generator purchased, they are a solid piece of equipment that should last a lifetime. These generators cost between $1700.00 to $7000.00. There are several companies on the Internet and many home improvement centers who offer these solar generators – make sure you investigate these sources for the best price and the best generator for your needs.

When running any generator unattended outside, get a heavy chain and lock and secure it where it cannot easily be stolen. Generator theft is popular during long power outages.

SOLAR PANELS

Solar panels are a form of active solar power that harvest sunlight and actively convert it to electricity. The solar cells on the surface of the panels are arranged in a grid-like pattern and collect sunlight during the daylight hours and covert it into electricity. The advantages of solar panels include being environmentally friendly, less electrical grid consumption, tax breaks, no noise and maintenance free operation. The disadvantages include an expensive start-up cost and panels only work while the sun is shining unless a battery is installed that stores electricity during the day for use during other times. Years of overheating and physical wear can also reduce the operation efficiency of the photovoltaic unit. Solar cells become less efficient over time.

The amount of power solar panels produce is influenced by the quality of the solar panel, the materials and technology used in making the solar panel, and the amount of time the solar panel has been in use. There are many families who have made the investment in solar panels and have been free of the electrical grid for years. When purchasing solar panels, look beyond size and look at the dollars/watt ratio.

WIND TURBINE

Wind turbines operate with tall, narrow airfoils that catch the wind while spinning around a vertical axis. As the rotor turns, a generator turns the energy into electricity and the inverter then converts the electricity from a direct current (DC) to an alternating current (AC) used in homes. The turbine is connected directly to the electric panel in your home and on through to the power grid operated by the local power company.

When the wind is blowing and the turbine is rotating, your electrical needs are being generated by the turbine. If the wind stops blowing, the turbine stops and your electric needs are transferred back to the power grid. One model offers a generator that stores electricity generated by the turbine for use when the wind is not blowing. Basically, the power grid would not be needed to generate electricity for the home using this particular model.

These turbines are expensive (costing between seven and fifteen thousand dollars plus the cost of installation). The primary residence must be in a location that creates at least 11 MPH winds. However, once installed, reliance on the power grid is greatly decreased and electricity would be available for home use.

GENERATOR (FUEL)

A backup generator (using fuel) is not for everyone but offers a reasonable and realistic alternative to electricity for many survival teams. When considering a generator, be aware they are noisy, emit deadly carbon monoxide fumes, must be properly installed and operated, and the fuel (gas, diesel, propane) is dangerous to store. A generator connected to the household electrical system **MUST** be installed by a licensed electrician and have a special device installed called a transfer switch that can be automatic or manually switched. These generators must be situated <u>outside</u> the house where there is adequate ventilation.

When selecting a fuel generator, consider the (1) power output rated in watts or kilowatts (one thousand watts), (2) the fuel to power the generator, normally gasoline, diesel, propane, or natural gas, (3) the time the unit will run on one tank of fuel, and (4) whether the unit is started from a battery, or uses a pull-cord to be manually started.

Generators are available in power output ranges, from a small 800-watt unit with handles, to huge units powering a hospital during a power outage (1500 kilowatts or more). An 800-watt unit would be capable of powering eight 100-watt light bulbs (or equivalent) at one time. A popular size generator readily available from local hardware or home improvement outlets is a unit built in a metal frame with power output of 4500 to 5000 watts. It is capable of powering most of your lights and some of the critical appliances in the primary residence such as the refrigerator, freezer, microwave oven, and 240-volt water well pump but will <u>not</u> run the air conditioner, heater, or electric stove.

Generators operating on gasoline are the least expensive, but are louder and wear out faster than diesel, propane or natural gas generators. A 5 kilowatt gasoline generator will run about five hours on a full tank of gas. When you suspect the gas is about to run out, power off everything in the house, shut off the generator and let it cool down before refilling the tank with gas. Gasoline on a hot generator engine could start a fire and/or explode!

SOLAR POWERED BATTERY CHARGER

There are several good (and inexpensive) solar powered battery chargers on the market that use the sun to charge AA, AAA, C, and D batteries. The batteries must be <u>rechargeable</u> types and not the average alkaline batteries purchased in department stores.

These batteries are rather expensive (around two to three dollars each for AA and AAA and around seven to ten dollars each for C and D batteries). The batteries claim to be able to be charged up to 500 times. Make the investment and purchase several (at least four each) of these batteries.

The chargers are available on the Internet, hardware and tool outlets, electronics stores and home department stores and cost anywhere from twenty dollars to forty dollars. There are some models that charge two batteries at a time and others charge four batteries at a time. Most models require the same type, i.e., AA, AAA, C, and D to be charged during one session. Make sure that you purchase a charger with a green light that shows when batteries are completely charged – some models don't have this option and it is important to make sure you have it on your charger.

When using these chargers, there must be full sun; otherwise, the ability to charge the batteries can be decreased by over fifty percent. Charging a battery using solar power is NOT as expedient as using an electrical charger and depending on the model purchased, weather conditions and the fullness of the sun, an AA battery can take two to four hours while a D battery can take up to 36 hours to charge. A solar powered battery charger is a good investment - once regular batteries are spent – you would be out of luck.

LIGHT

One of the elements largely affected by electric power disruption is providing light for our households or shelters during an emergency. It is important to have several *alternatives* or *layers* of light available such as:

- **Candles**
- **Flashlights (solar/hand crank/batteries)**
- **Lamps**
- **Lanterns (solar, battery and fuel)**
- **Light Bulbs (low watt squiggly kind)**
- **Light Sticks**
- **Matches**
- **Mirror**
- **Oil Lamps (including oil and wicks)**
- **Solar Battery Charger**
- **SOLAR GARDEN LIGHTS**
- **Sun**

> *Edison failed 10, 000 times before he made the electric light. Do not be discouraged if you fail a few times.*
>
> **- Napoleon Hill**

Flashlights

There are many types of flashlights. As a general rule, a working flashlight should be available in every room of the house and the location of these flashlights should be known by all survival team members. Establish rules about *when* and *where* emergency flashlights can be used and a schedule for inspections.

Make sure at least one of the flashlights in your home and the one assigned to your evacuation pack is a sturdy, heavy-duty model. Consider a solar or shake-and-charge flashlight that doesn't require batteries. You just put them in the light and/or shake them for a minute and they give light for about an hour. They can be shaken repeatedly and last for years. A standard-sized flashlight using two D-cell batteries will drain a fresh set of batteries in approximately seven hours of continual use, so consider them as a temporary light source rather than for long-term use.

Lanterns (Battery-Operated)

These lanterns are one of the best choices for <u>safety</u> and light. They are relatively bright and easy to use. One disadvantage is they generally require a significant number of batteries to operate. Lanterns with fluorescent bulbs will burn much longer than lanterns with incandescent bulbs.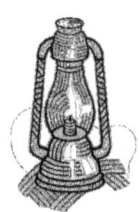

Light Sticks

A light stick can provide instant light just by shaking and bending the stick. They glow, but are not a bright light. Light sticks require little storage space, are lightweight and shelf stable. One disadvantage of light sticks is they are one-use items. You can't turn it off to conserve the light for another time. After it is lit, it will continue to glow for eight to twelve hours and will then go out.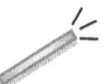

Candles

A candle is an inexpensive alternative but at the same time, can prove to be a dangerous option during a disaster. Candles must be located in safe, stable and out of the way locations. Purchase solid candleholders or bases to hold candles. There is a difference between emergency candles and decorative candles. Emergency candles are made with different wicks and wax in order to burn brighter and longer. Consider using tea lights or votive candles as nightlights. Candles should be stored lying flat with waxed paper in between them in a cool and dry place.

Oil Lamp

An oil lamp uses a wick and oil to create light. Begin by filling the reservoir of the lamp with fuel. The wick needs to soak up the oil before it will burn. Raise the wick to create a brighter light. The higher the wick, the more fuel is consumed. The price of lamp oil has become expensive and the oil comes in relatively small containers. Most oil lamps are glass and can break easily. Purchase ample lamp oil and additional wicks.

Pop Can Oil Lamp

The parts needed for this lamp can be found in every household - an empty aluminum pop can, an old cotton sock and a tablespoon of cooking oil. Cut the can completely in half. Use the bottom half of the pop can, and cut half inch deep slits spaced each half inch along the circumference of the can. Fold over to make a safe rim along the edge. Take the top half of the can and work the tab back and forth with upward pressure until it pulls off. Dispose of the top half of the can.

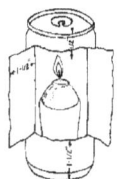

Cut a one inch by 3/8" slip of material from the old sock. Roll the material into a thick rope and feed it into the pull tab attachment hole. Pull through about half an inch so it sticks up while the pull tab rests upside down. Now pour a cap full of cooking oil into the bottom of the can. Place the upside down pull tab with the wick in the middle of the can and drape the cotton wick so it pulls the oil from the edge of the can. The length of the wick pulled through the tab hole will determine the height of the flame. A good quarter inch of wick will give a good flame with virtually no smoke. The wick should last about three to four hours with each tablespoon of cooking oil.

Candle Lamp

A candle lamp is made by cutting a standard aluminum pop can in half using a knife. To make a stable base for a short candle, place sand across the bottom to barely cover its center. The first candle burned will saturate and harden the sand making a permanent base or holder.

Lantern (Fuel)

Lanterns associated with camping and outdoor recreation work well in power outages and disaster situations. They are generally much brighter than battery-operated models and fuel is less expensive than batteries. Purchase ample fuel and mantles.

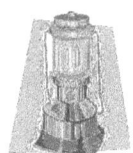

Solar Garden Light

The solar garden lights currently installed outside in the yard can be used at night to provide a light source in the primary residence, place of refuge, at work or even in the car. They are a renewable light source and do not require batteries or fuel. These lights will prove to be a valuable addition to all emergency pantries – the only energy source needed for operation is the sun. **AN EXCELLENT CHOICE FOR ALTERNATE LIGHT**!

Light Bulbs

If the purchase of a solar powered generator is part of your advanced planning for emergency preparation, make sure a good supply of light bulbs (swiggly type) is included in the pantry. The purchase of low watt bulbs is the better choice in order to ensure the generator can carry the load required to turn on the bulb(s).

Mirror

An idea that doubles lighting output is an ordinary mirror! If you do not have a mirror, aluminum foil will work but not as well. The mirror will reflect the light from an emergency light source giving you twice the illumination. Sit an oil lamp on the fireplace hearth and place a 14 x 16 inch mirror against the fireplace <u>behind</u> the lamp. This method will greatly increase the light in the room.

WATER

REMEMBER - THERE IS NO SUBSTITUTE FOR WATER. Having an ample supply of clean <u>drinking</u> water is a top priority in any emergency. A normally active person should drink at least two quarts (half gallon) of water each day. Individuals living in hot environments, children, nursing mothers, and sick people require even more water. Teams should store at least one gallon of drinking water per person/pet per day and consider storing at least a two-week supply of drinking water for each survival team member and pet. If supplies run low, minimize the amount of water the body needs by reducing activity and staying cool.

The body loses water through sweating, urinating and defecating. During average daily exertion at 68 Degrees Fahrenheit, the average adult loses and requires two to three quarts of water daily. Heat or cold exposure, intense activity, high altitude, burns or sickness can cause the body to become dehydrated resulting from insufficient replacement of lost body fluids. It decreases efficiency and, if injured, increases susceptibility to severe shock.

The loss of fluid in the body can have devastating affects, including:

- Five% loss results in thirst, irritability, nausea and weakness
- Ten% loss results in dizziness, headache, inability to walk and a tingling sensation in the limbs
- Fifteen% loss results in dimmed vision, painful urination, swollen tongue, deafness and numbness to skin
- Greater than fifteen% loss may result in death

The most common signs and symptoms of dehydration are:

- Dark and sunken eyes
- Dark urine with a very strong odor and low input
- Delayed capillary refill in fingernail beds
- Emotional instability
- Fatigue
- Loss of elasticity in the skin
- Thirst - you are already two percent dehydrated by the time the body craves fluids
- Trench line down center of tongue

Although the body is programmed to replace water, attempting to make up a deficit is hard and thirst is not a sign of how much water is needed. Most people cannot comfortably drink more than one quart of water at a time, so during an emergency, even if not thirsty, team members should drink small amounts of water at regular intervals each hour to prevent dehydration.

Increase water intake if under physical and mental stress or subject to severe conditions. Survival team members should drink enough liquids to maintain a urine output of at least ONE PINT every twenty-four hours. In any situation where food intake is low, drink six to eight quarts of water per day. In an extremely arid climate, the average person can lose 2.5 to 3.5 quarts of water *per hour*. In these conditions, team members should drink fourteen to thirty quarts of water *per day*.

The body also looses electrolytes (body salts) with the loss of water. Our diet can generally keep up with these losses but in a disaster, additional sources are needed. A mixture of ¼ teaspoon of salt to one quart of water will provide a concentration the body can absorb.

During an emergency, team members should drink water when eating since it is used as part of digestion and can lead to dehydration if not enough water is consumed. If necessary, ration water until a suitable source is found. A daily intake of ½ quart of a sugar-water mixture (2 teaspoons sugar per quart of water) will suffice to prevent severe dehydration for at least a week provided you keep water losses to a minimum by limiting activity and heat gain or loss. Limit sweat producing activities but continue to drink water.

INDIVIDUAL WATER REQUIREMENTS

As part of emergency preparation planning, the need of water for certain individuals and circumstances could require a larger amount of water being stored than just the minimum requirement. For example:

- **Activities** – increased physical activities and work could result in the need for additional water.

- **Babies** - consider how much water is needed for preparing formula, baby food and personal hygiene.

- **Foods** – depending on the type of food storage in emergency pantries, i.e., freeze-dried or dehydrated rather than canned and ready to eat, you will need additional water to prepare them.

- **Habit** – many people drink a lot of water as part of an overall health regiment and to dramatically cut back on this regiment, especially during a disaster, could result in physical complications.

- **Heat** – if living in an area with extreme heat during the summer months and if the crisis was to occur during this time, additional water would be required to meet minimal needs.

- **Invalids** – consider their need for increased water to take medications or for personal care.

- **Pets** – family pets and livestock will also need to have a fresh and ample supply of water.

- **Teenagers** – generally have more energy than adults and need more of water. As part of *planning in advance*, conduct serious discussions with teens on what the allowable water rations will be during a disaster and the necessary containment of activities that will be required.

PREPARATION OF WATER

To have the safest and most reliable <u>short-term</u> emergency supply of drinking water, purchase commercially bottled water, and store water in the original sealed container and observe the expiration or "use by" date. When preparing your own containers of water, purchase <u>food-grade</u> water storage containers used for water storage from surplus or camping supplies stores.

If re-using storage containers, use two-liter plastic soft drink bottles – <u>not</u> plastic jugs or cardboard containers with milk or fruit juice in them. Milk protein and fruit sugars cannot be adequately removed from these containers and provide an environment for bacterial growth. Cardboard containers leak and are not designed for long-term storage of liquids. No glass containers!

Avoid placing water containers in areas where toxic substances such as gasoline and pesticides are present since vapors may penetrate the plastic over time. Do not store water containers in direct sunlight. Select a place with a fairly constant and cool temperature.

> **ECONOMICS 101**: Remember how I told you that during an emergency, not everyone would be as nice as you? During the 1994 California earthquake, water was being sold for one dollar for 1/2 cup.

Preparing and Filling Water Containers

- Thoroughly clean bottles with dishwashing soap and water; rinse completely so there is no residual soap.

- Sanitize plastic soft drink bottles by adding one teaspoon of non-scented liquid household chlorine bleach to a quart of water. Swish the sanitizing solution in the bottle so it touches all surfaces. After sanitizing the bottle, thoroughly rinse out the sanitizing solution with clean water.

- Fill the bottle to the top with regular tap water.

If your water utility company treats your tap water with chlorine, you do not need to add anything else to the water to keep it clean. If the water comes from a well or water source that is not treated with chlorine, add one drop of non-scented liquid household chlorine bleach to each gallon of water.

WATER TYPES

Based on the severity of the disaster, it is likely water lines will be damaged or destroyed. There are several types of water sources that should be available for team members including (1) drinking, (2) cooking, (3) personal hygiene i.e. bathing, brushing teeth, washing hair, (4) laundry, (5) cleaning and disinfecting, i.e., cleaning counters and appliances and washing dishes, (6) toilet, and (7) water for pets, livestock and plants. Since the most vital water is used for drinking and depending on the level (1-3) of the disaster, you may be able to stay at the primary residence or the team may be forced to evacuate and seek alternative shelter. This alternative shelter may or may not have water sources available. Regardless of the level of disaster or whether the survival team members will be at the primary residence or located in another area, it is important to have several *alternatives* or *layers* of drinking and other water available such as:

White Water

White water used for drinking, cooking, brushing teeth and washing dishes comes from several safe and uncontaminated sources including:

- o **Wells** - safe water that comes from underground rivers or aqueducts and is pumped up to the surface of the ground by electric pumps and then forced into the home using water pipes. Water from wells service most individuals living in a country setting as well as many city residents.

- o **Reservoirs** - safe water flowing along natural or manmade pathways into natural or manmade depositories that hold water used by citizens living in the nearby area.

- o **Springs** - safe water from underground rivers or aqueducts that naturally comes to the surface of the ground.

- o **Toilet Tank** - safe water that flows *into* the toilet tank.

- o **Creeks and Streams** - safe water coming from either melting snow high in the mountains or from springs that have naturally come to the surface of the ground and now <u>rapidly</u> flow downhill. In order for this water to be safe for drinking, the water must flow swiftly enough to prohibit any animals or fish from being able to live, swim, walk, drink, defecate or urinate in the water.

- o **Rain** - safe water that falls <u>directly</u> into a sanitized water-safe container.

- o **Bottled** - safe water that is commercially available in plastic containers.

- o **Drums** - safe water that has been *previously* stored in large drums (55-gallon) or containers and contains a small amount of bleach.

- o **Hot Water Heater** - safe water stored in hot water heater.

- o **Juices** - from vegetable and fruit cans and bottles.

- o **Radiator** - safe water stored in the radiator.

- o **Hot Water Boiler** - safe water stored in a hot water boiler.

- o **Snow** - fresh and clean snow must be melted - avoid the yellow stuff!

- o **Underground Still** - safe water vapor in the air that condenses into water in an underground still.

As part of *planning in advance*, survival team members must recognize it is highly probable safe <u>white</u> water will be scarce. However, if there is **no doubt** there will be an adequate supply of white water available for the entire length of the disaster, then this water can and should be utilized; however, if there is **any doubt** whatsoever that white water is or will become scarce, <u>white</u> water that is *clean*, *sanitary* and *uncontaminated* should be used for only four (4) major tasks as follows:

- **Drinking*** - water used for human drinking
- **Teeth** - water used for brushing teeth and cleaning dentures
- **Eating** - water used for cooking food, making ice cubes or is required in the recipe
- **Dishes** - water used for washing and rinsing dishes

If white water is plentiful, there are three (3) additional tasks that can be included as follows:

- **Drinking** - water used for drinking by animals, pets and livestock
- **Cleaning**** - water used for general cleaning purposes including counters, spills etc.
- **Personal Hygiene**** - water used for showering, bathing and washing hair

*If necessary, water from natural resources such as lakes, rivers and streams could be used for drinking and cooking by humans provided water is correctly boiled, chlorinated or distilled.

**Although it is preferred to use white water for showering, bathing, washing hair and cleaning - it will more than likely be necessary to use gray water since safe white water may be scarce.

<u>Gray Water</u>

The water has previously been used for specific purposes **and/or** contains some contaminates that may be harmful if ingested. Gray water comes from several sources as follows:

Previously Used

- **Dishes** - water that was previously used for washing and rinsing the dishes
- **Laundry** - water that was previously used for washing clothes
- **Bath or Shower** - water that was previously used for taking a bath or shower
- **Water Bed -** water from a water bed treated with chemicals including bleach
- **Swimming Pool** - water from a swimming pool treated with chemicals
- **Hot Tub** - water from a hot tub treated with chemicals

Depending on the level and type of contamination or chemicals in the water, this previously used gray water could be used again for:

- **Personal Hygiene** - shower or bath - avoid water containing bleach or strong chemicals
- **Washing Hair** - washing hair - avoid water containing bleach or strong chemicals
- **Shaving** - shaving face/arms/legs - avoid water containing bleach or strong chemicals
- **Garden** (outdoor and indoor) - fruits and vegetables (avoid water containing bleach or strong chemicals)
- **Trees, shrubs and vines** - avoid water containing bleach or strong chemicals
- **Cleaning** - wiping floors, counters*, appliances*, spills*, garbage cans, toilet*
- **Toilet** - manual flushing

    *use disinfectant (if possible) after wiping

Contains Some Contaminates

- **Natural Sources** - water coming from dams, lakes, rivers, canals, ponds and streams
- **Rain** - water that falls on the roof of the house and then flows directly into a sanitized container
- **Toilet Bowl** - water from tank into <u>bowl</u> *with no urine, feces or bodily fluids*

Depending on the level and type of contamination or chemicals in the water, this semi safe water can be used for:

- **Drinking** - water for animals, pets and livestock
- **Personal Hygiene** - shower or bath
- **Washing Hair** - water used for washing hair
- **Shaving** - water used for shaving the face, underarms or legs
- **Laundry** - water used for laundry
- **Plants** (outdoor and indoor) - watering fruits, vegetables, trees, shrubs, vines, grass
- **Cleaning** - wiping floors, counters*, appliances*, spills*, trash cans, toilet*
- **Toilet** - manual flushing

    *use disinfectant (if possible) after wiping

NOTE: Safe water coming *into* the tank of a toilet is considered <u>white</u> water. However, once the water leaves the tank and flows into the bowl, it is considered <u>gray</u> water even though the water may contain no urine, feces or bodily fluids. The toilet bowl itself is unsanitary and contains countless bacteria and germs as well as other chemicals used to actually keep the toilet bowl clean. Once the bowl contains urine, feces or other bodily fluids, it is really not safe for any human use.

Black Water

The water has previously been used for specific purposes **and/or** due to a natural phenomenon, now contains contaminates that are unsafe for any human or animal use. Black water can come from several unsafe sources as follows:

- **Toilet Bowl** - water that flowed from the tank into the toilet bowl and now contains urine, feces, bodily fluids or other icky stuff

- **Rain** - water that is known to be *acid* rain

- **Ponds** - *standing* water that contains debris, trash, large amounts of dirt, dead humans and animals, feces, urine, etc.

- **Natural/Manmade Sources** - contaminated water with dangerous chemicals and/or toxins from manufacturing plants, or littered with debris, trash, dead humans or animals, feces, urine and other substances deposited by humans into lakes, rivers, canals, ponds and streams

- **Salt Water Sources** - contains salt including oceans, seas and lakes

During an emergency, and when water sources become scarce, there will be confrontations taking place between individuals and groups on rights to the water and being able to take water from a source. As part of *planning in advance*, know where all water sources are located in your area. For example, dams, lakes, rivers, creeks, streams and springs are obvious sources of water. Keep in mind that during a water shortage, many people will be lined up at these particular sources to get water. Locate other less obvious sources (natural springs or small creeks) adjacent to the primary residence and/or evacuation location.

> **Make sure you KNOW in advance where water from *natural* sources and especially flowing springs are located. During a serious disaster, a person's claim of owning the rights to the water will become insignificant. Make sure you have the tools and equipment needed to transport the water.**

Hidden Water at the Residence

There are safe drinking water sources in the primary residence including water in the hot-water tank, pipes and even ice cubes. Team members should protect water sources already in the primary residence from contamination if there are broken water or sewage lines, and if local officials advise you of a problem. To shut off incoming water, locate the main valve and turn it to the closed position. Be sure all adult survival team members know *in advance* how to perform this important procedure.

After shutting off the main value and to use the water in the pipes, let air into the plumbing by turning on the faucet in the home at the *highest* level. A small amount of water will trickle out. Now get water flowing out of the *lowest* faucet in the home. To use the water in the hot-water tank, make sure electricity or gas is off and open the drain at the bottom of the tank. Start the water flowing by turning off the water intake valve at the tank and turning on a hot-water faucet. Refill the tank before turning electricity or gas back on. If the *natural* gas is turned off, a professional will be needed to turn it back on and reinstate gas service to the house.

Other Possible Water Sources

Beach	Dig a hole deep enough to allow water to seep in; obtain rocks, build a fire and heat rocks; drop hot rocks in water; hold cloth over hole to absorb steam; wring water from cloth OR fill a container with water, build a fire and boil water, hold a cloth over the container to absorb steam and then wring the water from the cloth.

Desert	In the ground, dig holes deep enough to allow water to seep in and in a sand dune, any available water will be found beneath the original valley floor at the edge of the dunes. If a cactus is available, cut off the top of a barrel cactus and mash or squeeze the pulp. **DO NOT EAT THE PULP** – place pulp in mouth, suck out juice and discard the pulp.
Rain	Catch rain in tarps or other water-holding material, rain barrels, buckets or containers.
Snow and Ice	Do not eat snow and ice without melting which can reduce body temperature and will lead to more dehydration. Snow and ice is only as pure as the water which made it! I would strongly suggest that you do <u>not</u> use yellow snow!
Dew	Tie rags or grass tufts around your ankles and walk through dew-covered grass before sunrise. As the rags or grass tufts absorb the dew, wring the water into a container. Repeat the process until you have a supply of water or until the dew is gone.

There are several sources of water <u>not</u> <u>acceptable</u> as a water source for *drinking*. These include *alcoholic beverages* that dehydrate the body. *Urine* contains harmful body wastes and an excessive amount of salt. *Sea water* contains over four percent salt and takes over two gallons of body fluids to rid the body of waste from one gallon of sea water. By drinking sea water, you deplete the water supply in your body resulting in death. Finally, unless you are Dracula or the latest vampire on television or in the movies, *blood* is salty, requires additional body fluids to digest and can transmit deadly diseases.

Above Ground Still

To make an aboveground still, you need a sunny slope to place the still, a clear plastic bag, green leafy vegetation and a small rock.

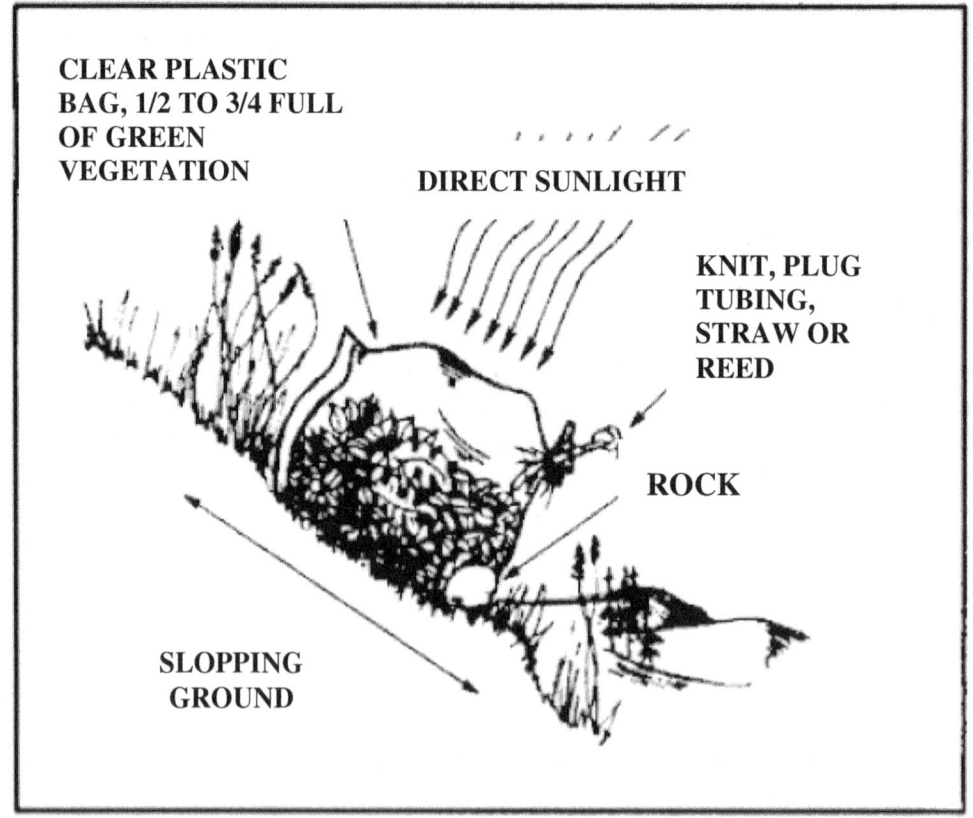

SOURCE: UNITED STATES ARMY

To make the still, use the following steps:

- Fill the bag with air by turning the opening into the breeze

- Fill the plastic bag half to three-fourths full of green leafy vegetation. Remove all hard sticks or sharp spines that might puncture the bag.

- Place a small rock in the bag.

- Close the bag and carefully insert one end of a piece of tubing, a small straw, or a hollow reed in the mouth of the bag. Securely tie the mouth as close to the end of the bag as possible to keep the maximum amount of air space. Tie off or plug the tubing so air will not escape. This tubing will allow you to drain out condensed water without untying the bag.

- Place the bag, mouth downhill, on a slope in full sunlight. Position the mouth of the bag slightly higher than the low point in the bag.

- Settle the bag in place so that the rock works itself into the low point in the bag.

- To get condensed water from the still, loosen the tie around the bag's mouth and tip the bag so that the water collected around the rock will drain out <u>or</u> unplug the piece of tubing and allow the water to drain out of the end. Retie the mouth securely <u>or</u> replug the tubing and reposition the still to allow further condensation. Change the vegetation in the bag after extracting most of the water from it. This will ensure maximum output of water.

Below Ground Still

To make a below ground still, you need a digging tool, container, clear plastic sheet, drinking tube and a rock.

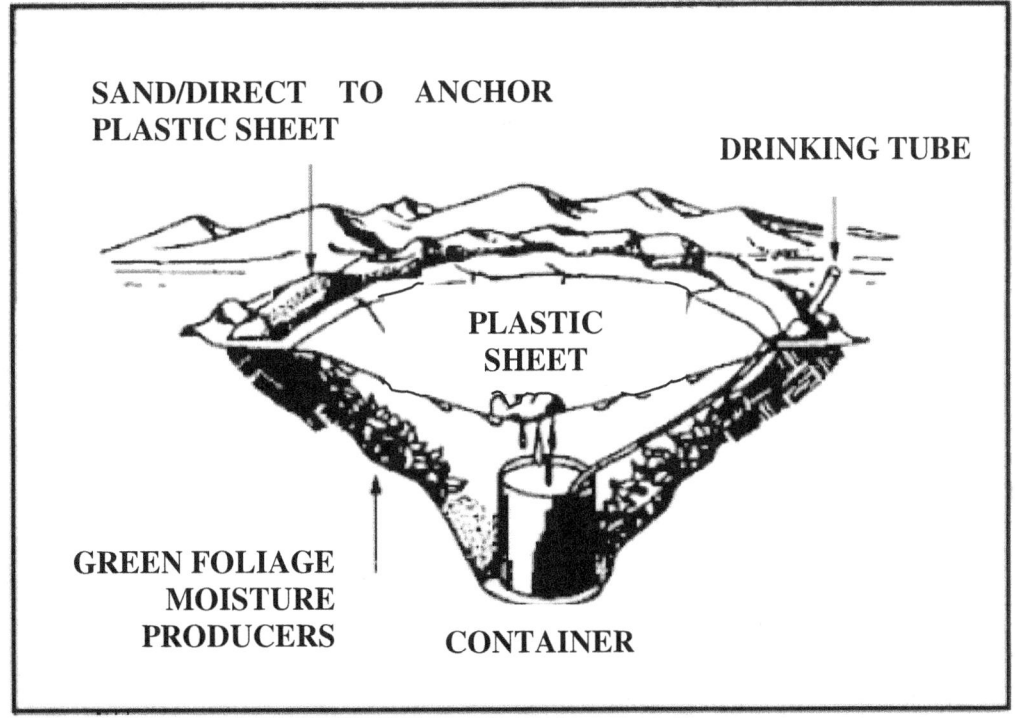

SOURCE: UNITED STATES ARMY

Select a site where soil contains moisture (a dry stream bed or low spot where rainwater has collected). The soil at this site should be easy to dig, and sunlight must hit the site most of the day.

To construct the still, use the following steps:

- Dig a bowl-shaped hole in the ground one yard across and two feet deep.

- Dig a sump in the center of the hole. The sump's depth and perimeter will depend on the size of the container you have to place in it. The bottom of the sump should allow the container to stand upright.

- Anchor tubing in the bottom of the container by forming a loose overhand knot in the tubing.

- Place the container upright in the sump and extend the unanchored end of the tubing up, over, and beyond the lip of the hole.

- Place a plastic sheet over the hole, covering its edges with soil to hold it in place and place a rock in the center of the plastic sheet.

- Lower the plastic sheet into the hole until it is about forty inches below ground level. It now forms an inverted cone with the rock at its apex. Make sure the cone's apex is directly over the container and the plastic cone does not touch the sides of the hole because the earth will absorb condensed water.

- Put more soil on the edges of the plastic to hold it securely in place and to prevent the loss of moisture.

- Plug the tube when not in use so that the moisture will not evaporate.

- Drink water without disturbing the still by using the tube as a straw. You may want to use plants in the hole as a moisture source by digging out additional soil from the sides of the hole to form a slope on which to place the plants.

> **Do not use poisonous plants when making the still. Do not drink the liquid if sticky, milky or bitter tasting. Do not keep the sap from plants longer than twenty-four hours as it begins to ferment and becomes dangerous as a water source.**

Taste and Appearance

Stored water tastes "flat" (as does boiled water) because it has no air in it. It does not harm the water in any way. Pouring it back and forth between two containers can add oxygen back into the water and make it taste better. Refrigeration, if available, also helps the taste. There are also taste-neutralizer tablets and commercial carbon filters on the market that will remove chemical odors and tastes.

TREATING WATER

If using bottled water, make sure the seal is not broken. Otherwise, water should be boiled or treated before use. Boiling water kills harmful bacteria and parasites and by bringing water to a rolling boil for one minute will kill most organisms. If you cannot boil water, treat water with chlorine tablets, iodine tablets or unscented household chlorine bleach (5.25% sodium hypochlorite).

> **Another method to carry water is to use a heavy-duty polyethylene trash bag and place it inside of a pillowcase. The trash bag serves as a water proof liner! Slick!**

If using chlorine tablets or iodine tablets, follow the directions that come with the tablets. If using household chlorine bleach, add 1/8 teaspoon of bleach per gallon of water if the water is clear. For cloudy water, add ¼ teaspoon of bleach per gallon. Mix the solution thoroughly and let stand for thirty minutes before using it. Treating water with chlorine tablets, iodine tablets or liquid bleach will not kill many parasite organisms. Boiling is the best way to kill these organisms. In addition to having a bad odor and taste, contaminated water can contain microorganisms (germs, bacteria, and viruses) that cause disease such as dysentery, typhoid and hepatitis. You should treat all water of uncertain quality before using it for drinking, food preparation or personal hygiene.

There are many methods to treat water and often the best solution is a combination of methods. For example, boiling or chlorination will kill most microorganisms but will not remove other contaminants such as heavy metals, salts and most other chemicals. Before treating, allow any suspended particles to settle at the bottom, or strain them through layers of paper towel, clean cloth or a coffee filter. The instructions below are for treating water of uncertain quality in emergency situations when no other reliable clean water source is available.

Boiling	In a large pot or kettle, bring water to a rolling boil for one full minute, keeping in mind that some water will evaporate. Let water cool before drinking. Boiled water will taste better if you replace oxygen by pouring the water back and forth between two clean containers. This will also improve the taste of stored water.
Chlorination	Use newly opened regular household liquid bleach containing 5.25 to 6.0 percent sodium hypochlorite. Do not use scented bleaches, color safe bleaches, or bleaches with added cleaners. Add 16 drops (1/8 teaspoon) of bleach per gallon of water, stir and let stand for thirty minutes. The water should have a slight bleach odor. If not, repeat the dosage and let stand another fifteen minutes. If the water still does not smell of bleach, discard it and find another source of water. Iodine or water treatment products (sold in camping or surplus stores) that do not contain 5.25 to 6.0 percent sodium hypochlorite as the only active ingredient should not be used.
Distillation	Distillation will remove microorganisms and heavy metals, salts, and other chemicals. Distillation is boiling water and collecting the vapor that condenses back to water. The condensed vapor will not include salt or other impurities. Fill a pot halfway full with water. Tie a cup to the handle on the pot's lid so that the cup will hang right-side-up when the lid is upside-down (make sure the cup is not dangling into the water), and boil the water for twenty minutes. The water that drips from the lid into the cup is distilled. Upside Down Dome Lid Condensed Water Rising Vapors Boiling Water POT

SOURCE: Federal Emergency Management Administration/United States Army

STORAGE OF WATER

Remember - the <u>minimum</u> supply of drinking water to be stored is one gallon per person and pet per day but you will also need water for food preparation, personal hygiene, brushing teeth, cooking, washing dishes and other tasks so store a seven day supply of water (at least seven gallons) for each person and pet. Water can be stored in large plastic fifty gallon barrels. This is a great option but a full barrel will weigh 440 pounds and will be difficult to transport unless a dolly or cart is included in your plan. A siphon hose pump will also be needed to remove the water from the barrel.

> *I got this powdered water - now I don't know what to add.*
>
> *- Steven Wright*

Rain Barrel

A good item to include in emergency supplies is a rain barrel. When water is scarce and at premium prices, a rain barrel full of water can give the survival team a valuable and important water resource. A rain barrel can be above or below the ground. The concept of a rain barrel is to collect rain water from the roof or directly from the clouds and into a barrel. Even a brief summer shower will quickly fill a rain barrel. A quarter-inch of rain falling on a 14' by 25' roof area will provide almost fifty gallons of water. This rain water can then used to water the garden, take showers, and other non-drinking uses.

Another use for a rain barrel is to collect rain water to be used for <u>drinking</u> purposes. In this case, the rain is directed into the barrel *before* it falls to the ground.

Rain barrels are available for purchase through commercial outlets and come with features that make saving water easy and convenient. The overflow outlet diverts excess water away from the house, safety grids on top of the barrel with removable debris screens keep leaves out of the water, a hose valve connects to a garden hose and the spigot provides the means to empty water from the barrel into a bucket. There are also linking kits where two or more barrels can be linked together. When one of the barrels is full of water, the rain automatically is directed into the second barrel allowing twice the rain to be captured at a time. A good rain barrel will cost around $100.00 and can hold 50, 75 or even 100 gallons of water.

An above ground rain barrel must be emptied and either stored inside or turned upside down and covered during the winter months to avoid water from freezing, expanding and then cracking the barrel.

> To clean algae from a large water barrel, empty out three-fourths of the water. Using a small funnel, add a full box of baking soda and a half-gallon of vinegar to the water. The water will begin to "boil and bubble". Put the plugs back in the barrel, lay it on its side and roll the barrel back and forth so that the mixture sloshes around in the barrel. Allow the barrel to sit for a day - roll and slosh it frequently. Make sure you turn the barrel upside down to get the inside top of the barrel. Drain the barrel on the lawn or driveway. Fill the barrel one-fourth to one-half full of clean water and rinse well by rolling and sloshing. Repeat several times until the barrel is clean. Any residual soda or vinegar will dissipate in the water. Refill the container with fresh water and replace the plugs.

SHELF LIFE OF WATER

Water can be stored for long periods of time - up to five years or more, if it does not react with the container or its components. Drinkable water stored in glass or polyethylene containers will remain safe, but may change in taste or odor. Although some of these qualities may be undesirable, they are not harmful. Check stored water every year to determine whether the containers have leaked or if any undesirable characteristics have developed. If so, the water needs to be replaced.

DISINFECTING WATER FOR MULTI-YEAR STORAGE

To store safe water and keep it safe for years, disinfect the container by rinsing it with a strong solution of chlorine bleach and then rinse it with safe water before filling it with the clear and safe water to be stored. Disinfect by adding household bleach containing 5.25% sodium hypochlorite as its only active ingredient. To five gallons, add one teaspoon of bleach. To prevent possible entry of air containing infective organisms through faulty closures, seal the container's closures with duct tape.

TRANSPORTING WATER

There are many types of containers that can be used to carry water. Whatever option(s) you choose, make sure it is clean, has a tight-fitting lid, and are specifically designed for food or water. Some options include (1) canteens, (2) back-pack flasks, (3) commercial bottled water, (4) water pouches, (5) water bottles, (6) water jugs, (7) gott, or (8) thermos. The canteens and flasks are good choices but only hold a small amount of water. One advantage of commercially bottled water is the containers are sealed. Individual 8-ounce pouches of water sold in sporting good stores and army/navy outlets could be used in conjunction with an evacuation kit but they are neither large nor refillable. The two, four or six quart water bottles with tight-fitting lids found in the house wares department will work with an evacuation kit. The sturdy plastic water jugs with handles and the gott with spigots are excellent choices to use as well but based on their size, they will be heavy when filled with water so you will have to *plan in advance* on how to transport it.

I bought a collapsible plastic "bucket" from a local sporting goods store. It folds up and takes very little space. It holds about two gallons of water. Good for auto and evacuation kits!

How much water you <u>should</u> carry is going to realistically be superseded by how much you <u>can</u> carry. As part of our focus on *planning in advance* for an emergency, fill some jugs or bottles with water and practice carrying them to your car, down the stairs or across the street. Even better, walk to your nearest natural source of water (river, lake, spring, well) with your bucket, fill the bucket with water, and carry the bucket filled with water back to your home. It may seem absurd now but during an emergency situation, team members do not want to learn how heavy a container of water can be or how it seems to increase in weight the further it is carried.

It is a good idea to have some mode of transporting heavy or large water containers, such as a luggage tote, dolly or hand truck. You can attach small water bottles to belts for easier carrying and carry water bottles in a backpack. As a guideline, consider that <u>one gallon of water weighs eight pounds</u> – govern yourself accordingly. If forced to leave the primary residence and evacuate to an alternative site, you will need a container to carry water from a main source to your personal or family area. If relocated in a public shelter or reception center with water still running in the faucets, it may still be necessary to carry water to your area. As part of evacuation kits, include a sturdy, heavy-duty container (bucket) and a funnel for transporting water.

SHUTTING OFF UTILITIES

Gas and Propane

For households using *natural* gas, an automatic valve (Earthquake Command System) is commercially available that turns the gas off in the event of an earthquake. After an emergency situation and especially an earthquake, do <u>not</u> use matches, lighters, appliances, or operate light switches unless certain there are no gas or propane leaks. Sparks from electrical switches can ignite gas or propane causing an explosion. If you smell the odor of gas or

83

propane or notice a large consumption of gas being registered on the gas meter, shut off the gas or propane immediately by finding the main shut-off valve, generally located on a pipe next to the gas meter (if using natural gas) and located on the top of the propane tank (if using propane). Use an adjustable wrench to turn the valve to the "off" position. Whether using natural gas or propane, *prepare in advance* by tying an adjustable wrench to the gas meter or propane valve. That way, you will not have to waste valuable time looking for a wrench when the gas needs to be turned off.

GAS METER AND SHUT-OFF VALVE

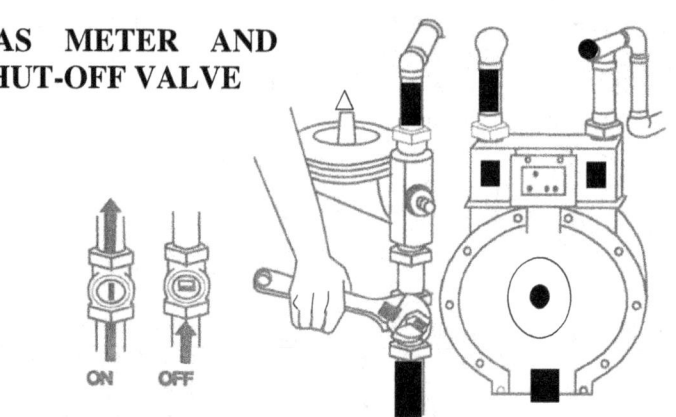

Before turning off natural gas, make sure that it is essential to do so to avoid an explosion. <u>Once turned off, only a professional from the gas company can turn it back on.</u>

The <u>natural</u> gas meter shutoff diagram shows the shutoff valve location on the pipe coming out of the ground. To turn off the valve, use a wrench to turn the valve clockwise one-quarter turn.

Electricity

After a major disaster, shut off the electricity. Sparks from electrical switches can create a shock or fire hazard. Carefully turn off electricity using the main breaker switch on the electrical panel in your home.

Water

For individuals using city water, water can generally be turned off at two locations: (1) the main meter, which controls water flow to the entire property, and (2) the water main leading into the home. Shutting off the water main retains the water supply in your water heater. For individuals using well water, water is turned off at the main valve located somewhere inside the house. Depending on your water source, make sure water valves are marked and easily identified as **INSIDE** and **OUTSIDE**. <u>Attach a wrench to the water line and/or valves.</u>

The OPERATION Element is considered as a top priority for emergency preparation. It involves some of the most important resources and supplies for survival - shelter, electricity, light, water, heat, tools and clothing - all essential components to maintain our health during a disaster. Take steps to ensure that pantries include alternatives and layers of OPERATION components. <u>Female team members must become self reliant and not depend on male members to protect them from the evils of a disaster. The loss of an alpha male in the survival team is possible, and during any level of disaster, any team member may die from natural causes or be killed by a natural or manmade force. Female members must be able to carry forward with the goal of maintaining health and surviving the crisis.</u> Communicate effectively so adult survival team members understand the overall emergency preparation plan. The loss of a team member who maintains and provides crucial information on the location of resources and supplies or has knowledge and skills used to operate and maintain machinery and equipment will severely impact the overall effectiveness of the survival team. If information and skills are learned and shared among team members – the loss would not be so traumatic for the entire team. PLAN AND PREPARE IN ADVANCE!

WHAT TO CONSIDER FOR THE OPERATION ELEMENT

WATER

- **BUCKET** - (3) heavy-duty (used to carry <u>white</u> water, <u>gray</u> water and <u>black</u> water)
- **CLOROX, IODINE TABLETS OR OTHER WATER TABLETS**
- **Rain Barrel** (for catching drinking and gray water)
- **WATER** from natural sources (rivers, streams, lakes)
- **WATER** from springs (flowing and non-flowing)
- **WATER** in sterile plastic fifty-gallon drums
- **WATER** purchased in bottles
- **WATER** purchased in gallon and five gallon containers

LIGHT

- **FLASHLIGHTS** (solar)
- Light Sticks
- **MATCHES**
- **MIRROR**
- **OIL LAMPS**
- **OIL** (for oil lamp)
- **SOLAR BATTERY CHARGER**
- **SOLAR GARDEN LIGHTS**
- **WICKS** (for oil lamp)

ELECTRICITY

- **Generator - Fuel Powered**
- **GENERATOR - SOLAR POWERED**
- **SOLAR BATTERY CHARGER**
- **SOLAR PANELS**
- Wind Turbine

SHELTER IN PLACE

- **Batteries**
- **BEDDING/SLEEPING BAG**
- **Books, Games, Cards**
- **FOOD** – ready to eat
- **FLASHLIGHT** (battery, **solar**, **hand crank**)
- **DUCT TAPE**
- **First Aid Kit** (small)
- **Heater** (if cold weather)
- **LANTERN** (**solar** or battery powered)
- **MEDICATIONS/PRESCRIPTIONS**
- **PLASTIC SHEETING** (windows and doors)
- **RADIO** (**solar/hand crank**/battery powered)
- **SCISSORS**
- **STAPLER AND STAPLES** (staple sheeting)
- Telephone
- **Towels**
- **WATER** (one gallon/person/pet per day)
- Weapon/Ammo

CLOTHING

- **BELT**
- **BOOTS**
- **GLOVES**
- **HATS COATS**
- **HOUSE SLIPPERS**
- **JACKETS**
- **RAIN GEAR**
- **ROBE**
- **SEWING SUPPLIES**
- **SHIRTS**
- **SHOES**
- **SLACKS**
- **SLEEPWEAR**
- **SOCKS PANTS**
- **SUNGLASSES**
- **SWEAT SHIRTS**
- **SWEATERS**
- **THERMAL UNDERWEAR**
- **T-SHIRTS**
- **UNDERWEAR**

BABY SUPPLIES

- Bath Soap
- Bathtub
- Bibs
- Blankets
- Body Suits
- Bottle Brush
- Bottles
- Carrier
- Coats
- Comb/Brush
- Crib
- Crib Sheets
- Diaper Bag
- Diaper Pins
- Diaper Rash Ointment
- Diapers (cloth)
- Diapers (disposable)
- Gloves
- Hats
- High Chair
- Lotion
- Medicine Dropper
- Medicine Spoon
- Mittens
- Oil
- Pacifiers
- Pajamas
- Plastic Pants
- Potty Chair
- Powder
- Quilts
- Rattle
- Shampoo Shoes
- Sleepers
- Slurpy Cup
- Socks
- Stroller
- Swaddles
- Swing
- Teething Rings
- Toys
- Training Pants
- Underwear
- Utensils
- Washcloths

TOOLS

- **AXE**
- Bars
- Bolt Cutter
- **Bolts**
- Cement Trials
- **Chisels**
- Clamps
- Crimpers
- **Duct Tape**
- Files
- Glass Cutter
- Glue
- **HAMMERS**
- **HATCHET**
- **HOE**
- **KNIFE** (putty, utility)
- **KNIFE SHARPENER**
- **LADDERS**
- Level
- Lopper
- Lumber
- **Mallet** (rubber)
- Miter Box with Saw
- **Nails**
- **Nut Drivers**
- **Nuts**
- Paintbrush
- **Pick**
- **Pitch Fork**
- Planers
- **PLIERS**
- Plow
- **Pruner**
- **Pruning Saw**
- Punch
- Putty
- **RAKES**
- **Ratchets/Sockets**
- Sander
- Sand Paper
- **SAWS**
- Scrapers
- **SCREWDRIVERS**
- **Screws**
- Shears
- **SHOVEL**
- **Sledge Hammer**
- Snips
- **Spades**
- Spikes
- Squares
- Tape Measure
- Vise
- **Washers**
- Wedge
- Weeder
- **WRENCHES**

HEAT

- **AXE** (for cutting wood)
- Barbeque and Briquettes – (heating hot water)
- **BEDDING** (quilts and blankets)
- **Carbon Monoxide Detector**
- Card Table (for making a tent)
- Catalytic Heaters
- Chemical hand and feet warmers
- **Coal** (for fireplace and stove)
- **Fire Alarm (battery operated)**
- **Fire Extinguisher**
- **Fireplace** (wood-burning)
- **FLINT FIRE STARTER TOOL**
- **GENERATOR (SOLAR)** or Generator (Fuel)
- Heating pad
- Hot water bottle
- **MATCHES**
- **Plastic (Heavy-Duty) Sheeting**
- **Rain Gear**
- **SLEEPING BAGS** (tested for cold weather)
- Space Heaters (electric and/or butane)
- **Stapler and Staples (Heavy-Duty)**
- **Tent** (pop tent not require staking)
- **WARM CLOTHING** (cold climate and seasons)
- **Wood** (for fireplace and stove)
- **Wood Burning Stove**

CHAPTER FOUR

MEDICATION

A critical component in an emergency preparation plan is to have <u>current</u> medical, medication and immunization needs fully addressed <u>prior to any emergency</u> to reduce overall medical needs that may arise during a disaster. For example, as I am writing this paragraph – a tooth on the upper right side of my mouth has shown the first symptoms of tooth decay and I am experiencing more sensitivity in the tooth every day. Of course, being an extremely intelligent and logical person, I plan to wait until the tooth is entirely decayed and infected so the excruciating throbbing forces me to scream out in pain. Only then will I actually make the appointment to see the dentist. Sometimes I amaze myself at just how clever I really am . . .

On a continuous basis and with few exceptions, we all tend to experience some type of "body malfunction" – whether it is dry or itchy eyes, stuffy nose, chapped lips, dry skin, water retention, heartburn, back or joint pain, or even a pesky hangnail. At some time in our lives, we all had a headache or perhaps a painful migraine, constipation, diarrhea, earache or a toothache. Women enjoy the delightful experience each month of menstrual cramps and menopause later in life. All babies experience the pain associated with cutting new teeth. In order to relieve our ailments, there is a buffet of products that provides relief in soothing and reducing the agony – eye drops, decongestant, lip balm, lotion, pain reliever and fingernail clippers. Depending on our individual health condition, we try to have a supply of medications, ointments and potions on hand to serve our needs.

I cannot stress enough the importance of being proactive in getting treatment for any type of medical ailment or injury in a <u>timely</u> manner and stocking any products or supplies used to treat body malfunctions! During a serious disaster, due to contaminated water and food sources and sewage backups, there will be plenty of medical ailments and serious injuries without worrying and dealing with a painful toothache, dry skin, chapped lips or a headache.

Depending on the disaster level (1-3), the consequences to the various elements, i.e., **Operation**, **Medication**, **Immunization**, **Communication** etc., and the length of time the elements are damaged or destroyed – some members who are injured as a result of the disaster may not survive. Depending on the availability of transportation, survival team members may not even be able to reach medical facilities. Self-sufficiency could make the difference between life and death.

After a major disaster, we must assume most first responders, clinics, hospitals, pharmacies and other medical institutions in the area would be out of action and/or overwhelmed. In fact, it is likely outside assistance may not be available for days, weeks or even months after the disaster. Depending on the severity of <u>current</u> medical conditions and specific medications taken by survival team members – life-saving medical treatment or prescription medications may not be available. <u>Remember, during many disasters, there will be casualties due to injuries and lack of available medical and pharmaceutical treatments</u>. During serious or long-term disasters, there will also be suicides. Prepare mentally and psychologically for these casualties.

Another factor to consider when preparing for an emergency involves technological advances in medicine we have made over the past years. Although these extraordinary advances in medicine have been valuable to us as a civilization, it can also prove to be a determent during a disaster. For example, during times <u>without</u> disaster, and if we are in poor health, we simply make an appointment with a physician. Once in the doctor's office, a blood and urine sample is taken and perhaps an x-ray, MRI or CAT scan, depending on the symptoms. These tests are performed by complicated medical instruments that provide information, statistics and reports for the attending physician concerning the patient. Based on the final reports, the physician and medical staff can <u>then</u> determine the specific disease or cause of illness. At this point, medication can be prescribed or other techniques and procedures are performed to make the patient well again. If necessary, surgery can be performed – again using complicated equipment as part of the procedure. During a serious and long-term disaster, medical equipment could be damaged or destroyed.

Over the past twenty-five years, the objective of all medical schools (at least in this country), is to teach medicine using the latest technology and advancements in medical science. Medical schools have focused on using complicated computers, instruments, tools and equipment to instruct up-coming physicians on how to diagnose disease and heal injuries. These physicians who have entered the work force over the past twenty-five years have been taught to use <u>machines</u> to practice medicine and not to practice medicine as previous physicians have done over the centuries. As a result, many practicing physicians have compromised their ability to diagnose disease and treat injuries without the use of electronics and medical equipment.

It could be legitimately argued that physicians who practiced medicine fifty to one hundred years ago would be better able to serve patients in an emergency than those who practice today. During a serious and long-term disaster, medical services may be compromised because of the inability of physicians to practice medicine without advanced technology.

EMERGENCY PREPARATION GUIDELINES

There are several guidelines that can be incorporated into an overall emergency plan to prepare for and in some cases eliminate medical issues that could become prevalent during an emergency situation. For example:

- Sign up for CPR, FIRST AID or CERT training courses and learn the procedures for basic lifesaving techniques including mouth-to-mouth resuscitation and the Heimlich maneuver.

- Learn alternative methods for treating wounds, burns, infections, blisters, diarrhea, constipation and nausea.

- Study and learn alternative methods for using herbs and other natural sources to heal the body and keep the body healthy.

- All supplies in the first aid kits should be freshly stocked, not expired and in good working condition.

- A "word of wisdom" to everyone – maintain a healthy weight, eat nutritious food, exercise, avoid tobacco, alcohol, and illegal drug use and abuse of prescription and over-the-counter drugs.

- Know the exact location of nearby hospitals and medical treatment centers and have a list of phone numbers for your physician, dentist and other medical personnel in a convenient and safe place in the home, car and work (consider laminating the list).

- Keep all medical equipment (wheelchairs, crutches) in good working condition.

- Keep all <u>electronic</u> medical equipment and supplies (diabetic) in good working condition.

- Ensure that all prescription and over-the-counter medicines have not expired (and if so, replace them).

- Keep all <u>prescriptions</u> filled and attempt to keep at least a three-month supply.

- Everyone should schedule a yearly overall <u>medical and dental</u> examination.

- Anyone with <u>vision</u> problems should have regular examinations and up-to-date prescriptions for glasses and contacts and have an extra pair of glasses including sunglasses.

- Maintain a list of all medications in wallet or purse including drug name, strength, dosage, and schedule.

- Wear a medical-alert bracelet or necklace at all times and/or keep any other medical information device up-to-date and readily available.

- Any medications used to stabilize an existing medical condition or keep a condition from worsening (medications for asthma, seizures, cardiovascular disorders, diabetes, psychiatric conditions, HIV, and thyroid disorders) should be carried with you, if possible, in a purse or briefcase in labeled containers.

- Do not store medications in areas susceptible to extremes in heat, cold, and humidity (e.g., car, kitchen or bathroom) as this could decrease the effectiveness of the medication.

- If children or pets are in the home, use child-resistant containers, and secure all medicine cabinets, purse, wallet and briefcase.

- Rotate medications whenever prescriptions are refilled to use them before the expiration date.

- Refill prescriptions while still having a 5-7 day supply of medication. Keep in mind that some sources, such as mail-order pharmacies, have a longer refill lead time.

- If your child takes medications, talk to the school and learn their emergency preparedness plans.

- If being treated with a complex medication regimen, talk to your physician or pharmacist to create appropriate emergency preparation plans. Such regimens include injectable medications, including those delivered by pumps (e.g., insulin, analgesics, chemotherapy), medications delivered by a nebulizer (e.g., antibiotics, bronchodilators) and dialysis.

SENIOR CITIZENS

Seniors have complex medication regimens, often involving multiple medications prescribed by several physicians that make them vulnerable to accidental poisonings. Patients should immediately contact their physician if they experience an adverse reaction to their medicines. If the physician is not available, contact the local poison center using the toll free number (800) 222-1222. Keep this number readily available by the telephone. Eighty percent of directors and half of all staff members at poison control centers are pharmacists and health care professionals who are trained and highly educated on the complexities of today's medications.

Senior patients should:

- **Keep a written record** of medications you take including drug name, dosage, and frequency. This list should be kept current and stored in purse or wallet, the glove compartment in the car(s) and on the refrigerator in the home.

- **Communicate**. Inform your doctor and pharmacist of all medications you are taking, including non-prescription medications and dietary supplements; this will help reduce chances of an interaction.

- **Learn about your medications**. Ask your doctor or pharmacist to explain *why* you are taking the medication, the food and medicines you should avoid and possible reactions and side effects.

- **Use one pharmacy**. Many seniors receive prescriptions from more than one doctor. By using one pharmacy, all prescriptions are consolidated and the pharmacist can check for possible interactions between medications.

- **Keep a journal**. Make notes of all symptoms and especially after taking your medications. Painful or unexpected side effects may signal a need for adjusting the medication treatment.

- **Maintain a schedule**. A routine can decrease the chances of missing dosages or taking more than needed.

- **Organize**. Purchase a seven-day pill box for medication taken each day in an individual compartment.

CHILDREN

The Centers for Disease Control report that approximately nine out of ten accidental poisonings occur in the home, a staggering sixty percent of these victims are children younger than age six years old, and close to half of poisonings in children of this age group involve a misuse of medicines. Parents of infants rarely feel totally comfortable leaving them alone with anyone. Provide the babysitter or caregiver with complete emergency medical information about the child. Authorize the caregiver (in writing) to seek medical attention if the child becomes ill and have the document notarized. Keep in mind that any child can be treated <u>without</u> authorization in an emergency situation, but it often has to be a true life-threatening emergency.

Provide the following information and keep it in a practical location, such as by the phone, so the babysitter or caregiver has the right information in case of an emergency.

- How to activate your area's emergency medical services, especially if it isn't done by calling 9-1-1
- Number for Poison Control - (800) 222-1222 or the regional hospital in your area
- Emergency contact information (work and cell numbers and any additional numbers and contacts)
- Child's doctor's name and phone number
- Child's dentist's name and phone number
- Health insurance information, including the plan and policy number
- Child's full name and date of birth
- Child's medical history (allergies, medications, all medical problems)
- Any special instructions
- Address and number for your home
- Landline telephone number for your home
- Other important emergency information

Below are guidelines every parent, caregiver and grandparent should use to prevent accidental poisonings:

- Avoid taking medications in the presence of children as they often try to imitate adults
- Do not refer to any medicine as "candy"
- Use child-resistant closures on medicine and other products
- Keep all medications (both prescription and nonprescription) in their original child-resistant containers
- Always turn on the light when giving or taking medicine
- Check medications for expiration dates and if not dated, consider it expired six months after purchase
- Avoid putting medications in open trash containers in the kitchen or bathroom
- Be aware that vitamins, particularly those containing iron - can be poisonous if taken in large doses
- In case of poisoning, call 800-222-1222, the national phone number for poison control centers

MEDICAL INFORMATION FOR RESPONDERS

Recalling the details of medications, diseases or disabilities does not come easily during a medical emergency and especially during a serious disaster. Emergencies happen when we least expect it, so it is important to prepare ahead of time. Here are some products and services designed to assist in preparing for an emergency. Regardless of which one you use, be sure to *regularly* update medical information. Outdated information may be *more* dangerous than none at all.

E-HealthKEY from MedicAlert Foundation International (www.medicalert.org)

The E-HealthKEY is a product from MedicAlert that keeps all personal medical information available on a portable USB device attached to a key ring. The device is supported by a database at MedicAlert headquarters. Medical information is made available using any PC with an Internet connection. A computer not connected online can access the emergency section in the device. The cost is approximately $40.00. *The Problem:* Many ambulances do not have computers.

Medic Tag USB Device

Medic Tag is a Windows PC compatible USB device (portable flash drive) that does not use the Internet to access personal medical information. They are easy to use with nothing to install and has preloaded software. Most devices have 256 megabytes of memory to store medical information and contact lists. Over 95% of emergency responders will check for a bracelet, necklace or key chain for medical information. A first responder can easily view and print out the list. The cost is approximately $30.00. *The Problem:* Most ambulances are not equipped with portable computers to access these devices.

Personal Medical Jewelry

Medical bracelets or necklaces have basic personal medical information engraved on the back of the jewelry and emergency workers can immediately see important conditions or allergies. Jewelry may also be used to address end-of-life decisions. Some jewelry is supported with databases that can be accessed by emergency workers. The cost is approximately $10.00. *The Problem:* You have to wear it!

Wallet Cards

A simple laminated personal medical information card for first responders can be carried in the wallet or purse. It does not need to be detailed, but should cover basic information:

- *Name / Birthdate*
- *Drug or food allergies*
- *Prescription Medications*
- *Medical Conditions*
- *Emergency Contacts*

Whether you print the information on a card with a computer or by hand, make sure it is legible. *The Problem:* Ambulance personnel will probably not look in your purse or wallet. The card will be found at the hospital.

Cell Phone on ICE (icesticker.com) or 1425 Market Blvd, Suite 330-155, Roswell, GA 30076

ICE stands for "In Case of Emergency." Putting "ICE" next to a number in the cell phone's contact list will tell medical or law enforcement personnel which number to call in an emergency. A sticker on the outside of the phone will alert emergency workers that there is an emergency contact identified in the contact section of the phone. By accessing the website, you can purchase the stickers. Prices range from $2.00 for one sticker, $7.50 for 5 stickers, $10.00 for 10 stickers, $25.00 for 50 stickers and $60.75 for 250 stickers. *The Problem:* Ambulance personnel may not look in your phone. They will take the phone to the hospital where workers may find it and can call the emergency contact.

Vial of Life (www.vialoflife.com) – (888) 724-1200

The *Vial of Life Project* is free to use and provides a decal and form to fill out with medical information. Fill out the Vial of Life form and answer all or any pertinent questions. Make blank copies of the form to keep information current or go to the website to maintain and store updated information. Attach a decal to the front of a heavy-duty plastic baggie. You may also consider placing a copy of an EKG, living will or equivalent, DNR (Do Not Resuscitate) and a recent photo of yourself. Securely tape the plastic baggie at eye level to the front of the refrigerator door. Place a second decal on the front door or window for easy visibility by anyone responding to a medical emergency.

The Vial of Life system can work in the automobile and at work. In the automobile, place a decal in a secure location <u>inside</u> of the car, i.e., windshield or visor. Then place the baggie (with a decal on the front) in the glove compartment. At work, the baggie can be placed in a conspicuous location in your office area and/or given to a trustworthy and responsible individual in the office. *The Problem*: **None - good choice**!

Scroll Identification

The scroll is a keychain device with a small scroll inside for personal medical information. It carries the same type of personal medical information as a wallet card. One method to draw attention to the keychain is to identify the outside of the container as a medical information device using some type of medical sticker. Identification issues are eliminated by putting the owner's picture on the scroll. The cost is approximately $5.00. *The Problem:* This product is not as well known and rescuers may not recognize this object as a medical information device.

DISEASES AND INJURIES OF DISASTER

During peaceful times, the "diseases of disaster" may be rare in this country, but a disaster carries with it increased sanitation issues which in turn may activate many dormant diseases that normally would not affect the general population. In other cases, disease is simply spread from one person to another through close contact with others. For example, strains of flu can quickly become epidemic in schools and then travel throughout other areas including the home, church, office, movie theater, shopping mall, stores and locations where citizens tend to congregate in large numbers.

A buffet of injuries can also occur due to falling objects, falling down or being careless when cleaning up. Depending on the severity of the disaster, there could be countless injuries, diseases and even deaths due to lack of vaccines, medical facilities or treatment options.

The Centers for Disease Control (CDC) provide a list of <u>some</u> of the diseases and injuries that can become prevalent and deadly during a disaster including:

Influenza

According to the Centers for Disease Control, even with annual vaccinations, the flu kills more than 40,000 people, puts over 200,000 in the hospital each year and costs over ten billion dollars in this country. A pandemic or worldwide outbreak of a new influenza virus could overwhelm the health and medical capabilities of this country. In 1918, there were forty million deaths, in 1957, there were two million deaths, and in 1968, there were one million deaths from influenza worldwide.

The CDC further states that the next pandemic is likely to come in waves, each lasting months and pass through communities of all sizes across the nation and world. In a worst case scenario, the general public would stay in their homes with no work, school or shopping for up to three months. To reduce the spread of flu, get a flu shot every year and be prepared to follow public health recommendations that may include limiting attendance at public gatherings and travel for several days, weeks or even months.

Cholera

Cholera is an acute, diarrheal illness caused by a bacterial infection in the intestine. The infection is often mild or without symptoms but can sometimes be severe. Approximately five percent of infected persons will have profuse watery diarrhea, vomiting and leg cramps. In these people, rapid loss of body fluids leads to dehydration and shock and without treatment, death can occur within hours.

The cholera bacteria are <u>usually found in water or food sources that have been contaminated by feces</u> from a person infected with cholera. Cholera is most likely found and spread in places with <u>inadequate water treatment, poor sanitation and poor hygiene</u>. The cholera bacteria may also live in brackish rivers and coastal waters.

Cholera can be successfully treated by immediate replacement of fluid and salts lost through diarrhea using an oral rehydration solution - a prepackaged mixture of sugar and salts mixed with water and drunk in large amounts. All persons (visitors or residents) in areas where cholera is occurring or has occurred should observe the following recommendations:

- Drink only bottled, boiled, or chemically treated water and bottled or canned carbonated beverages. When using bottled drinks, make sure the seal is not broken. Avoid tap water, fountain drinks and ice cubes.

- To disinfect your own water: boil for one minute or filter the water and add two drops of household bleach or ½ iodine tablet per quart of water.

Dysentery

Dysentery is an inflammatory disorder of the intestine and colon and is usually caused by a bacterial or protozoan infection or infestation of parasitic worms, but can also be caused by a chemical irritant or viral infection. If left untreated, dysentery can be fatal.

In developed countries, dysentery is generally a mild illness with symptoms consisting of mild stomach pains and frequent passage of feces. Symptoms appear after one to three days and are usually no longer present after a week. The frequency of urges to defecate, the volume of feces passed, and the presence of mucus and/or blood depends on the pathogen causing the disease. Vomiting blood, severe abdominal pain, fever, shock and delirium can also be symptoms.

> *We have made of ourselves living cesspools, and driven doctors to invent names for our diseases.*
>
> - **Plato**

To reduce the risk of contracting dysentery during a disaster, the following precautions are suggested:

- Wash hands with soap and water *prior* to handling, cooking and eating food, handling babies, feeding young or elderly people, using the toilet or coming in contact with an infected person

- Avoid contact with someone known to have the disease

- Wash laundry using the hottest water possible (may not be possible)

- Avoid sharing personal items such as towels and face cloths

- Dispose of feces and urine in a sanitary manner to prevent contamination of water and food sources

- Use bottled, boiled, or chemically treated water to drink, wash dishes, brush teeth, wash and prepare food or make ice

- Eat foods that are packaged or freshly cooked and served hot and do <u>not</u> eat raw and undercooked meats or seafood and unpeeled fruits and vegetables

Sexually Transmitted Diseases

There is one very simple method to avoid sexually transmitted diseases and that is to avoid sex – but it is not a realistic choice. Did you know that during disasters, the sexual activity of individuals living in the area actually increases and sure enough, nine months later, the hospitals are inundated with pregnant women? Make careful and smart choices with regards to your sexual activity. Married couples should honor their vows and remain monogamous to one another and single persons should behave responsibly and use protection to avoid contracting these diseases. By avoiding a sexually transmitted disease – it is one less obstacle to address during serious disasters. **BEHAVE YOURSELF**!

Infection

Due to increased medical emergencies during a disaster, infection becomes widespread. Any breach in the skin provides the opportunity for infection and due to sanitation problems, superficial abrasions or deep and large wounds could easily become infected. There are several signs that occur when a wound is infected, including:

> *Never does Nature say one thing and wisdom another.*
>
> **Johann CF von Schuller**

- Chills and fever
- Increased pain and swelling
- Limited movement
- Persistent and elevated temperature
- Pus draining directly from the wound or collecting in an abscess or boil under the skin
- Redness surrounding or spreading from the wound
- Swollen lymph nodes

As part of your overall emergency preparation planning, *learn in advance* what steps to take to treat infection caused by wounds or other injuries.

Burns

Burns will be a very common injury during a disaster. There are three classifications of burns, including:

- *First Degree* – burn appears on outer layer or epidermis of the skin. The skin appears mildly red, swollen and painful. There are no blisters. An example of a first degree burn is *sunburn*.

- *Second Degree* – burn passes through epidermis and extends into the dermis or secondary layer of the skin. The pain and swelling is moderate and blisters are present.

- *Third Degree* – burn reaches into the underlying fat and muscle tissue of the body. The skin appears charred and leathery and is numb to the touch.

How much of the body is burned, as well as the location and degree of burn will determine how the patient will be treated and the odds for survival. Burns to the face, neck, hands, feet, genitalia and buttocks are serious. Facial burns can result in serious damage to the respiratory tract and cause breathing problems. Burns that completely encircle the body can have a tourniquet effect on the victim. A person experiencing serious or third degree burns requires *immediate* hospitalization or they will likely not survive due to damaged capillaries that allow blood serum to leak into the burned tissue. This fluid loss reduces the blood volume of the body and rapidly causes shock. People with severe burns require massive amounts of intravenous fluids in order to survive.

Diarrhea

During an emergency, a common problem is diarrhea caused by a number of variables including stress, intestinal infections from contaminated water, food poisoning from eating spoiled food and allergies. There are two types of diarrhea, including:

- *Traveler's diarrhea* generally caused by the E.coli bacteria with an incubation period of twelve to forty-eight hours and will last between two and five days. Symptoms include abdominal stress, cramps and watery stools. This type of diarrhea can generally be treated with Pepto-Bismol or Imodium AD.

- *Bacterial diarrhea* includes additional symptoms of chills and fever, and blood, pus or mucous in the stool. This type of diarrhea is very serious and would be treated with anti-microbial medication and NOT Pepto-Bismol or Imodium AD as these medications will prolong the illness.

Severe diarrhea (ten bowel movements per day) and the resulting severe dehydration can kill young, old or weaker team members. The replacement of fluids and electrolytes (sodium and potassium) is vital for all victims of diarrhea. Remember that fruit juices and sodas make diarrhea worse. Most adult dehydration caused by diarrhea, vomiting or fever can be improved by drinking plain water.

In an emergency, this homemade oral rehydration solution can be used for those who may need more than simply water to rehydrate a sick body:

- **½ teaspoon salt**
- **½ teaspoon baking soda**
- **3 tablespoons sugar**
- **1 quart of room temperature drinking water**

> **Make sure to <u>accurately</u> measure the ingredients.**

Mix the above ingredients in the quart of water and drink the entire contents.

Affected people under three years old, over sixty five years old, who are pregnant or who have had severe diarrhea for more than 48 to 72 hours with abdominal tenderness should seek medical care as soon as possible.

Constipation

The normal length of time between bowel movements ranges widely with some people having bowel movements three times a day while others only one or two times a week. Going longer than three days without a bowel movement makes the stool or feces harder and more difficult to pass. Constipation is usually caused by a disorder of bowel function rather than a structural problem.

Many of the causes of constipation occurring during a disaster include:

- Antacid medicines containing calcium or aluminum
- Depression
- Disruption of regular diet or routine
- Inadequate activity, exercise or immobility

- Inadequate fiber in the diet
- Inadequate intake of water
- Medicines (especially strong pain medicines)
- Overuse of laxatives (stool softeners)
- **STRESS**

Chronic constipation - at least two of the following for at least three months:

- Hard stools more than 25% of the time
- Incomplete evacuation more than 25% of the time
- Straining during a bowel movement more than 25% of the time
- Swollen abdomen or abdominal pain
- Two or fewer bowel movements in a week
- Vomiting

If constipated, consider the following treatments:

- Eat prunes, dates and figs
- Exercise on a regular basis
- Use a very mild stool softener or laxative
- Avoid caffeine and soft drinks
- Add fruits, vegetables, legumes, whole grains and bran to the diet
- Drink two to four extra glasses of water every day (unless fluid restricted)
- Drink warm liquids - especially in the morning (coffee helps many people)

> **Did you know that the only time you apply a tourniquet is as a very last resort?** You have tried everything else, and the victim is going to die soon because you can't stop the bleeding. Using a tourniquet will cause the victim to lose their limb below the point of the tourniquet. If they lose a limb but save their life, it may be worth it. But if their life was not ever in question, using a tourniquet consigns them to living the rest of their life as an amputee for no reason. One paramedic of thirteen years said he had never needed to use a tourniquet.

Blisters

During a serious emergency, transportation may present a problem and team members may be required to walk from place to place. As part of *planning in advance*, all survival team members should have good and sturdy walking shoes in order to avoid blisters on the feet. A ruptured blister is an invitation to infection so the instant a blister appears on the foot – **stop** – take off your shoes – dry out your socks – and apply a bandage or tape (first aid or duct tape) over the hot spot.

Upon discovery of a small blister - do not open it because an intact blister is safe from infection. Apply padding material around the blister to relieve pressure and reduce friction. If a blister bursts, clean and dress it daily and pad around it. Leave a large blister intact. Once the blister is cleaned, run a sterilized needle and thread through the blister, detach the needle, and leave both ends of the thread hanging out of the blister. The thread will absorb the liquid inside which reduces the size of the hole and ensures the hole does not close up. Pad around the blister.

Bee and Wasp Stings

If stung by a bee or wasp, remove the stinger and venom sac by scraping with a fingernail or a knife blade. Do not squeeze or grasp the stinger or venom sac since squeezing will force more venom into the wound. Wash the sting site with soap and water to lessen the chance of a secondary infection. If allergic to insect stings, always carry an insect sting kit with you. Relieve itching caused by insect bites by applying one of the following treatments:

Cold Compresses	**Coconut Meat**	**Dandelion Sap**
Mud and Ashes	**Garlic Cloves (crushed)**	**Onions**

Rash

To treat rashes, use the following guidelines:

If it is moist, keep it dry - If it is dry, keep it moist - Do not scratch it

To treat a skin rash - learn what is causing it. Use a compress of vinegar or tannic acid (derived from tea, or boiling acorns or the bark of a hardwood tree) to weeping rashes. Keep dry rashes moist by rubbing a small amount of rendered animal fat or grease on the affected area. Treat rashes as open wounds and clean and dress them daily.

Wounds

There are many "natural" treatments available for use as antiseptics for wounds (including a rash):

- *Baking Soda:* Prepare a paste of baking soda and water
- *Bee Honey:* Use it straight or dissolved in water
- *Garlic:* Rub on a wound or boil to extract the oils and use the water to rinse area
- *Iodine Tablets:* Use five to fifteen tablets in a gallon of water to produce a good rinse
- *Salt Water:* Use two or three tablespoons per gallon of water to kill bacteria
- *Sphagnum Moss:* Found in boggy areas, it is a natural source of iodine and used as a dressing

Intestinal Parasites

Ugh!! To avoid worm infestations and other intestinal parasites, take preventive measures and never go barefoot! The most effective way to prevent intestinal parasites is to avoid uncooked meat and raw vegetables contaminated by raw sewage or human waste used as a fertilizer. There are home remedies that work on the principle of changing the environment in the gastrointestinal tract that kills the parasite - but none are fun choices.

- *Kerosene* - drink two tablespoons of kerosene *but no more.* If necessary, repeat this treatment in twenty-four to forty-eight hours. Do not inhale the fumes and by all means, do not smoke! The kerosene may cause lung irritation. (Try not to blow yourself up) ☹

- *Nicotine* - eat one to one-and-a-half cigarettes. The nicotine in the cigarette will kill or stun the worms long enough for your system to pass them. If the infestation is severe, repeat the treatment in twenty-four to forty-eight hours *but no sooner.* ☹

- *Peppers* - *spicy* peppers are effective only if they are a steady part of the diet. You can eat them raw or put them in soups or rice and meat dishes. They create an environment that prohibits parasitic attachment. ☹

- *Salt Water* - dissolve 4 tablespoons of salt in 1 quart of water and drink. Do <u>not</u> repeat this treatment. ☺

ANTIBIODICS

In the United States, many drugs requiring a prescription can be purchased in other countries <u>without</u> a prescription. Obviously, there are certain medications that <u>definitely</u> require oversight by the medical profession and should rightfully be controlled and distributed only with authorization by a qualified medical professional using a prescription. However, once a patent has expired on a prescription drug, the drug can be manufactured and distributed over the counter. A good example is Prilosec which was a prescription medication for acid reflux and heartburn. Once the patent ran out – Prilosec was available over the counter. In most cases, the over-the-counter version is the exact chemical compound and is less expensive. The problem – insurance companies will not cover over-the-counter medication.

There are several medications requiring a prescription in this country that should be included in all emergency supply pantries (primary residence, place of refuge, work, car and evacuation kits). During any level of disaster, but especially during long-term catastophes that limit any outside medical, pharmecudical and first aid assistance, these particular drugs will prove to be critical life-saving supplies.

It seldom fails – during an emergency, we can count on <u>someone</u> getting a cut, slash, scrap or slice from falling debris, falling down or falling into some sharp object. Survival teams who have *planned in advance* will have adequate first aid supplies to tend the wound. On many occasions, no matter how carefully a wound or injury is treated – an infection is very possible. For these type of infections, an <u>antibiotic</u> may be able to kill the infection and heal the wound. Unfortunately, antibiotics require a prescription in this country and depending on the circumstances surrounding the disaster, getting a prescription from a doctor, getting to the pharmacy to fill it and actually having the drug available at the pharmacy may be impossible. The prudent choice is to include antibiodics in the emergency supplies.

An <u>easy</u>, <u>safe</u> and <u>legal</u> way to get antibiodics <u>without a prescription</u> is to purchase them from sources outside of the country. However, most insurance companies and government sponsored programs (Medicare and Medicaid) <u>will not cover</u> prescriptions purchased outside the country. When purchasing drugs from outside sources, one must personally pay for the medication using either a debit or credit card.

In my experience, I have used the Internet to search for companies in CANADA (<u>not Mexico!</u>) who offer antibiodics for sale without a prescription. It is important to thoroughly investigate the various companies and compare prices. There are numerous legitimate companies that offer antibiobics at reasonable prices. Depending on the drug and the company, the actual drug is generally manufactured in Switzerland, India or countries in Europe. Some companies include free shipping and handling and others charge for these services. The drugs are shipped from the manufacturer to your home within several weeks. There are several types of antibiodics offered in various strengths and used for different types of infections. For example, the antibiotics sold over the Internet in this manner are used to kill *bacterial* infections and not *viral* infections, such as the common cold. Do your homework first before making a purchase.

I have also discovered that many drugs <u>requiring a prescription</u> can be purchased from legitimate companies in Canada at a significantly reduced price. Again, the entire cost would be paid by you, but in many cases, insurance companies are requiring outrageous co-payments for certain prescription drugs – one example is Nexium which is used for acid reflux and heartburn. In order to get a three month supply, my co-payment was over eight hundred dollars – the insurance company countered by reminding me that the total price was over twelve hundred dollars and I should be exceedingly grateful that they would pick up the additional four hundred dollars. I got on the Internet and found a *legitimate* company in Canada that would sell me a three-month prescription of Nexium or an acceptable generic brand for a total price of one hundred and twenty dollars for the brand or one hundred dollars for the generic brand.   I contacted my physician and he faxed the prescription to the Canadian company. Within three weeks, I had my prescription delivered to my door.

ALL SURVIVAL TEAMS SHOULD INCLUDE <u>ANTIBIODICS</u> IN THEIR EMERGENCY SUPPLY PANTRIES – including primary residence, place of refuge, work and auto kits and all evacuation kits.

STORAGE

Emergency medical supplies should be stored in a location providing easy access and protection from outside elements, i.e., water, sun, cold, humidity, fire and structural damage. For the home, all or some of the supplies could be stored in a medicine cabinet, or if you prefer, stored in a container with a tight lid such as a tool box, plastic container or fish tackle box.

Regardless of the storage method used, <u>the container should be clearly marked and identifiable as the first aid kit</u>. The medical supplies for the car and work should be stored in a compact container and also clearly marked and identifiable as the first aid kit. Inspect supplies in the home, car and work regularly and keep them freshly stocked. Important medical information and most prescriptions can be stored in the refrigerator that also provides excellent protection from fires.

Many people store medications in the bathroom, but this popular spot is actually one of the <u>worst</u> places to keep medicine. Bathroom cabinets tend to be warm and humid, an environment that speeds up a drug's break down process. This is especially true for tablets and capsules. Unnecessary exposure to heat and moisture can cause drugs to lose potency prior to the labeled expiration date.

For example, a warm, muggy environment can cause aspirin tablets to break down into acetic acid (vinegar) and salicylic acid, both of which are potential stomach irritants. Instead, keep medicines in a <u>*cool*, *dark*, and *dry* place and out of children's reach</u>. If you must keep them in the bathroom, always keep the containers tightly closed and never repackage them. If medicines must be stored in a kitchen, store them away from the stove, sink, and any heat-releasing appliances.

In rare cases, medicine improperly stored can actually become toxic. To prevent danger, follow these tips:

- Don't leave the cotton plug in a medication bottle that can draw moisture into the container
- Check the expiration date when taking a drug and throw out/replace any medications that are out of date
- Never use a medication that has changed color, consistency or odor regardless of the expiration date
- Throw away capsules or tablets that stick together, are harder/softer than normal, or cracked/chipped
- Ask your pharmacist about any specific storage instructions

OVER THE COUNTER DRUGS

If you stock the first aid kit with over-the-counter drugs, the following list examines each type of drug you may or may not want to include in your first aid kits.

PAIN RELIEVERS AND FEVER REDUCERS

Pain relievers and fever reducers are the most basic drugs to put in the first aid kit. These drugs provide relief for many minor aches, pains and illnesses. Three kinds of pain relievers may be considered for first aid kits: (1) non-steroidal anti-inflammatory drugs (NSAID), (2) acetaminophen, and (3) topical anesthetic. NSAID's and acetaminophen can also reduce fevers. All three have distinct strengths and weaknesses.

<u>Non-Steroidal Anti-Inflammatory Drugs (NSAIDs)</u>

This class includes ibuprofen, aspirin, and naproxen. All three are available as over-the-counter drugs, can relieve pain and reduce fevers and are also notorious for causing gastric upset in some people.

- *Ibuprofen* is the safest for all ages. It relieves muscle aches and pains and reduces fever.
- *Naproxen* is tough on the stomach, but it is a strong pain reliever lasting up to twelve hours.
- *Aspirin* thins the blood and may cause bleeding problems. Not for use in children - linked to Reye's Syndrome.

<u>Acetaminophen</u>

Acetaminophen reduces pain and fever without reducing inflammation, which means it does not help with swelling or redness caused by injury. Acetaminophen has also been shown to be hard on the liver. An example of acetaminophen is *Tylenol*.

<u>**Topical Anesthetic**</u>

Topical anesthetics like *benzocaine* or *lidocaine* are applied directly to skin surfaces or mucous membranes (inside the mouth) to cause numbing and reduce pain. These drugs do not reduce inflammation or fever and do not last very long. They can easily wash off with water. They are useful for a quick treatment of minor scrapes, toothache and bug bites.

ALLERGIES

Allergies are common and during a disaster, additional allergies can occur due to changes in the environment and traveling to a location with new allergens. Lotions are available to treat itching from plants or other skin irritants.

- *Diphenhydramine* - provides relief from all types of allergic reactions. The biggest side effect is drowsiness and is so common that it is also sold as a sleeping aid. Buying it as an allergy medication is cheaper than a sleep aid so be sure to read the labels. It is also available as a cream and often combined with calamine lotion to treat bug bites, poison oak or poison ivy. It is not for use in children under six years old.

- *Loratadine* - doesn't cause drowsiness and may work better as an allergy medication but is newer to the market and is usually more expensive.

NAUSEA

Antihistamines are used for allergies but are also used as nausea medications - especially for vertigo or motion sickness. There are several over-the-counter nausea medications on the market. Nausea medications often cause drowsiness, blurred vision, dry mouth, and may cause spasms in the neck, jaw or tongue.

- *Cyclizine* - the oldest of the antihistamines approved as nausea medications. It causes drowsiness and is not for use in children under six years old.

- *Dimenhydrinate* - the most common over-the-counter nausea medication but used primarily to combat motion sickness. It causes drowsiness but can be used in children as young as two years old.

- *Meclizine* - a nausea medication has long been used as a prescription for vertigo. It is also useful for non-medical causes of motion sickness. It is not for use in children under twelve years old.

DIARRHEA

It's a good idea to include diarrhea medication in first aid kits. Unfamiliar organisms in food and water will often result in gastric upset. Loperamide is the active ingredient in almost all diarrhea medications on the market. Some examples are Imodium or Pepto-Bismol.

HEARTBURN

Antacids are a good idea for a first aid kit including Rolaids, Tums and Alka Seltzer or a generic over-the-counter medication.

A vigorous five mile walk will do more good for an unhappy but otherwise healthy adult than all the medicine and psychology in the world.

- Paul Dudley White

COMBINATION DRUGS

Almost anytime a drug claims to treat more than one symptom; it usually has more than one active ingredient. Read the labels and look for drugs with only a *single* active ingredient.

- Combination drugs only last as long as the drug that expires first. If two drugs with different shelf life are combined, they'll expire together when the shorter one is past its prime. You don't always want all the affects of a combination drug.

- If you need a drug for fever, and all you have is a drug combining a fever-reducer with an antihistamine, you may end up feeling drowsy. Stocking singles means you can combine them when necessary or take them separately.

- Single drugs are less expensive. Milligram for milligram, combination drugs are usually more expensive. Combination drugs are also less likely to be sold as generics, a proven way to get cheaper medications.

BIRTH CONTROL

Depending on personal beliefs, the subject of birth control must be considered when *preparing in advance* for emergencies – and especially during severe and long-term disasters. As I have travelled around the world, I have witnessed unimaginable poverty of decrepit slums filled with shacks and boxes used for homes and rancid and disease-infested pools of water used for drinking, laundry and personal hygiene. I have watched in horror as mothers stare into the void searching for a means to feed the five starving children by her side. I have witnessed the countless children running in the streets of a village - orphaned because of AIDS and other rampant diseases overtaking the region. The eyes of children appear hopeless – desperate and doomed to a short and unfulfilled life.

Many parents believe that a child is a blessing from God – but a child is also a responsibility for both the mother and father. When considering the role of birth control in emergency planning – survival team members should recognize that a child born in the middle of a serious and long-term disaster will command the right to be sheltered, fed, clothed and cared for by the parents through infancy, childhood and up to adulthood. It is not the responsibility of others to provide emergency rations for you and your children. **Be responsible and accountable for sexual and reproductive decisions and actions.**

> *It's supposed to be a secret, but I'll tell you anyway. We doctors do nothing. We only help and encourage the doctor within.*
>
> - Albert Schweitzer, MD

MEDICAL SUPPLIES

A first aid kit is similar to having health insurance. You pay high insurance premiums over and over again for a possible service in the future. You may never use it – but just in case - you need to have it if there really is an accident, a serious illness or a death. You are then very grateful for continuing to pay those premiums month after month after month. When you are **FINALLY** fortunate enough to be injured, diseased or dying - you are taken to the hospital only to find out that your insurance policy covers **EVERYTHING EXCEPT YOUR SPECIFIC CONDITION**. Figures!!!!! To prepare a top notch first aid kit that provides maximum coverage in the event of a serious injury during a disaster – it is going to cost you a hefty premium. Medical and first aid supplies are expensive – you can pay a hefty premium for a small amount of product.

> **Drug dealers, legal or illegal, do not profit from healthy people. Most physical and mental diseases are consequences of unhealthy lifestyles, poor choices, unhappy relationships and not taking responsibility or accountability for your actions. CLEAN UP YOUR MESS!**

I would strongly recommend you investigate *wholesale* medical supply outlets. Simply go on-line and search for these outlets in your area. Do some comparative shopping and get the best price for the items you purchase at each outlet. In many cases, you can order the items from the on-line catalog and the company will ship the order to your home for a minimal charge. Consider partnering with other survival teams when purchasing first aid supplies from a wholesale dealer. For example, if there are three teams involved – buy one box of triangular bandages (50/box) and then split the contents three ways. This will give all three teams an adequate supply of this type of bandage.

When asked my opinion about first aid kits for the primary residence, place of refuge, work, auto and evacuation pantries, I offer the following advice:

> *"The primary residence should have a larger assortment of first aid items available for the survival team members. Depending on how many members are on the team will determine the amount of first aid supplies to include in the kit. Include __basic__ first aid supplies in your place of refuge, work, auto and evacuation kits."*

Most injuries to the body occur as a result of falling and flying debris such as bricks, rocks, trees, concrete or metal parts during many natural and manmade disasters. Another factor to consider when selecting the type and amount of supplies to include in the first aid kits: (1) where you live (2) profession (3) where you spend most of your time and (4) what type of disaster is likely or possible to happen in your area. For example, if you live in California and work six days a week in downtown Los Angeles on the fifteenth floor of a skyscraper, the probability of being injured by falling debris during an earthquake is a pretty good bet. On the other hand, if you live in Idaho and work seven days a week out in the middle of the country growing and harvesting potatoes – there is a fairly good chance you won't need to worry about getting hit in the head by a falling brick – even during an earthquake.

It is difficult if not impossible to decide exactly **WHAT** items to include in these first aid pantries. Obviously, the injury will determine the appropriate first aid supplies needed for treatment. The problem is whether or not survival team members will even __be__ injured, and if so, WHAT injury and HOW severe will it be? Perhaps a simple bandage will solve the problem – perhaps not. The wound may be so serious that a medical hospital, qualified surgeons, physicians and complex equipment will be mandatory to treat the injury. These medical resources may or may not be available during the disaster. There is no way to tell and your carefully planned first aid kit contains **EVERYTHING EXCEPT WHAT YOU NEED FOR YOUR SPECIFIC INJURY**.

Try to have a variety of different types of bandages, gauze, pads, swabs, wound closures, medications, tools and other items on this list – especially for the primary residence but don't over-indulge in purchasing large quantities of first aid supplies and equipment. When budgeting for the medication and immunization elements – you will be better served by making sure every survival team member has all up-to-date immunizations recommended by the Centers for Disease Control. Consider yourselves warned and prepare yourselves.

Here is a list of emergency medical supplies that could be included in first aid kits for the primary residence, place of refuge, evacuation, auto and work kit:

BANDAGES

- Adhesive tape rolls
- Bandages - elastic
- Bandages – strips (various sizes)
- Bandages – triangular (various sizes)
- Bandages – fingertip (various sizes)
- Bandages – butterfly (various sizes)
- Bandages - knuckle
- Brace - Ankle
- Brace – knee

- Brace – wrist
- Compress (hot and cold)
- Dressings – burn (various sizes)
- Gauze – rolled (various sizes)
- Gauze – squares (various sizes)
- Gauze sponges (various sizes)
- Pads – abdominal (various sizes)
- Pads – eye
- Pads – non-adherent (various sizes)
- Splints (various sizes)
- Wound Closures – butterfly (medium/large)

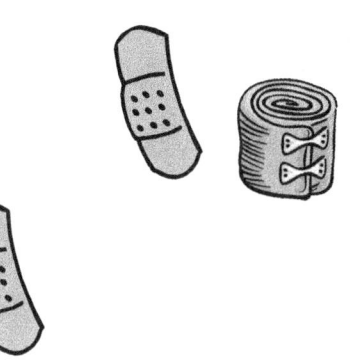

MEDICATIONS AND MISCELLANEOUS

- *Antibiotics*

- *Activated Charcoal* - for poisoning (Kaopectate)

- *Analgesics*
    o Aspirin
    o Acetaminophen (Tylenol)
    o Ibuprofen (Advil or Excedrin)

- *Antacid* (Rolaids, Alka Seltzer, Prilosec, Nexium)

- *Antihistamine* (Benadryl)

- *Antiseptics and Topicals*
    o Calamine Lotion
    o Hydrocortisone Cream
    o Hand Sanitizer (antiseptic)
    o Hydrogen Peroxide
    o Liquid Soap (Dial)
    o Minor Burn Cream
    o Rubbing Alcohol (bottle and wipes)
    o Triple Antibiotic Ointment (Neosporin)
    o Wipes (antiseptic/individually wrapped)

- *Birth Control* (pill or device)
- *Cough Suppressants and Throat Lozenges*
- *Diarrhea* (Imodium or Pepto-Bismol)
- *Eye Drops* and/or *Eyewash Solution*
- *Laxative* (Milk of Magnesia)
- *Toothache Remedies* (Eugenol or Anbesol)

> Prepare <u>in advance</u> FIVE separate first aid kits as follows: (1) primary residence (2) place of refuge (3) evacuation (4) auto and (5) work. The kits prepared for the auto, work, place of refuge and evacuation kits need not be as broad or comprehensive, however, all or some items should be included.

TOOLS AND OTHER ITEMS

Baby Supplies	Heating Pad	Safety Pins
Blanket and Pillow	Hot Water Bottle	Scissors
Cold Pack	Ice Pack	Shampoo – (lice killing)

- Compression Socks/Stockings
- Cotton Balls and Swabs
- CPR Microshield
- Dust Masks
- Epson Salts
- Eye Glass Repair Kit
- Feminine Supplies
- First Aid Manual
- Gloves (latex)
- Heat Pack
- Matches (for sterilization)
- Medicine Dropper/Spoon
- Nail Clippers
- Needles/Thread
- Noxzema
- Paper Cups
- Petroleum Jelly
- Plastic Bags - Small
- Pocket Knife
- Rubber Syringe
- Sunscreen
- Suppositories
- Swabs - alcohol
- Swabs - cotton-tipped
- Swabs - insect bite
- Thermometer
- Tissues
- Tongue Blades
- Tweezers
- Vapor Rub (Vicks)

HERBAL REMEDIES

I believe there is a simple recipe that will cure every type of ailment known to man, but I don't know the recipe. Could it be three cups of dandelion greens and three tablespoons of green moss? Perhaps if I add some bee pollen, I will have the solution. There are many methods that can be utilized to heal our bodies. In addition to medical science, there are aromatherapy treatments, herbal remedies, energy healing, spiritual, emotional, holistic and acupressure healing techniques.

During serious and long-term disasters, it may be necessary to utilize various methods or remedies used for healing purposes. It is wise to prepare *alternatives* that could be used for eliminating or reducing diseases and symptoms. One of these methods is using herbs for treating ailments. Depending on the circumstances, physicians, drugs and standard medical facilities may not be available. As part of *preparing in advance*, consider purchasing an herbal remedies guide at your local bookstore.

> *The famous herbalist Samuel Thompson used mainly two herbs - Cayenne and Lobelia. With those two herbs, it is estimated he helped 3.5 million people recover from their illnesses.*
>
> **- Dick Shulze, N.D. M.H.**

Consider combining forces when buying first aid supplies! Contact other survival teams and share the load. For example, each survival team may only want to purchase ten finger bandages but they come in a box of fifty if purchased at a wholesale medical supply outlet. Split the cost of one box with five other survival teams and divide up the bandages – each team gets ten finger bandages to be stored at the respective five primary residences. The same approach can be taken with prescription and over-the-counter drugs. A good approach for getting supplies you <u>want</u> and <u>need</u> – without spending extra money on getting too much of a good thing! Clever!

Bird Flu – RUN FOR YOUR LIVES!

AHEM . . . AAH-CHOOO!

CHAPTER FIVE

IMMUNIZATION

In the United States, smallpox and polio have been virtually wiped out and cases of measles, mumps, tetanus, whooping cough (pertussis) and other life-threatening illnesses have been reduced by more that 95 percent. Immunization against influenza and pneumonia prevent tens of thousands of deaths annually among elderly persons and those who are chronically ill. As a result, millions of lives have been saved. But don't let the success of vaccines fool you into thinking we no longer need them. Most vaccine-preventable diseases are not gone. In the event of a serious disaster – diseases we think have been eradicated can appear in epidemic proportions.

Depending on the level of the disaster (1-3), there could be a severe breakdown of medical facilities and supplies in this country. There could be increased injuries, contaminated food and water and other factors that can awaken dormant diseases in a matter of days. Remember – the main goal and objective in preparing for an emergency is to safeguard and maintain our HEALTH. NOW is the time to make sure survival team members have all necessary immunizations. KEEP THEM UP TO DATE. BE PREPARED!

Vaccines stimulate our bodies to make antibodies that specifically recognize and target the bacteria and virus against which the vaccines are designed and remove them from the body when we encounter them. Without vaccine protection, we can easily contract and transmit infectious diseases. It may only take one person to start the spread of a disease - a team member, another family member, a neighbor, or a visitor from another country.

Some adults incorrectly assume that vaccines they received as children will protect them for the rest of their lives. Generally this is true, except that:

- Some adults were never vaccinated as children
- Newer vaccines were not available when some adults were children
- Immunity can begin to fade over time
- Higher susceptibility to serious disease caused by common infections (flu, pneumococcus)

The table below lists some diseases that can be contracted by persons who are not vaccinated. During a serious and long-term disaster, these disasters will show up throughout the general population. All survival team members must *plan in advance* to avoid these diseases – get immunized now!

DISEASE	AFFECTS	CAUSE	SPREAD	SYMPTOMS/AFFECTS
Diphtheria	Throat Lungs Heart Nerves	Bacteria	Person to person by breathing, sneezing, coughing and talking	Causes thick covering in back of throat, breathing problems, paralysis, heart failure, nerve damage, death
Hepatitis A	Liver	Hepatitis A Virus (HAV)	Found in the stool of infected persons and easily spread to hands and objects. Contracted through close personal contact and by eating contaminated food or drinking water.	Mild flu-like illness, jaundice, severe stomach pains, diarrhea, liver damage, death

DISEASE	AFFECTS	CAUSE	SPREAD	SYMPTOMS/AFFECTS
Hepatitis B	Liver	Hepatitis B Virus (HBV)	Contact with blood or body fluids of infected person	Loss of appetite, diarrhea, vomiting, jaundice, muscle pain, liver damage, death
Human Papillomavirus	Genitals Throat Cervix	Virus	Sexual contact	Warts in genital area or throat. Attributed to cervical cancer in women
Influenza	Lungs Throat Ears Stomach Bowels	Virus	Person to person by breathing, sneezing, coughing and talking	Fever, sore throat, headache, cough, muscle aches, loss of appetite, tiredness, ear infections, stomach ache, vomiting, diarrhea
Measles	Skin	Virus	Person to person by breathing, sneezing, coughing and talking	Rash, cough, runny nose, eye irritation, fever, ear infection, pneumonia, seizures, brain damage, death
Meningococcal (Meningitis)	Brain Spinal Cord	Bacteria	Person to person by breathing, sneezing, and coughing. Can also be spread through direct contact with infected persons.	Infection brain and spinal cord fluid as well as blood infections, pneumonia
Mumps	Ears Glands Genitals	Virus	Spread through the air by sneezing, coughing or breathing infected droplets. Can also be spread through direct contact with infected droplets or saliva.	Fever, headache, earache, tenderness under the jaw, swollen glands, deafness, meningitis, painful swelling of testicles or ovaries, death
Pertussis (Whooping Cough)	Lungs Brain	Bacteria	Spread through the air by coughing, sneezing and breathing infected droplets.	Coughing spells, vomiting, disturbed sleep, pneumonia, seizures, weight loss, incontinence, rib fractures, brain damage, death
Pneumococcal (Pneumonia)	Lungs	Bacteria	Transmitted directly from person to person through close respiratory droplets contact.	Fever, cough, chest pain, blood-tinged sputum, headache, shortness of breath
Polio	Muscles	Virus	Enters body through the mouth	Paralysis and death
Rubella (German Measles)	Skin	Virus	Person to person by breathing, sneezing, coughing and talking	Rash, fever, arthritis, impaired eyesight
Tetanus (Lockjaw)	Muscles Mouth	Bacteria	Enters the body through cuts, scratches or wounds	Painful tightening of muscles all over the body. Lockjaw – victim can not open mouth or swallow Leads to death in two out of ten cases.

DISEASE	AFFECTS	CAUSE	SPREAD	SYMPTOMS/AFFECTS
Typhoid	Blood Intestines	Bacteria	Bacteria lives only in humans. Disease is spread by eating food or drinking beverages that have been handled by a person who is shedding bacteria or if sewage contaminated with bacteria gets into the water used for drinking or washing food.	Fever, weakness, stomach pains, headache, loss of appetite, rash
Varicella (Chickenpox)	Skin	Virus	Spread from person to person through the air (breathing, coughing, talking, sneezing) or by contact with fluid from chickenpox blisters	Rash, itching, fever, tiredness, skin infection, pneumonia, scars, brain damage, death
Zoster (Shingles)	Skin	Virus	Only someone who has had chickenpox can get shingles. You cannot catch shingles from another person who has shingles.	Skin rash with blisters, fever, headache, chills, upset stomach, blindness, hearing problems, pneumonia, brain inflammation, death

SOURCE: United States Department of Health / Centers for Disease Control

The recommended immunization schedules for adults, young adults and children for 2013 are listed below. **Be sure to check with your physician before getting *any* type of vaccination or immunization**. The cost of immunization varies and in many cases, medical insurance will cover all or part of the cost. In addition to receiving the vaccinations from your physician, most states offer these vaccines through their respective health departments and in many cases, will directly bill your insurance company.

The list of recommended immunizations (2013) for <u>adults</u> is listed below:

VACCINE	DOSES	SCHEDULE	DURATION
Hepatitis A*	2 doses	1 - 2	Life
Hepatitis B*	3 doses	1 - 2 - 6	Life
Human Papillomavirus**	3 doses	1- 2 - 6	Life
Influenza	1 dose	One time	1 year
Measles/Mumps/Rubella	2 doses	1 - 2	Life
Meningococcal (Meningitis)	1 dose	One time	Life
Pneumococcal (Pneumonia)	1 to 2 doses	1 - 2	Life
Polio	1 dose	One time	Life
Tetanus, Diphtheria and Pertussis (Whooping Cough)	1 dose	One time	10 years

VACCINE	DOSES	SCHEDULE	DURATION
Typhoid***	1 dose	One time	5 years
Varicella (Chickenpox)	2 doses	1 - 2	Life
Zoster (Shingles)	1 dose	One time	Life

SOURCE: UNITED STATES DEPARTMENT OF HEALTH - CENTERS FOR DISEASE CONTROL

*	There is a combination vaccine for Hepatitis A and B with three doses required – Month 1 - Month 2 – Month 6.

**	There is a vaccine for males to protect women from contracting cervical cancer (Human Papillomavirus)

***	Although a Typhoid vaccination is not included on the list approved by the ACIP, it is highly recommended you get this immunization.

The recommended immunization schedule for persons aged 7 through 18 years – United States 2013 approved by the Advisory Committee on Immunization Practices, the American Academy of Pediatrics, and the American Academy of Family Physicians is as follows:

VACCINE	7-10 YEARS	11-12 YEARS	13-18 YEARS
Hepatitis A	all children	all children	all children
Hepatitis B	catch-up	catch-up	catch-up
Human Papillomavirus		all children	catch-up
Influenza	all children	all children	all children
Measles/Mumps/Rubella		catch-up	
Meningococcal (Meningitis)	high risk	all children	catch-up
Pneumococcal (Pneumonia)	high risk	high risk	high risk
Polio	catch-up	catch-up	catch-up
Tetanus, Diphtheria and Pertussis (Whooping Cough)		all children	catch-up
Typhoid		catch-up	catch-up
Varicella (Chickenpox)	catch-up	catch-up	catch-up

Range of recommended ages for all children

Range of recommended ages for certain high risk groups

Range of recommended ages for catch-up- immunization

The recommended immunization schedule for persons aged <u>0 through 6 years</u> – United States 2013 approved by the Advisory Committee on Immunization Practices, the American Academy of Pediatrics, and the American Academy of Family Physicians is as follows:

VACCINE	BIRTH	1 Month	2 Months	4 Months	6 Months	12 Months	15 Months	18 Months	19-23 Months	2-3 Years	4-6 Years
Hepatitis A						HEP A (2 doses)				HEP A Series	
Hepatitis B	HEP B	HEP B			HEP B						
Rotavirus			RV	RV	RV						
Influenza					Influenza (Yearly)						
Measles Mumps Rubella						MMR					MMR
Meningococcal (Meningitis)										MCV4	
Pneumococcal (Pneumonia)			PCV	PCV	PCV	PCV					
Polio			IPV	IPV	IPV						IPV
Diphtheria Tetanus Pertussis			DTaP	DTap	DTaP	DTaP					DTaP
Typhoid										ViCPS	ViCPS
Varicella (Chickenpox)						VAR					VAR
Haemophilus Influenza			Hib			Hib					

Range of recommended ages for all children

Range of recommended ages for certain high risk groups

IMMUNIZATION is so important to advanced planning for emergency preparation. Team members should seriously consider getting all pertinent immunizations for their respective age groups. It is easy to assume during a serious disaster, Americans will be immune from diseases currently affecting millions of people around the world. Basically, we have been fortunate in that our society offers vaccines that have either eradicated or reduced many diseases.

However, a serious disaster can quickly compromise sanitation causing rampant diseases that can spread throughout the region. Check with your physician or local health department to obtain important information on recommended immunizations for all team members, and remember - keep them up to date.

CHAPTER SIX

COMMUNICATION

During local, state, and national emergencies, the importance of our country's communication system, including telecommunications, television, radio, cable, newspapers and satellite systems becomes clear. We use our phones to call 9-1-1 or call our family members, neighbors and friends to make sure they are safe. We turn on our televisions and radios or access the Internet to get information updates. Unfortunately, a disaster situation rarely provides prior warning and the affect of the emergency can overwhelm normal information sources in this country and around the world. Although our country has an adequate communication system, unusual conditions can create a strain on communication resources so it is crucial to recognize the part communication will play in the survival of the team. It will be necessary to receive accurate and consistent status on world, national, state and local issues as well as the status of individual team members.

Depending on the communication source, the information could be merely sensationalism, partial truths or outright lies perpetrated by networks to gain higher ratings or by reporters desperate for the first story on the disaster. Another problem is how to "consider the source" of family members, friends, neighbors or other citizens who provide information. For example, during peaceful times, think of individuals you know to be unreliable in providing accurate, realistic or truthful information. It could be they quite simply do not know how to tell the truth or are so out of touch with reality, they don't know the truth. Others may simply exaggerate the real facts in an attempt to appear important or knowledgeable.

Some persons may be able to provide accurate information when calm, but during hectic or stressful times, they become confused, disoriented or bewildered in their facts. We must be able to determine whether any information people provide during an emergency can be trusted, followed or used so we can make critical decisions based on their information.

EMERGENCY PREPARATION PRINCIPLES

In an emergency preparation plan, *communication* needs and concerns should be addressed <u>prior to any emergency</u> to reduce overall problems in communicating with family members and organizations that may be helpful in providing important disaster information and knowledge about the emergency and location of emergency supplies. Depending on the severity of the disaster, communication could easily be disrupted due to household destruction, power outages and fuel shortages.

> *In day-to-day commerce, television is not so much interested in the business of communications as in the business of delivering audiences to advertisers. People are the merchandise, not the shows. The shows are merely the bait.*
>
> **- Les Brown**

There are <u>five</u> principles that can be incorporated into your overall emergency plan to prepare for and in some cases eliminate communication issues that could become prevalent during an emergency situation. For example:

- **<u>During many serious disasters, and if you are one who is located in the area of the disaster, the rest of the world will likely know the details of the disaster before you do – those unfortunate enough to be in the cross-fire generally loose communication sources</u>**.

- Be wary about anyone providing information - take ALL people's information, instructions and advice with "a grain of salt" – use your instincts and common-sense to determine the accuracy or truthfulness of statements.

- Whenever possible, use communication equipment that does **not** require electricity or batteries.

- When creating your communications emergency plan, use preparation methods that include **alternatives** or **layers** of sources and items so that if one fails or is not available or realistic to use, another item or source may be used instead.

- Don't count on the Internet or cell phones for medium to long-term disasters.

NEIGHBORHOOD

It becomes obvious to individuals serious about *preparing in advance* for an emergency that two heads are better than one – thus, the importance of a survival team. As your team becomes more disciplined and prepared for a disaster, the team is able to accomplish much more than a single person. In addition to the survival team, the group can be expanded to include the neighborhood. Any neighborhood that can be cultivated to prepare together for emergencies will be a well-developed and muscular force during a disaster - especially when combining forces to protect persons living in the neighborhood, the homes and emergency supplies. It could likely be the neighborhood force that would do what governmental agencies and private companies would be unable to do.

It is important for all persons living in a neighborhood to become acquainted with their neighbors and to know and understand their basic patterns and habits of movement. Everyone should pay attention to unusual situations or circumstances occurring around the homes. For example, if someone's mail box suddenly becomes piled up, if a moving truck suddenly appears in the driveway of a family who is supposed to be on vacation, if the elderly woman down the street doesn't come out to water her flowers etc.

It is just as important to pay attention and investigate individuals living in your neighborhood who could pose problems during a disaster. For example, while living in California, we resided in a neighborhood where gang members lived. The mother was a single parent and her teenage sons were continually in trouble with the law. The teens had been charged with drug possession, robbery and rape, and in fact, two of the gang members had been imprisoned for auto theft and were out on parole at the time.

It was smart for all neighbors to keep their doors locked at all times. Unfortunately, one evening, we were going to work and forgot to lock the back door. When we arrived home, our house had been robbed. Although we were unable to prove who had robbed our home – the entire neighborhood knew who had done it. The teenagers were later caught robbing another home and were killed in an ensuing gun battle with the police. The important lesson to learn throughout the neighborhood – take the time to pay attention to the good witches and the bad witches in the neighborhood - and keep in touch.

If a solid foundation among neighbors has not been reached *prior* to a disaster, and once the situation becomes unmanageable, it will be difficult to restore any useful communication or cooperation with others. In essence, human nature under pressure is perhaps the biggest ambiguity in a crisis.

A good first step in getting to know your neighbors is to begin a Neighborhood Watch Program. It will give everyone the opportunity to meet all of the neighbors (including the kids). Once a good foundation has been established, an overall emergency plan could be created among neighbors to identify common and general guidelines to follow during a disaster.

When discussing information with neighbors, let caution, common sense and intuition be your guarding light as you interact with your neighbors. Although it is important to communicate basic information, in this current day and age, loose lips can sink ships. Travel these waters very carefully.

FAMILY

The knowledge of knowing where your survival team members are located *before*, *during* and *after* a disaster will become so paramount that it may even impede more important considerations such as shelter, heat, light, water and food.

Our human nature will demand information to guarantee all survival team members and other family members and friends are safe and secure. We will be driven to get this information – sometimes at all cost. If we have the information, it will be easier for us to deal with circumstances of disaster and we would likely be able to focus on the tasks at hand. There are several methods that can be considered to assist in locating and communicating with survival team members, neighbors, friends, relatives and other family members.

W^5 PLAN

Although we cannot possibly know the whereabouts of our family members and other loved ones all the time, we can initiate an effortless plan to at least provide a starting point in locating and hopefully communicating with the team members and other loved ones after a disaster. The W^5 Plan is simple – you provide the following information to another survival team member when leaving the area for <u>at least</u> one day:

- **Where** you will be going
- **When** you will return
- **What** transportation mode you will be using
- **Who** is in your party
- **Why** you are taking the trip

Although this practice may seem to be monotonous and even unnecessary – think about having a serious disaster that wipes out power, roads and communication. The big ticket item on everyone's mind will be: **WHERE IS CRAIG?** This method is especially important for teenagers - in fact, teens should inform adults where they are going any time they leave the house - even if it is for just an hour.

BLOCK CAPTAIN

Every neighborhood should appoint a block captain who agrees to serve as an "overseer" in the event an emergency occurs in the neighborhood. A neighborhood could be considered as a residential block or even an apartment complex. Regardless of how the area is divided, all neighbors, including the block captain should know the area under the "emergency control" of the block captain. This person should hopefully be someone who is home (or close by) during both day and night hours, someone who is responsible and mature enough to carry out the assigned duties and someone who is able to quickly canvas the entire neighborhood area by walking or driving from house to house. In the event of an emergency in the neighborhood, the block captain would be responsible for checking each house to make sure everyone is safe and if necessary, aid those individuals needing assistance.

HOME SIGNAL

During a crisis situation, one of the easiest and most effective methods to alert first responders and neighbors about the status of survival team members is to use a pre-determined signal device in the home. Using a signal as a means to communicate is a common-sense system that can save precious time and resources. For example, every neighborhood could devise a plan where a <u>large</u> (so it can be clearly seen from the street) white "flag" (or large white poster board) is hung from the front window or door of the home with a large black shape signifying a condition inside of the residence.

For example, purchase white poster boards and cut in half. On one side, glue a large black circle that signifies **SAFE** and on the other side, glue a large black rectangle that signifies **HELP**. Make sure the words "**SAFE**" and "**HELP**" are also on the poster board so residents know which shape is correct for the situation. Then, laminate the entire poster board. Pass out a completed poster board flag to each neighbor in the area and explain the procedure to be used in the neighborhood to display the flags. As emergency response personnel, block captains or neighbors scan through the neighborhood, the situation of each home and survival team becomes immediately evident.

- White rectangle with large black circle - team is **SAFE**
- White rectangle with large black rectangle – team needs **HELP**

NO COLORED FLAGS! Some responders or survival team members may be colorblind and will not differentiate between the colors – or their meaning. Using a shape in the flag eliminates this problem.

Whether it is your state, county, city, church, charitable organization or neighborhood who is overseeing the emergency preparation plan in your area, and as part of *planning in advance*, the people in each vicinity should devise a neighborhood signaling system, selected a block captain, make sure each survival team has been trained and has the specific flags or signaling device ready to use during an emergency.

EMERGENCY ALERT SYSTEM

During a serious disaster (and sometimes even during a Level 1 emergency), instructions from various governmental agencies will be provided to citizens through the Emergency Alert System (EAS). Almost all radio and television broadcast stations, including cable companies, are required to carry EAS messages. These stations and especially those with emergency power generators and equipment, provide extensive information about local disaster conditions, warnings, instructions and guidelines on how to locate missing family members. Providing the Emergency Alert System is working and whether power is available at their end and at your end, it is designed so local city or county dispatchers can contact the stations with specific crisis-related information which is then broadcast to the general population in the area, i.e. open and closed transportation routes, location of public shelters, power outages and weather conditions. These broadcasts are where you would receive the most reliable information and instructions. During a disaster, tune to the local television/radio stations for information.

COMMUNITY WARNING SYSTEMS

Depending on the circumstances, there may be other community warning systems available in your area. For example, the use of bullhorns and sirens may be utilized by police or fire departments to notify citizens of impending danger. Another method of communication used by government agencies is door-to-door notification by fire, police, National Guard or trained CERT volunteers. If you are warned by local authorities to take certain actions, you should explicitly and immediately follow their instructions.

UNITED STATES POSTAL SERVICE

Although the United States Postal Service is a government entity, it is one of the few agencies that must be self-sufficient – it is not subsidized by the federal government. However, the United States Postal Service does have one enormous advantage over the other carriers. During a widespread disaster in the country, the federal government would grant the right-of-way to the post office at the expense of all other carriers. The theory is simple. If all other communication systems were down – either for the short-term or long-term, the federal government would use its resources to provide some type of communication system. The United States Postal Service could be instrumental in delivering hard-copy correspondence and packages during a crisis. The old saying "the mail always gets through" may become true during a widespread disaster.

ESTABLISHING A PRIORITY LIST

Take time *before* an emergency to write an <u>emergency priority list</u>, including important items to be hand-carried by you, items to be removed by car or truck if one is available, and things to do if time permits, such as locking doors and windows, turning off utilities, etc.

Place the list in a secure location. Include on your list the following information:

- Important telephone numbers (police, fire, paramedics, and medical centers)
- Telephone numbers of electric, gas/propane, sewer and water companies
- Name and telephone numbers of neighbors
- Name and telephone number of landlord or property manager
- Radio and television broadcast stations to access for emergency broadcast information

OUT OF STATE CONTACT

One of the most important keys to receiving and sending information to family members who may be in different places when a disaster occurs is through an out-of-state contact. This person is a trusted friend or relative designated to handle messages should you not be able to call or locate local family members. While most local private phone lines may be out of order for hours after a disaster, <u>pay phones are usually working much sooner</u>. The out-of-state contact receives and relays messages from family members.

<u>Tips for Communication</u>

- Establish *in advance* who will be your out-of-state contact and make sure everyone knows who it is – including the out-of-state contact!

- Everyone should carry with them a <u>laminated</u> card with the out-of-state contact's name, address, and day and evening phone numbers. Include the following information: (1) emergency meeting place with the address (outside the home); and (2) alternate meeting place and address (outside the neighborhood).

- Let teachers know who the out-of-state contact is for your team. That way, if children are at school and you cannot pick them up, school representatives will know who to contact concerning your children.

- Each family member should know where the public phone booths are located in the area, and carry a phone card or enough change for several phone calls.

> **If possible, try to select an out-of-state contact who is not a first responder in their area and who does not live directly on the San Andreas Fault, next door to a nuclear missile silo or in tornado alley. Although it is difficult to predict the disaster level or the type that causes it, i.e., earthquake, nuclear bomb, tornado or hurricane, attempt to increase your odds of your contact person being ready, willing and able to receive and transmit calls to and from your survival team members.**

HAM RADIO OPERATORS

It will be helpful to find out *in advance* if you have a ham radio operator in your area. They are very helpful and can deliver messages from both private and community sources *before*, *during* and *after* a disaster. If a pay telephone isn't readily available, and your out-of-state contact is several states away, you can communicate via this type of relay system. Your local ham operator can contact another ham operator that will contact another ham operator, and so on, until they find one within your out-of-state contact's area. The ham operator closest to your contact could then hopefully phone the contact and deliver any messages. Consider becoming a ham operator.

FAMILY STATUS REPORT LETTER

A family status report is a valuable and worthwhile consideration for each survival team. The concept is simple – each teenager and/or adult team member carries a one-page status report form that can quickly be filled out and mailed to the out of state contact or other contacts located outside the vicinity of the primary residence.

The information on the form can advise family members or loved ones living in a far away location, i.e., another county or state, about the status of survival team members. The form should be very quick and easy to fill out and yet still provide the recipient with critical information about the status of the survival team members.

Ensure team members have continual and immediate access to a blank copy of the form in the (1) primary residence (2) place of refuge (3) auto (4) work and (5) evacuation kits. If possible, female team members should carry a form in their purse and those individuals who use wallets or briefcases should also consider carrying a blank form.

Place the form in an envelope and address the envelope to your intended recipient(s). Make sure your return address

FAMILY STATUS REPORT FORM
There has been a disaster in our area as follows:

As the designated out of state contact for our survival team, this letter will serve to advise you that our condition is as follows:

WHO	STATUS	INJURIES	LOCATION

ADDITIONAL COMMENTS:

Please advise other survival team members who contact you of the status of other team members as this information becomes known to you and provide additional instructions as necessary.

_____   _____
SIGNATURE   DATE

is included on the envelope. Place a "forever" stamp on the envelope. Try to have a sharpened pencil or pen available as well. After the disaster, fill out the form with pertinent information on survival team members, attempt to find a United States Postal Service **blue mailbox** and drop the letter in the slot. If there is any chance at all for your letter to be delivered – the United States Post Office would be a good bet.

HIDDEN MESSAGE BOX

Another excellent method to communicate with survival team members is to create a hidden message box. The message box will serve as a depository for survival team members to leave and receive messages from one another. There are several "do" and "do not" guidelines when preparing the box, including:

DO -

- Container **MUST BE** water proof, dirt proof, insect proof and rust proof
- Container that is six inches long, six inches wide and six inches deep would be a perfect size
- Container should be made out of heavy duty plastic, galvanized metal or material that keep contents dry

- Container should have air-tight lid but should be easy for team members to open and close – **NO LOCKS**
- Container should contain several small notebooks and at least 5-10 <u>sharpened</u> pencils – **NO PENS**
- Container should be <u>hidden</u> and **BURIED** in the ground somewhere on or near the primary residence
- A heavy duty baggie or trash bag could also be wrapped around it for added protection from the elements
- Located where it will <u>not</u> be disturbed, discovered or moved by anyone

DO NOT -

- Put container in a shed, barn or other structure – these buildings could collapse or be swept away
- Put container near standing water and/or water drainage areas
- Put container <u>directly</u> next to primary residence, power lines, sewer lines, gas lines or propane tanks
- Bury it under a tree –tree could be easily uprooted and the box could be difficult if not impossible to locate
- Bury it so deep in the ground it is hard for team members to reach it

Special attention and thought should be taken in picking the location for the hidden message box. Some recommended locations could be adjacent to a fence, across the street in a field, next to a large boulder or rock, or even out in the middle of the backyard lawn. Whatever location is selected, it must be in a location that is easy to remember and easy to access.

In general, the location of this message box should be known only to **SURVIVAL TEAM MEMBERS**. Bringing outsiders into the secret, regardless of good intentions, tends to confuse and complicate the flow of communication. Also, only share the secret with team members who are mature enough to maintain the secret of the location, understand its significance and purpose and be able to utilize the box if needed during and after a disaster. If a disaster occurs and some of the survival team members at the primary residence are forced to flee to an alternate site or refuge, any remaining survival team members who later arrive at the primary residence can check the message box for any messages.

Likewise, any member can check and/or leave messages so other team members will be informed of their status, location and other important information. All team members using the box should be instructed and trained to tightly close and rebury the box to avoid contamination after accessing the message box and either receiving or leaving messages. Team members should be watchful when accessing the box to make certain outsiders are not observing their action.

COMMUNICATION EQUIPMENT

Many types of communication equipment require a power source. During any level of disaster, it is likely power will be out. For obvious reasons, when planning for communication devices and equipment, attempt to purchase solar powered, rechargeable battery-operated (including solar powered battery charger) or alternative power forms that are <u>not</u> subject to an electrical power grid. Again, always remember to plan for *alternatives* or *layers*.

<u>AM/FM Radio</u>

As part of emergency planning for communications, every survival team <u>MUST</u> have a basic AM/FM radio that does not require conventional electricity. One choice is a battery-operated radio, but <u>another excellent alternative is a solar-powered radio or hand crank to generate power</u>. These radios are good because you will always have power. Make sure when selecting the radio, it is powerful enough to pick up weak signals – especially in a remote area. As part of *planning in advance*, <u>make sure your radio works for your location</u>. Remember that AM broadcasts will override FM broadcasts for disaster news and many can be picked up from a very long distance.

If a widespread emergency occurs, civil defense-affiliated stations are generally set up to broadcast survival information on the <u>AM</u> broadcast band. These radios should be specified for *emergency use only* and off-limits for all other use. <u>I cannot emphasize enough the importance of making sure you have several *alternatives* or *layers*</u>

of radios available for emergency situations. These radios would very likely be your **ONLY MEANS** of receiving emergency news and other important information concerning the outside world.

Don't forget to provide radios for the place of refuge, evacuation, auto, and work kits.

When purchasing emergency radios, consider these guidelines:

- Purchase brand-name and reliable radios
- Purchase smaller radios instead of large radios with lots of bells and whistles
- Purchase several types of radios including AC/DC, battery, solar power, hand crank or shaking models
- Use these radios for emergency situations ONLY – not for recreational listening
- During an emergency, limit the use of the radio(s) for disaster information only
- Keep plenty of FRESH batteries stored for use with emergency battery-operated radios
- Check batteries and/or replace on a regular schedule, i.e., every six months
- Purchase a solar-powered battery charger and rechargeable batteries for solar powered radios

Phones

A cell phone has become a common communication device throughout the world. In fact, as a society, we have become so dependent on them, it is practically impossible to conduct business or manage our personal affairs without having one close by throughout the day and night. The cell towers that operate our cell phones rely on regular AC power for operation. During times of serious disasters, the towers and/or backup power systems could be damaged or destroyed. The cell phone itself involves complexities with moving parts. The batteries are short-lived and sensitive to fluctuations in temperature and geographic location.

The land line phones also create a problem during a disaster. Depending on the level of the disaster (1-3) and the circumstances surrounding the crisis, telephone poles and wires go down, switch stations can be destroyed, transmitting and receiving cells can be damaged – and in an instant – landline telephone communication can be shut off. Remember that when the power is out, a cordless land line phone will not operate, but a corded phone could still work (depending on the circumstances) without power to support it. **Only an ill-advised person would rely on any phone to support communication during any level of disaster**.

Internet

There is no doubt the Internet can be considered as one of the most important technological advancements in the last one hundred years. It has literally changed the way we do business and conduct our personal lives. The Internet has afforded us the privilege of accessing information from around the world in a matter of minutes. We can access news, weather, sports, entertainment and general academia. We can deliver an email within seconds by the power of an email system.

Alas! The Internet is an incredible communication tool – as long as the power is working and that, my friends, is the bitter pill. The Internet relies on the electrical grid – either directly or indirectly to operate the system. The battery that operates your computer would at some time have to be recharged – using electrical power. The Internet parallels the cell phone dilemma in that towers, cables and lines supporting Internet relies on regular AC power for operation, and just like a cell phone, these towers and lines could easily be damaged or destroyed. Even Internet powered by satellite can be affected by weather conditions or other logistical complications. Again, do **NOT** count on the Internet for communication – even during a Level One disaster. If you rely on the Internet for important products or services – have other alternatives available in the event the Internet is not working. If you can get "on-line" – great! Just don't consider the Internet as a reliable source of communication during a crisis.

CB Radio

There are over fifty-five million CB users throughout the United States. A CB radio is considered to be one of the most accessible modes of communication for the general public. The range for a CB radio is generally about ten to twenty-five miles, depending on the geography in the area. One of the problems with a CB radio is during an emergency; interference from other users can be common since users share only a few channels. And again, another pesky setback is their reliance on a direct or indirect electrical power source. One of the good points about a CB radio is that they are useful as a neighborhood communication system or in the car when on the road to get real-time information from other drivers about roads and highways or other hazards. On a CB radio, Channel 9 is the official nationwide channel for emergency use and traveler's information. The Radio Emergency Associated Communications Team (REACT) is a volunteer group who monitors Channel 9 continuously all across the country.

Walkie Talkie

A walkie talkie – or two-way radio – is a good communication device when communicating with a minimum amount of interference and the person is only a short distance away. A walkie talkie comes in a wide variety of styles, channels, power outputs and prices. The uses are varied, for example, they can be used on road trips between multiple vehicles to keep in contact with the other car or on camping trips when two hikers want to keep in contact with one another. A walkie talkie could prove invaluable during an emergency situation if two members of a survival team need to communicate and both were in a close proximity to one another. Again, one of the major setbacks with a walkie talkie is their reliance on a direct or indirect electrical power source.

Shortwave (Ham) Radio

A shortwave radio system allows you to be in touch with the unfiltered world of international radio whether you live in a small town or large city. Depending on the equipment, a shortwave radio system can also be used for two-way communications instead of just listening to conversations. Users of shortwave radios are also called "ham operators". During any emergency situation, the ham operators are vital to receiving and dispersing valuable information to citizens. Basically, the ham radio system has towers or receivers located at high points around the world. If a ham radio operator from Los Angeles, California wishes to communicate with someone in Sydney, Australia, his signal and conversation "bounces" from one receiver to another until it finally reaches its destination.

Ham operators use many frequency bands across the radio spectrum - these frequencies are allocated by the FCC for amateur use. Non-hams can "**listen in**" via their own receivers or radio scanners. Hams operate from just above the AM broadcast band to the microwave region in the gigahertz range. Many ham bands are found in the frequency range above the AM radio band (1.6 MHz) to just above the citizens band (27 MHz). During daytime hours, 15 to 27 MHz is a good band for long-distance communications. At night, the band from 1.6 to 15 MHz is good for long-distance communications. These bands are often referred to historically as **short-wave** bands (as in "short-wave radio").

You need an easy-to-learn license to transmit on an amateur radio frequency. License tests cover electronics theory and amateur radio rules and regulations. Study guides are readily available on the Internet or in book stores. There is no age restriction. Each country has its own licensing arrangements. Many countries share many of the same frequency bands with hams in the United States. Each license class allows operation in certain bands using certain modes. The higher the class of license, the more allowable frequency bands are available for use. A typical ham radio is a transmitter and a receiver, usually purchased as one unit, called a transceiver and an antenna. The cost of a ham radio system can be fairly inexpensive ($200) or can cost thousands of dollars.

Scanners

A scanner allows you to receive broadcasted information from police, sheriff, ambulance, fire, Border Patrol agents, United States Customs, the Federal Emergency Management Administration (FEMA), the National Oceanic and Atmospheric Administration (NOAA) and ham radio operators. During an emergency, and depending on the severity of the crisis, these governmental agencies will generally have important information on the disaster and would broadcast much of this information on scanners. At the very least, a listener would be able to learn the knowledge base of local agencies, their plan of action and more importantly, the priorities established by each agency. There are regulations governing the use of scanners which mostly revolve around using the intercepted communications for personal gain or discussing it with others. A good recommendation is a VHF police, marine, aircraft, and weather band scanner. Attempt to purchase a more recent model that can demodulate trunked traffic and if you have the budget, purchase a digital model.

Paper and Pencils

It is hard to believe that although our world has a buffet of technical gadgets to communicate effectively around the world – we must have the grace to blush in recognizing that all of these electronic gadgets and complicated equipment must be fed using electrical power. Once again, we as a society will be humbled into accepting an age-old method of communication – a simple piece of paper and a pencil. Although pens are fine - remember they can run out of ink AND the ink can become frozen (when cold) or old. Pencils, on the other hand, seem to write just fine - providing they are sharpened. As an integral part of emergency preparation kits, have an abundant supply of paper, pens and pencils. These items should be included in emergency pantries including: (1) primary residence, (2) place of refuge, (3) auto and (4) evacuation kit. It is assumed that these office supplies would already be available at your worksite.

Typewriter

It is very difficult to find a manual typewriter in any office supply outlet but they can be found on-line and can be purchased using a ribbon or a ball for about $120.00. Ribbons cost about $10.00 each. This typewriter will serve as a means to communicate using a simple piece of paper during a serious disaster, when electric typewriters, word processors and computers will be standing silently by watching the real typing master at work!

Bull Horn

Somewhat of a crazy idea – I'll admit – but the individual holding a bull horn can be heard over the crowd and throughout the neighborhood! Survival team members who are assigned to serve as team leaders or block captains during a disaster in the neighborhood, at the church or in the community should consider the purchase of a bull horn. Someone speaking with a bull horn is much more likely to be heard, recognized and accepted than someone screaming and shouting in the wind.

Whistle

All survival team members should have a good whistle in their evacuation pack. This whistle could serve as a means of communication in the event some member becomes lost or disoriented during the chaos that may be prevalent during the evacuation. As part of *planning in advance*, teams could devise various "codes" that could be used to identify specific issues, i.e. one whistle means safe, two whistles mean hurt and needs assistance, etc.

ITEMS TO CONSIDER FOR THE COMMUNICATIONS ELEMENT

AM/FM RADIO (hand crank or battery)   **PAPER, PENCILS AND PENS**
Bullhorn   **PENCIL SHARPENER**
CB Radio   Scanner
HAM Radio   Typewriter (manual) and ribbons
Hidden Message Box   Walkie Talkie
                                            WHISTLE

CHAPTER SEVEN

DOCUMENTATION

All members of the survival team have important documentation that must be preserved during an emergency. These documents include legal, financial, religious, medical and insurance documents. Unfortunately, most of us have these important documents stored in various locations throughout the house. It is vital to *prepare in advance* to manage important documents during an emergency situation, whether the survival team remains at the primary residence or is forced to evacuate the primary residence and transport to an alternate location or place of refuge. During an emergency is **NOT** the time to be gathering up all of this critical documentation.

As the severity and duration of a crisis is increased, the possible loss and destruction to documentation increases as well. For example, during a fire at the primary residence, documents could easily be burned and destroyed. If the survival team is forced to locate to a public shelter, these documents could be stolen or destroyed by others in the building. It is important to recognize that during **LEVEL ONE** and **LEVEL TWO** disasters, most documents are significant to guarantee your rights, prove ownership or to file insurance claims for losses caused by the disaster. However, at the end (one year) of a cataclysmic or catastrophic **LEVEL THREE** disaster, the importance of documentation would diminish due to lack of enforcement, validity, legitimacy, legality and authority the documents would contain at the time.

EMERGENCY PREPARATION PRINCIPLES

There are <u>eight</u> guidelines that can be incorporated into an overall emergency plan to prepare for and in some cases eliminate documentation issues that would become prevalent during an emergency situation:

- Purchase a good safe that is fire and water resistant - place important documentation in the safe.

- Make and continually update an inventory of all possessions including jewelry, guns and clothing.

- Consider storing documents that cannot be replaced in a location away from the primary residence such as a safe deposit box at a nearby bank.

- Consider personal property insurance.

- Update scrapbook and photo albums. Consider leaving sentimental photos and negatives or duplicate photos in storage or with a relative. Put photos on CDs!

- Make duplicates of all documentation including personal address lists.

- Consolidate all documentation into one location, including personal records, financial documents, school records, etc.

- Plan for pets. Keep pets' records updated and with you during an evacuation that includes you and your pets.

There are several methods that can be utilized to safeguard important documents and paperwork during an emergency. By *planning in advance*, the survival team members would have a good prospect for maintaining and accessing important documentation during a crisis situation.

1. Gather all important documents and make *three* GOOD copies of each. If necessary, have each document notarized. Place all <u>original</u> documentation in a safe deposit box at a bank near the primary residence.

   Distribute the three copies as follows:

   o If your alternate place of refuge is a long distance away from the primary residence, put a copy of all documentation in a safe deposit box at a bank near the alternate site.

   o Maintain a copy of the complete set of documentation at the primary residence in a fire-proof, water-proof, and dinosaur-proof container or safe – with a combination lock.

   o Mail a copy (using certified mail) of the complete set of documentation in a clearly marked and sealed envelope to a trusted friend or relative who lives outside the area of your primary residence (perhaps the out-of-state contact) – preferably in another state across the country.

2. Make a list on <u>one</u> sheet of paper of all policy numbers, contract numbers, account numbers and identification numbers on all the documents. Include names, addresses and phones numbers of the institutions where the accounts are located. Make two copies of the list. Mail one copy to a friend or relative who lives outside the area of your primary residence (out-of-state contact) – preferably in another state across the country. Laminate the second copy and tape it to the *inside* of your evacuation kit.

3. Make a list on <u>one</u> sheet of paper of all policy numbers, contract numbers, account numbers and identification numbers on all the documents. Include names, addresses and phones numbers of the institutions where the accounts are located. On this list however, write all numbers <u>backwards</u>; in other words, if the correct policy number is 12345, write it down as 54321. Make three copies of the list. Laminate the lists and place one under the driver's seat of the car(s), tape one list on the bottom of a drawer in your desk at work and put another one in your wallet or purse. If using the car for evacuation or if you are stuck at work or are stranded at the store during an emergency, you would have the list. If the car, wallet or purse is stolen at any time, or if a co-worker finds the list in your desk - no problem – the numbers would not be valid – only you will know how to decipher the accounts.

4. Assemble <u>copies</u> of all documentation into one heavy-duty and waterproof container (locking file box with handle). Consider this container as an additional evacuation unit that must be transported with the rest of your evacuation supplies. If the place of refuge is a public shelter, survival team members must be vigilant to guard the safety and security of its contents.

5. Scan copies of all important documentation. Make sure that each page of the documents and photographs can easily be viewed and read. Copy the scanned documents and photographs onto four CD's. Store the first one in the safe deposit box at your local bank, the second one at the safe deposit box at a bank near the alternate site, the third one with a trusted friend or relative who lives outside the area of your primary residence (out-of-state contact) – preferably in another state across the country, and the fourth one in your evacuation kit.

6. After scanning all the documents and photographs, email them to your private email address. Create a folder called "**EMERGENCY DOCS**" and move them to this location. Make sure they will not be automatically deleted – as some email systems are programmed to do after a specific length of time. Now – leave them alone. Depending on the crisis, it may be possible to access a computer, printer and the Internet near your location of refuge. You can simply bring up your email, access the folder and print out the files containing your important documentation.

NOTE: When emailing documentation to your private email address, attach the documents assigned to the same category in one email, i.e., send all medical documents under one email. Depending on your Internet provider, you may be limited on the amount of data that can be transmitted.

When all emails arrive at your private account, set up sub-folders for each category under the **EMERGENCY DOCS** folder.

For example:

EMERGENCY DOCS (Main Folder)

Legal
Financial
Records
Will
Bank Deposits
Insurance
Religious
Medical
Utilities
Miscellaneous

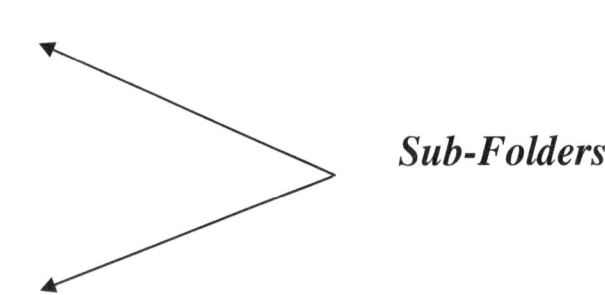

Sub-Folders

WHAT TO CONSIDER FOR THE DOCUMENTATION ELEMENT

Legal	Monthly Expenses
- *Marriage Certificate* - *Vehicle Plate Number* - *Birth Certificate* - *House Title / Deeds* - *Divorce Papers* - *Lease* - *Naturalization Papers* - *Mortgages* - *Vehicle Title* - *Drivers License* - *Car Registration* - *Social Security Card* - *Vehicle ID Number* - *Passport*	- *Budget* - *Bills* - *Outstanding Debts*
Will	**Bank/Credit Union Deposits**
- *Will* - *Living Will* - *Power of Attorney* - *Guardianship*	- *Safe Deposit Box Information* - *Checking – bank, phone, account number* - *Savings – bank, phone, account number* - *IRA – bank, phone number, account number* - *CD - bank, phone number, account number*
Financial	**Utilities**
- *Income for both spouses* - *Assets/ Debts* - *Stocks and Bonds* - *Income Tax Returns* - *Property Tax Statements*	- *Electric - name, phone, account number* - *Water - name, phone, account number* - *Gas - name, phone, account number* - *Propane – name, phone, account number* - *Sewer - name, phone, account number* - *Phone – name, phone, account number*

Insurance - *Life – agent, phone and policy number* - *Auto – agent, phone and policy number* - *Other – agent, phone and policy number* - *Home – agent, phone and policy number* - *Medical – agent, phone and policy number*	**Religious** - *Religious Books and Scriptures* - *Patriarchal Blessing* - *Genealogy Records* - *Membership Identification Number* - *Temple Recommend*
Medical - *Past Histories – diseases, surgeries, dates* - *Current Histories – current treatments, etc.* - *Medication – dosage, schedule, reason* - *Immunizations – type, date, purpose* - *Hospital – name, address, phone* - *Physician – name, address, phone, specialty* - *Dentist – name, address, phone, specialty* - *Other - name, address, phone, specialty*	**Important Miscellaneous** - *Recent photos* - *Fingerprints of children* - *Local Phone Book (if applicable)* - *Neighbors/Friends/Relatives* - *Police – address and phone number* - *Fire – address and phone number* - *Personal property – description, value, photo*
Records - *Employment – name, address, phone number* - *Military – dates, title, military number* - *School – name, address, phone, student*	**ALWAYS STORE ORIGINAL DOCUMENTS IN A FIREPROOF LOCATION, I.E., SAFE, SAFE DEPOSIT BOX, ETC. DOCUMENTATION TO BE PLACED IN YOUR EMERGENCY PANTRIES AND KITS SHOULD BE COPIES ONLY. CONSIDER ANY AND ALL SECURITY ISSUES BEFORE PLACING DOCUMENTS IN YOUR PANTRIES AND KITS.**

CHAPTER EIGHT

RECREATION

There will be many projects and tasks to do during an emergency situation. If one is fortunate enough to have advanced warning about the upcoming disaster, a multitude of tasks will be prioritized and accomplished in order to avoid bodily injury and destruction of property. Likewise, during the actual chaos, everyone will be preoccupied with staying alive and after the disaster is over, the population will stick their head out from under the rock where they were hiding, step out into the open, review the situation and begin the undertaking of making a recovery.

> *If bread is the first necessity of life, recreation is a close second.*
>
> -   **Edward Bellamy**

There has been increased recognition among aid agencies, donors and governments that supporting recreational activities closely following a disaster provides a means to enhance a calm, serene and peaceful environment during the down time of a crisis and can guarantee a sense of stability or reassurance to team members – and especially children. The actual location and strength of the disaster will more than likely determine the amount of time and effort needed by each individual to return to normal conditions, but there will be times when the human body will need to rest from the work. Not only will the physical body need to relax, but the mental and psychological spirit will need to recuperate as well. Is recreation absolutely essential to survival? No. You won't hear anyone screaming "The tornado is coming! Quick! Grab the ping-pong paddles!" Recreation is not life-saving in an emergency, but it is very important.

It is during these times that a form of recreation will be welcome to relieve the team members from the affects of the disaster. Actually, even during short periods of time when an emergency situation could take out the power supply, recreation materials would prove to be a welcome diversion from the inconvenience, fear and nuisance that a lack of electrical power can create in a household. It is important, as part of *planning in advance*, to have adequate recreational items available for all team members.

As part of the overall recreation pantry, and depending on the level of the disaster, we must also assume that all or part of our everyday recreational items could be damaged or destroyed or temporarily "out of service". For example, in the event the electricity is out, most electronic or electrical toys, games, videos, television, radio and computers in the home would be useless and within a short period of time, the battery-powered items would also run down. All entertainment facilities throughout the region would be out of service including movie theatres, bowling alleys, gaming arenas and amusement parks.

A large majority of citizens in the United States have become obsessed and dependent on having others entertain us. For example, in the past when electricity goes out in my neighborhood, I have actually become despondent and agitated because I was unable to watch television or put on a movie to watch while I waited for the power to return to the house. Over the years, as I have recognized my dependency on being entertained by others, I have attempted to return to my childhood habits of being able to "play by myself". As children in the neighborhood, we spent many hours creating our own fun and entertaining ourselves throughout the day. We would invent games to play including favorites like Hide-and-Seek, Tag, Red Rover and Kick-the-Can.

My mother would give me a large quilt or blanket and I would drape it over a card table and spend the day in my makeshift tent. My best friend and I would spend hours playing on a Tarzan rope we made out of twine and tied in a large tree over a canal. We would play in the family barn and pretend it was our castle. Her mother had a large assortment of old skirts and blouses up in the attic and we would spend entire days dressing up in these old clothes. Frankly, I can never remember a better or more entertaining time in my life – and I firmly believe it had nothing to do with being a child but everything to do with getting down to a basic and simple lifestyle.

EMERGENCY PREPARATION PRINCIPLES

As we prepare for future disasters, it will be necessary to return to a basic and simple lifestyle when preparing for the **RECREATION** Element. There are several basic principles that would apply when gathering recreational items:

- Items should not require any electricity or batteries to operate
- Items should be geared toward the recreational preferences of team members, i.e. everyone loves to read
- Items should be geared toward the ages of team members
- Items should be non-breakable, compact and easy to store
- Items should provide a balance between cooperative group games, traditional sports and individual play
- Items may be stored for <u>future</u> use in the event of an emergency and not for everyday use
- Some type of recreational item(s) should be included in all emergency pantries
- Include recreational items that already exist in the home as part of the plan

FUN BOXES

The first item of business will be the "Fun Box" that stores the recreational items. The number and size of these fun boxes will depend on the number of team members, the age of members, the significance that recreation plays in their everyday lives, money, and the opinions of how recreation would support an emergency situation.

It is important to include a <u>variety</u> of items that can be utilized for recreation. For example, after a hard day of cleaning up debris, repairing broken lines and finding food and water, the team may find that some quiet and calm relaxation may be more suitable than an aggressive sporting event. Sitting down and reading a good book or working on a puzzle may be more preferable than playing a game of soccer with other team members. On the other hand, there will be times during the aftermath of the disaster when a neighborhood baseball game would be able to bring all teams together with a supportive and cooperative spirit that comes only from team sports.

Here are some items that could be easily incorporated into recreational pantries including the following:

- **Games (board, arcade, lawn, yard, sport)**
- **Cards**
- **Toys**
- **Puzzles**
- **Books**
- **Writing Materials**
- **Sewing**
- **Musical Instruments**
- **Crafts**

> *Games lubricate the body and the mind.*
>
> - **Benjamin Franklin**

GAMES

There are five major types of games that could be included in the recreation pantry as follows:

<u>**Board**</u> – board games are commercially sold at large department or toy stores although individuals can make board games that serve the same purpose. There are board games designed for all age groups and depending on the age of team members, a variety of board games could be gathered that can be enjoyed by everyone. Many families already have a selection of board games in their home - great! These board games should definitely be included in the overall recreation pantry - but perhaps the addition of one or two new board games may be a good idea to provide a fresh appeal to family fun during trying times.

There are several suggestions that may appeal to survival team members:

CHILDREN

* **Ants in the Pants**
* **Battleship**
* **Candy Land**
* **Chutes and Ladders**
* **Connect Four**
* **Cootie**
* **Don't Break the Ice**
* **Don't Spill the Beans**
* **Hi Ho! Cherry O**
* **Hungry Hippos**
* **Memory**
* **Mousetrap**

ADULTS

* **Backgammon**
* **Checkers**
* **Chess**
* **Clue**
* **Cribbage**
* **Life**
* **Monopoly**
* **Risk**
* **Scrabble**
* **Trivial Pursuit**
* **Yahtzee**
* **Sorry**

Lawn and Yard – lawn and yard games are played outdoors by one or more persons and confined to a lawn or yard area. These games have equipment that is used as part of the game. A selection of lawn games could be included such as:

* **Badminton**
* **Bean Bag Toss**
* **Bocce**
* **Croquet**
* **Frisbee**
* **Lawn Golf**

* **Horseshoes**
* **Ladder Ball**
* **Lawn Darts**
* **Ring Toss**
* **Washers**

There are other lawn and yard games that do not require equipment to play. These are the classic yard games including Kick-the-Can, Red Rover, Tag, Hide-and-Seek and sack races.

Sports – sporting games are generally played outdoors by a group of persons with a larger area used as the playing field. These games have equipment used as part of the game.

* **Baseball**
* **Basketball**
* **Football**

* **Golf**
* **Soccer**

* **Tennis**
* **Volleyball**

Arcade – arcade games are found in entertainment centers or billiard parlors where a player attempts to score points by manipulating one or more balls on a playfield. Although many arcade games are now electronic devices and require some sort of power device to operate, there are still manual arcade games. For example, in some stores, you can find small pinball machines that can be played on a lap or on a table. Additional arcade-type games include **table tennis**, **pool** and **foosball**.

There are other games that could also be included in the recreational pantry such as:

* **Bingo**
* **Darts**
* **Dominos**

* **Hangman**
* **Hop Scotch**
* **Jacks**

* **Jump Rope**
* **Marbles**
* **Pick Up Sticks**

* **Pin the Tail on the Donkey**
* **Twister**

There are countless board, lawn, yard and sports games available on the market. Again – the important thing to remember is having a good supply of games and equipment for all team members and all age groups to enjoy during disaster situations.

CARDS

A good supply of card games is an excellent choice for team members to enjoy during troubling times. There are card games more suitable for adults, others for children, and still others for the entire family. A deck of cards is inexpensive, takes up very little room, and in some cases, one deck of cards can support several different games.

- **Blackjack**
- **Bridge**
- **Crazy Eights**
- **Cribbage**
- **Go Fish**
- **Gin**
- **Hearts**
- **Old Maid**
- **Pinochle**
- **Poker**
- **Uno**

TOYS

A selection of toys for children would already be in place at the home, and hopefully, all or many of these toys would survive a disaster situation. However, many of these toys may require electricity or batteries to operate and may not work. There are some classic toys, however, that could be considered for the recreational pantry requiring no electricity or batteries. They take up little space, are fairly inexpensive and fun to play for children of all ages.

- **Action Figures**
- **Balls**
- **Blocks**
- **Dolls**
- **Hand Puppets**
- **Kites**
- **Lego's**
- **Lincoln Logs**
- **Mr. Potato Head**
- **Paints and Brushes**
- **Paper Dolls**
- **Play Dough**
- **Pop Beads**
- **Sand Pails**
- **Slinky**
- **Silly Putty**
- **Stickers**
- **Tinker Toys**
- **Tops**
- **Yo Yo**

Additional items to consider in the recreational kit focuses on education including *slates*, *pencils*, *erasers*, *rulers*, *drawing tablets*, *books*, *whiteboards*, *blackboards*, *scissors*, *glue*, *colored paper*, *flashcards* and *scotch tape*. These educational items can be used to continue educational development even during emergency situations.

PUZZLES

A good selection of puzzles is an important item for recreation during hard times. These puzzles could include jigsaw puzzles for children and adults as well as logic and intellectual puzzles, brainteasers and crossword puzzles.

BOOKS

Books would become one of the most important items in the recreation pantry. If space allows, a large selection of books should be available for all team members to read including books for children, young adults and adults. Depending on the interests and preferences of team members, the emergency library could include a combination of fiction and non-fiction, biographies and reference materials. Although eBooks are certainly popular, remember that during some short-term emergencies and most long-term disasters, a power source would be required to continue eBook usage. Unless that power source is reliable and continuous - eBooks would not be available on the electronic devices needed to support them. For emergency preparation - I would suggest only hard or soft copy printed books.

During disaster times, a selection of religious books could also be very comforting to the group and could include works that provide hope, guidance, encouragement and support to team members.

When I was preparing my emergency book library, I decided to access the Internet and compile a list of books considered to be classics by various establishments and organizations around the world. I have always enjoyed reading the classics, i.e., *Great Expectations*, *Pride and Prejudice*, *The Fountainhead*, *Wuthering Heights*, *Of Mice and Men*, etc.

As I reviewed these Internet lists and prepared my own list, I discovered much to my chagrin, there were many classics I had not yet read during my lifetime. In many cases, the same book would appear on many of the lists – and depending on my own preferences, I would add or eliminate the book from my own list. In addition to reading a good mystery or the latest top seller, I also enjoy specific authors such as Dan Brown who wrote the *Di Vinci Code*, Michael Crichton who wrote *Jurassic Park* and Colleen McCullough who wrote *The Thorn Birds*. I made sure these books were also on my list.

Once I had compiled my list of books I wanted to include in my emergency preparation library, I began the search to gather them. I established several guidelines used in the purchase of these books including:

- *I would only purchase used printed books*
- *I would attempt to purchase only paperback books*
- *I would not read them until the time of a disaster situation*

I wanted to find the best buy on each book. In the beginning, my search obviously included the Internet. There are many sites on-line that offered new and used books at reasonable prices but there were expensive shipping and handling charges.

I continued my search at charitable outlets, second-hand book stores, book stores selling both new and used books and garage sales, and was surprised to discover that many of those same books I found on the Internet for $4.00 were only $1.00 or $2.00 at these other locations. I was also able to find other good books that were not on my list for only twenty-five or fifty cents. I also had the advantage of being able to examine each book prior to purchase to guarantee I was satisfied with the condition. Over the course of two years, I was able to find and purchase a majority of the books on my list.

As I purchased these books, I would place them in a large plastic container. I personally made the decision <u>not</u> to read *most* of the books now but to wait until there is a power outage or even a more serious emergency situation. In this way, I would have new materials to occupy my time and help alleviate the boredom that comes with not having the "power" to watch television! Of course, there were some books that I couldn't wait to read and will read again in the future with the same amount of enthusiasm.

For adults and young adults, a collection of *magazines* and *comic books* could also be included in the pantry. For teams that include small children, there should be an ample selection of *activity books*, *coloring books* and *crayons*, *song books* and other items that can entertain children during these times.

Reference Books

There is another type of book that *must* definitely be included in the emergency pantries of all teams – I am talking about *printed copy* <u>reference books</u>. These books include reference materials on <u>specific</u> emergency-related topics. Although the purchase of these books does not necessarily merit the need to buy new books, these reference materials should be in good condition and command an accessible location in the primary residence (including the shelter-in-place).

These books should be read and studied *prior* to an emergency, should be located in an area that has a high possibility of surviving a disaster and should be easily accessible to all adult team members. You will have plenty to do *before*, *during* and *after* an emergency without having to read and understand comprehensive reference books that can and will aid in your survival.

Many of these books and pamphlets can be obtained on-line or at book stores offering both new and used books. A valuable resource of information is through federal, state and local agencies including the Federal Emergency Management Administration (FEMA), the Armed Forces, and the extension service at most universities.

The type of reference books and materials to be included on the library shelf in the primary residence include the following:

- **Cookbooks** – these books should include simple and realistic recipes using dutch oven cooking, campfire cooking, wood stove cooking, barbeque cooking, solar oven cooking, canning and freezing, etc.

- **Medical** – these books should include comprehensive first aid methods and techniques, alternative healing, medicines and methods including plants, herbs, vitamins, minerals, salts etc.

- **Gardening** – these books should include comprehensive information on growing and harvesting a vegetable garden, sprouting, and growing fruit trees, berries and grapes. Make sure you have materials that provide information on insect pests, ground preparation and tools.

- **Survival** – these books could include information on survival in <u>specific</u> disaster scenarios including nuclear war, earthquake, biological and chemical warfare and weather related disasters (drought, cold, wind, fire and rain). There are also "how to" books and pamphlets available on how to build a root cellar, how to drain water pipes, etc. It is also important to have books on wilderness survival teaching the types of wild plants that are edible, non-edible and/or can be used for medicinal purposes, the locations and types of shelters that can be built in the wild as well as general rules and guidelines that must be followed for survival in a wilderness environment.

- **Operation** – these <u>manuals</u> should provide detailed and technical information on how to operate, maintain and repair various equipment, tools and machinery in your possession.

- **Maps** – a combination of local and regional maps in your area including a general highway map, topical maps, etc.

Journal

There is another type of book I have included in my recreation pantry – a journal. The journal should be new and unused and contain a <u>sufficient</u> number of blank pages to maintain a complete and comprehensive diary for the duration of the crisis. This record will provide valuable information during the emergency and a record of the challenges and opportunities prevalent during the course of the disaster. Don't forget the pen and/or pencil.

WRITING MATERIALS

An extensive assortment of writing materials could also be included in the recreation pantry. These writing materials actually serve multiple purposes. For example, writing tablets could be designated as a communication device – during an emergency, it is likely communication systems and devices will be down and writing a note or letter may be the only means of communication. Writing tablets would also be used by team members to keep lists and make notes of tasks and assignments or locate equipment and team members.

The writing tablets assigned to the recreation pantry would allow all team members – both adults and children – to have the means to write stories or poetry or draw scenes or objects as a way to relax and unwind after a hard day of dealing with disaster issues. Depending on the type of disaster – and duration – it is likely that numerous writing tablets would be used by team members as a relaxation tool. As part of the equipment to be included in writing materials, make sure there are pens, pencils, crayons and markers and a manual pencil sharpener.

SEWING

For individuals who enjoy sewing and embroidery work, have several projects available for disaster situations. The projects should be for <u>hand sewing only</u> and should include ample supplies. Embroidery work can be purchased in packages containing everything you need to create works of art. Sewing projects could include crocheting, knitting, weaving, quilting or embroidery work. Make sure you have yarn, floss, thread, crochet hooks and knitting needles in stock to continue and complete the work.

MUSICAL INSTRUMENTS

The importance of music in our lives is demonstrated again and again in every society since the beginning of time. The ancient people would devise handmade instruments used to create musical sounds. Singing and chanting has always been a method used by human beings to tell our stories. During a disaster, however, the music we enjoy today could be seriously and irrevocably thwarted by the lack of electrical power! Without electricity or a continual battery power, our boom boxes, iPods, radios, televisions, stereo systems and many musical instruments would be silent.

As part of a recreation pantry, a supply of musical instruments not relying on electrical or battery power would provide the means to enjoy music during a time when it would be needed and appreciated by all team members.

The instruments would normally be those that team members actually play but other instruments could also be included to entice and challenge the team to learn a new way of creating music. In general, the instruments should be small or able to be easily and securely stored. In addition to the musical instruments, it is also important to include sheet music.

Some possible musical instruments might include:

• **Accordion**	• **Flute**	• **Piano**
• **Banjo**	• **Guitar**	• **Tambourine**
• **Drums**	• **Harmonica**	• **Ukulele**
• **Fiddle**	• **Horn**	• **Violin**

For children, there are numerous sites on the Internet providing detailed instructions for <u>making</u> musical instruments that can be used to create an outstanding neighborhood band. For the most part, the supplies can be gathered around the house or purchased at the local hardware store. In the toy section of most department stores, parents will find toy versions of instruments including pianos, drums, horns, guitars, harmonicas and more. As part of *planning in advance*, teams with small children may want to include the kids in the preparation by making these musical instruments *now* and storing them away for *future* use during an emergency. Drums, flutes, horns, bells and other instruments can be easily and cheaply made using common household items.

CRAFTS

During an emergency, sitting down and working on a craft project can be fun. There are many craft projects that could be *prepared in advance* for a crisis including wood carving, pottery making, weaving, basket making, sand sculptures and painting. Make sure supplies are available for all team members depending on individual interests, preferences and aptitudes.

ADDITIONAL RECREATIONAL ACTIVITIES

There are other recreational activities for the survival team or could include other survival teams and neighbors. These activities serve to include everyone as a group and can certainly provide the means for individuals to bond together during hard times. For the most part, these activities do not require any advanced planning or equipment. For example:

- **Charades**
- **Dancing**
- **Talent Contests**
- **Tournaments**
- **Plays**

Remember! **RECREATION** is an element that could be shared between more than one survival team. For example, if there are five separate survival teams living in the same neighborhood, each team could be assigned specific recreation items and supplies to include in their primary residence pantry. During a disaster, and when it's time for a break, all five survival teams could share their recreation items with the other teams. In this way, all five teams can save money by not having to purchase so many recreation items. In the event that one of the teams makes a decision not to share with the others - there is really no major harm done to the other teams - because after all, survival is not contingent on whether you have a board game, guitar, football or deck of cards at your primary residence. Recreation supplies are certainly important, convenient and desired, but may not be considered critical *need* items. However, if your team has small children and/or teenagers, recreation supplies can offer a means to eliminate stress, anxiety and boredom for not only the kids, but the adults as well.

> **REMEMBER! DURING DISASTER SITUATIONS, SURVIVAL TEAMS CAN COMBINE FORCES AND PURCHASE, GATHER AND SHARE RECREATION SUPPLIES WITH MEMBERS OF OTHER TEAMS AND GROUPS.**

WHAT TO CONSIDER FOR THE RECREATION ELEMENT

Supplies, items and resources that could be considered for the **RECREATION** Element include the following:

- **Books (pleasure, reference)**
- **Cards**
- **Crafts**
- **Games**
- **Journal**
- **Musical Instruments**
- **Pencil Sharpener**
- **Puzzles**
- **Sewing Projects**
- **Toys**
- **Writing Materials (paper, pens, pencils etc.)**

SUMMARY

In the Bible and other religious scriptures, we have been counseled by ancient and modern prophets to prepare for the last days. Over the past five decades, we have been encouraged by religious, scientific and community leaders to prepare for future disasters. Today, all you need to do is turn on the television or read the newspaper to see continual and escalating emergencies and disasters occurring all over the world.

Over the past thirty years, as I have been practicing advanced planning for emergency preparation, I have discovered that I cannot do it alone. **There is a God. There is a Supreme Being and Creator of this earth.** I have found that if I continue to look to a Higher Power for guidance and assistance in this daunting task – it becomes easier – <u>and possible</u>.

As a beginning student to emergency preparation, you may see a foreboding obstacle in the path – lack of time, lack of funds and lack of organizational skills to accomplish the task. We all have to begin somewhere – and you are now off to a good start – by committing to learn what steps to take to <u>begin</u> your emergency preparation pantries. In the beginning – take small steps. As you move forward in Volumes 2 and 3, you will discover additional supplies that can be added to your pantries.

REMEMBER - YOU <u>CAN</u> DO HARD THINGS

ONE BY ONE
DAY BY DAY

BUT NEVER STOP FILLING THOSE PANTRIES

BIBLIOGRAPHY

Advisory Committee on Immunization Practices (ACIP)
American Academy of Family Physicians
American Academy of Pediatrics
American Association of Retired Persons (AARP)
American Medical Association
American Red Cross
Centers for Disease Control (CDC)
Federal Emergency Management Administration (FEMA)
Gerber Corporation
Lundin, Cody, *When All Hell Breaks Loose*
United States Department of Commerce
United States Department of Defense
United States Department of Energy
United States Department of Health and Human Services
University of Utah, Poison Control Center
Utah Department of Health
World Health Organization (WHO)

APPENDIX A - EMERGENCY PREPARATION WORKSHEET

ITEM	ELEMENT	NEED/WANT	PRIORITY	HOUSEHOLD TEAM MEMBERS	LENGTH OF TIME	PRIMARY RESIDENCE	PLACE OF REFUGE	AUTO	EVACUATION KIT	WORK	TOTAL ITEMS NEEDED	ON HAND	STILL TO PURCHASE	PACKAGING	UNIT COST	TOTAL COST

ITEM	ELEMENT	NEED/WANT	PRIORITY	HOUSEHOLD TEAM MEMBERS	LENGTH OF TIME	PRIMARY RESIDENCE	PLACE OF REFUGE	AUTO	EVACUATION KIT	WORK	TOTAL ITEMS NEEDED	ON HAND	STILL TO PURCHASE	PACKAGING	UNIT COST	TOTAL COST

SUPPLIES	EL	SUPPLIES	EL	SUPPLIES	EL
Activated Charcoal	M	Candles	OG	Fire Alarm (battery-operated)	OG
Adhesive Tape Rolls	M	Canned Heat	OG	Fire Extinguisher	OG
Alcohol (Rubbing)	M	Car Registration	D	Fire Starter	OG
Allergies (Sinus/Decongestant)	M	Card Table	OG	Fireplace - wood burning	OG
Aluminum Foil	OG	Cards	R	Fireplace Tools	OG
Analgesics	M	Cell Phone	C	First Aid Kit and Manual	M
Antacids	M	Cement Trials	OT	Flashlight	OG
Antibiotic Ointment	M	Certificate of Deposit	D	Flint Striker	OG
Antibiotics	M	Chains	OG	Funnel (water)	OG
Antihistamine	M	Chair (folding)	OG	Games	R
Antiseptic Wipes	M	Chisel	OT	Garbage Bags -13 gal	OG
Axe	OT	Clamps	OT	Garbage Can (large)	OG
Baby Supplies	OG	Clock	OG	Garden Hose	OG
Baggies (variety of sizes)	OG	Coat (heavy-duty and/or warm)	OC	Gauze - rolled	M
Bandages - butterfly	M	Cold Medicine	M	Gauze - sponges	M
Bandages - elastic	M	Cold Press (instant)	M	Gauze - squares	M
Bandages - fingertip	M	Compass	OG	Generator (gas)	OG
Bandages - knuckle	M	Compression Socks	M	Generator (solar)	OG
Bandages - strips	M	Cooking Oil	OG	Glass Cutter	OT
Bandages - triangular	M	Cornstarch	OG	Gloves – (Plastic)	OG
Band-Aids	M	Cotton Balls	M, OG	Gloves (heavy-duty and/or	OC
Batteries (rechargeable)	OG	Cotton Swabs	M	Gloves (Latex)	OG
Battery Charger (Solar)	OG	Cough Suppressants	M	Gloves (light duty)	OC
Belt	OC	CPR Microshield	M	Glue	OT
Binoculars	OG	Crafts	R	Gott (hold water)	OG
Birth Certificate	D	Crimpers	OT	Guardianship Papers	D
Birth Control	M	Crow Bar	OT	Hand Cart	OG
Blankets	OG	Deeds	D	Hand Dolly	OG
Bolt Cutter	OT	Dental Records	D	Hand Warmer	OG
Bolts	OT	Diapers (adult and/or baby)	OG	Hat (heavy-duty and/or warm)	OC
Bond Certificates	D	Diarrhea Medication	M	Hat (light-duty)	OC
Books (journal)	R	Divorce Decree	D	Hatchet	OT
Books (reading)	R	Dressings - burn	M	Heartburn Medication	M
Books (reference)	O, R	Drivers License	D	Heaters (electric and/or fuel)	OG
Books (survival, emergency)	O, R	Drum (heavy-duty 55 gallon)	OG	Heating Pad	OG
Boots (heavy-duty)	OC	Duct Tape	OG	Hidden Message Box	C
Box Cutter	OT	Dust Mask	OG	Hoe	OT
Brace - ankle	M	Epson Salt	M	Home Signal Flag	C
Brace - knee	M	Extension Cords	OG	Hospital Information	D
Brace - wrist	M	Eye Drops	M	Hot Press (instant)	M
Briquettes (Charcoal)	OG	Eyeglass Repair Kit	M	Hot Water Bottle	M
Bucket - drinking (heavy-duty)	OG	Eyeglasses (extra pair)	M	House Slippers	OC
Burn Ointment/Spray/Cream	M	Eyewash Solution	M	Hydrocortisone Cream	M
Buttons	OG	Fan (hand-held)	OG	Hydrogen Peroxide	M
Calamine Lotion	M	Feminine Hygiene Supplies	M	Ice Bag	M
Calendar	OG	Files (Tool)	OT	Immunization Records	I

SUPPLIES	EL	SUPPLIES	EL	SUPPLIES	EL
Immunization-Chickenpox	I	Medical Equipment (walker)	M	Property Tax Statements	D
Immunization-Diphtheria	I	Medication - prescription	M	Pruner	OT
Immunization-Hepatitis A	I	Medicine Dropper	M	Pruning Saw	OT
Immunization-Hepatitis B	I	Medicine Spoon	M	Punch	OT
Immunization-Influenza	I	Military Records	D	Putty	OT
Immunization-Meningitis	I	Mirror	OG	Puzzles	R
Immunization-MMR	I	Miter Box with Saw	OT	Quilts	OG
Immunization-Papillomavirus	I	Mortgages	D	Radio - CB	C
Immunization-Pertussis	I	Musical Instruments	R	Radio - Ham	C
Immunization-Pneumonia	I	Nails (various types and sizes)	OT	Radio (battery-operated)	C
Immunization-Polio	I	Naturalization Papers	D	Radio (crank/solar)	C
Immunization-Tetanus	I	Nausea Medication	M	Rain Barrel	OG
Immunization-Typhoid	I	Needles	M	Rain Gear	OC
Immunization-Zoster	I	Newspaper Logs	OG	Rake	OT
Income Tax Returns	D	Notebooks	OG, R	Ratchets	OT
Insurance - Auto	D	Noxzema Cream	M	Religious Materials	OG, R
Insurance - Home	D	Nozzle	OG	Religious Records	D
Insurance - Life	D	Nut Drivers	OT	Robe	OC
Insurance - Medical	D	Nuts (tool)	OT	Roller Skates	R
Insurance - Other	D	Pads - abdominal	M	Rope	OG
Iodide Tablets (thyroid)	M	Pads - eye	M	Row Boat	R
Ipecac Syrup	M	Pads - non adherent	M	Rubber Syringe	M
IRA Account Paperwork	D	Pain Relievers	M	Safety Glasses	OG
Jacket	OC	Paint Brush	OT	Safety Pins	OG
Keys (extra sets)	OG	Pants and Slacks	OC	Salt	OG
Knife or Scapel	OT, M	Paper	R, C	Sand paper	OT
Knife Sharpener	OT	Paper Bags (brown)	OG	Sandbags	OG
Ladders	OG	Passport	D	Sander	OT
Lamp Oil	OG	Pens/Pencils	R, C	Savings Account Records	D
Lantern (battery-operated)	OG	Permanent Markers	C	Saw	OT
Lantern (oil)	OG	Pet Records	D	Scanner	C
Lantern (propane/butane)	OG	Petroleum Jelly	M, OG	School Records	D
Lanyards	OG	Photographs - recent	D	Scissors	OG, R
Lawnmower (manual)	OG	Pick	OT	Scrapers	OT
Laxative	M	Pill Holders	M	Screwdrivers	OT
Leases	D	Pillows	OG	Screws	OT
Level (tool)	OT	Pitch Fork	OT	Sewing Kits (thread, pins)	OG, R
Light Bulbs (low watt)	OG	Planers	OT	Sewing Projects	R
Light Sticks	OG	Plastic Grocery Bags	OG	Shampoo - lice	M
Lighters	OG	Plastic Sheeting	OG	Shears	OT
Lip Balm	M	Plastic Ties	OG	Shirts	OC
Living Will	D	Pliers	OT	Shoe laces	OC
Lumber	OT	Plow	OT	Shoes - light-duty	OC
Mallet (rubber)	OT	Pocket Knife	OT	Shoes - sturdy	OC
Marriage License/Certificate	D	Power of Attorney	D	Shovel (regular)	OT
Matches	OG	Prescription Lists	M, D	Shovel (snow)	OT

SUPPLIES	EL	SUPPLIES	EL	SUPPLIES	EL
Skateboard	R	Tow Rope	OG		
Sledge Hammer	OT	Toys	R		
Sleeping Bag (heavy-duty)	OG	Treadle Sewing Machine	OG, R		
Sleeping Bag (light-duty)	OG	T-Shirts	OC		
Sleepwear	OC	Twine	OG		
Snake Bite Kit	M	Typewriter (manual) and ribbons	C		
Snips	OT	Umbrella	OC		
Social Security Card	D	Underwear (boxers, panties etc)	OC		
Sockets	OT	Underwear (thermal)	OC		
Socks (heavy-duty and/or	OC	Vapor Rub	M		
Socks (light-duty)	OC	Vehicle Registrations	D		
Solar Garden Lights	OG	Wagon	OG		
Solar Panels	OG	Walkie-Talkies	C		
Spikes	OT	Washers	OT		
Splints	M	Water - bottled	OG		
Squares	OT	Water - containers	OG		
Stapler (heavy-duty)	OT	Water - natural sources	OG		
Staples (heavy-duty)	OT	Water Can	OG		
Status Letter/Stamp	C	Water Purification Tablets	OG		
Stock Certificates	D	Waxed Paper	OG		
Sunglasses	OC	Wedge	OT		
Sunscreen	M	Weeder	OT		
Suppositories	M	Wheelbarrow	OG		
Swabs - alcohol	M	Whistle	C		
Swabs - cotton-tipped	M	Wicks (for oil lamps)	OG		
Swabs - insect bite	M	Wills	D		
Sweat shirts	OC	Wind Turbine	OG		
Sweaters	OC	Wire Screen Mesh (repairs)	OG		
Table (small folding)	OG	Wound Closures	M		
Tacks	OT	Wrenches	OT		
Tape Measure	OT	Writing Materials	C, R		
Tarp Clips	OG				
Tarps	OG	**ADDITIONAL ITEMS**			
Tea Kettle	OG				
Telephone Book	C				
Tent (heavy-duty)	OG				
Tent (light duty) - popup	OG			**LEGEND**	
Thermometer (medical)	M			*C - Communication*	
Thermometer (outside)	O			*D - Documentation*	
Thermos (insulated)	N			*I - Immunization*	
Throat Lozenges	M			*M - Medication*	
Titles (home, vehicles etc)	D			*OC - Operations - Clothing*	
Tongue Blades	M			*OG - Operations - General*	
Toothache Medicine	M			*OT - Operations - Tools*	
Tourniquet	M			*R - Recreation*